THE PUBLIC RECORD OFFICE AND JOHN MURRAY

DOCUMENTS FROM

THE ERA OF THE SECOND WORLD WAR

**HUGH GREANY   PAUL GREY
ROSEMARIE LITTLE   TONY LLEWELLYN
RACHEL MACFARLANE   DAVID SMITH**

Series Editor: IAN COULSON

JOHN MURRAY

Acknowledgements

Crown copyright material in the Public Record Office is reproduced by permission of the Controller of Her Majesty's Stationery Office.

Illustrations by Art Construction, Taurus Graphics

The authors and publishers would like to thank the following for permission to use copyright material:
pp. 28, 30, 36(F), 48, 67(Sources 1 and 2), 85, 97(A): *Illustrated London News.*
p.49(Source 6): Kent Messenger Group.
p.55(Source 2): Hulton Deutsch Collection.
p.58(Source 4): *Daily Mail*/John Frost Historical Newspapers.
p. 101: *The Guardian.*

Every effort has been made to trace all the copyright holders, but if any have been inadvertently overlooked the publishers will be pleased to make the necessary arrangement at the first opportunity.

Text © Ian Coulson, Hugh Greany, Paul Grey, Rosemarie Little, Tony Llewellyn, Rachel Macfarlane, David Smith, 1993

First published 1993
by John Murray (Publishers) Ltd
50 Albemarle Street
London W1X 4BD
in collaboration with the Public Record Office

Reprinted 1994

Typeset by Litholink Ltd.
Printed by St Edmundsbury Press, Bury St Edmunds, Suffolk.
Bound by Hunter & Foulis, Edinburgh.
A CIP catalogue record for this book is available from the British Library

ISBN 0-7195-5236-2

CONTENTS

For many years it has been the norm for school textbooks to include original source material. However, this has usually been transcribed and simplified and all too often the feel, the texture, the look and the challenge of the original are totally lost. This series aims to bring the documents into the classroom in a form similar to the original.

The PRO Sourcebooks provide fascimile documentary sources from the unrivalled British Government archive – the Public Record Office. The documents have been selected to support National Curriculum History teaching, particularly of the core units in Key Stages 3 and 4.

This series offers the first publications ever to trawl the enormous collections of the Public Record Office (there are for example seven **miles** of shelving devoted to documents from the Second World War!) for resources specifically targeted at National Curriculum History.

Original sources

Unlike almost all National Curriculum coursebooks, this series presents entirely original sources. The extracts have not been edited, simplified or translated. With the exception of a couple of almost totally illegible originals, the documents have been photographed in their original form to give pupils a genuine taste of the delights (and occasional frustrations) of a historian's work.

The majority of the sources have never been published before – in any form.

Language

While presenting the documents in an unedited form, every attempt has been made to select documents accessible to pupils of a wide range of abilities. Some of the documents will stretch the very best readers. Others will be accessible to all. Guidance on accessibility is given in the Teacher's notes.

Classroom potential

The documents have been selected by practising teachers for their classroom potential. They are presented as ready-to-use worksheets, complete with questions, activities and assignments alongside the documents themselves. Detailed teacher guidance on using the questions and activities is also given in the back of each book.

Investigations

Most documents are presented as part of an extended 'investigation'. In each investigation a selection of documents and questions lead pupils through a clear line of enquiry related to a key historical issue. The investigations allow pupils to reach their own conclusions and develop their own informed interpretations of the past.

Flexibility

Because the investigations are self contained, they can be incorporated into any course you are following. The books are deliberately geared to the main elements in the focus statements of the National Curriculum Programmes of Study so that they remain central to any course – published or home-grown – and to any system of assessment that you may follow.

The self-contained worksheets can be used for classroom projects, homework, in cover lessons, group work, revision and in many other ways. They can be used as stimulus material to raise pupils' interest in a particular subject or for sustained investigation over a number of lessons.

Variety

The Public Record Office holds a vast array of records, from letters, telegrams, minutes, reports and interviews through to magazines, newspapers, posters, cartoons and photographs. The series aims to reflect this wide range of material so that pupils have the fullest possible opportunities to develop their source-handling skills.

People in history

The official records of the government include records which give us a glimpse into the lives of many people of the past. This series focuses upon the lives of these people – the ordinary, the great, the good and the not-so-good.

The Attainment Targets

The series has learned from the experience of early years of National Curriculum teaching. It is built on the principle that the first aim of our history teaching is to help pupils ask and answer valid historical questions. In answering these key questions, pupils have to acquire and use a large amount of knowledge and use all the skills described in the Attainment Targets. In other words the key questions naturally introduce pupils to the skills and concepts required in historical investigation. In the process, pupils develop the skills described in the Attainment Targets.

Considerable emphasis is obviously placed on source-handling skills, particularly those needed for AT3 work. However, they key questions lead pupils into all areas of ATs 1 and 2.

AIMS

We aim to achieve four main things in this book:

1 to address the key historical questions raised by the focus statement in the Programme of Study for the Era of the Second World War
2 to stimulate pupils' interest in document-based research and to enable them to enjoy using the documents
3 to provide access to a wide of range of material, representative of the variety of records held by the Public Record Office
4 to enable pupils to see how historians try to piece together the story of the past – and how the skills of source analysis are used to achieve the wider aim of answering genuine historical questions.

This is not a core text, although you will see from the contents list on page 1 and the matrix on page 11 that the Programme of Study and each strand of the Attainment Targets are very widely covered. It does not, however, tell the story of the Second World War, or try to tell you or your pupils everything they need to know about the causes and consequences of the War.

Instead it selects a number of themes suggested by the focus statement in the Programme of Study and uses these as a basis for pupil investigation.

THE PUBLIC RECORD OFFICE AND THE ERA OF THE SECOND WORLD WAR

The focus statement from the Programme of Study for the Era of the Second World War states that:

'Pupils should be taught about the causes, nature and immediate consequences of the Second World War. The focus should be on the developing conflict between democracies and dictatorships in Europe in the 1930s, the impact of the war on soldiers and civilians and post-war reconstruction.'

The focus therefore is on causes, experiences and consequences of the war. The PRO archives are strong on all these issues, particular on the British perspective. So one has to select very carefully, bearing in mind the particular strengths and weaknesses of the archive.

Causes of the Second World War We have focused on two themes: British assessments of Hitler and British reactions to German rearmament and territorial expansion in the 1930s. Through the investigations pupils can see the policy of appeasement in action; they can appreciate the ebb and flow of British optimism about world peace in the 1930s. They can also see how the Great War and the Treaty of Versailles still influenced government policy on key issues.

Experiences of the Second World War The PRO holds many records relating to each of the armed services and detailed accounts of the arenas of war in which British servicemen and women were in action. It also houses the records concerning Home Defence, the regulation of civilian life and the harnessing of industry and agriculture to the war effort. Finally it documents in detail the activity of Britain's wartime leader, Winston Churchill. This amounts to a rich resource for investigating the varied experiences of soldiers, civilians and wartime leaders. The bulk of this book (Themes 3–10) is concerned with this area of the Programme of Study.

Immediate consequences of the War Theme 11 covers aspects of post-war reconstruction. The PRO is more limited in its scope for this subject than for the previous two. Some of the relevant documents (for example those dealing with Britain's nuclear weapons) are not yet open for public scrutiny or publication. In addition, many documents dealing with the UN or with the Cold War are long, complex and dry, and not suited to classroom work. We have therefore selected only a small number of documents to support teaching on post-war reconstruction.

Research at the PRO

If this book gives you a taste for using original sources, there is nothing to prevent you going to the PRO yourself. There is open access to the original records at the PRO at Kew from Monday to Friday and to the census returns at Chancery Lane from Monday to Saturday. You can apply for a reader's ticket when you get there. All you need is some proof of identity. However, if you are interested in doing specialised research of your own at the PRO, you are strongly advised to plan your visit carefully and if possible to talk to the officers responsible for education beforehand.

The record sheet opposite will be useful for both planning your research and recording your findings.

In the detailed Teacher's notes for each investigation, we have provided the PRO reference for each document, for example INF 3/400 (page 119). The **letters** (known as the group letters) relate to the government department which created, received or stored this document. In this case INF stands for the wartime Ministry of Information.

The **first number** (known as the class number) defines an area within the Ministry of Information records. INF 3 together describes a set of documents relating to the propaganda put out by the Ministry of Information during the War.

The **final number** (400) is the piece number. This is specific to an item that can be ordered. It will often be a bound volume, a looseleaf file, or (in this case) a portfolio of posters.

If you were to go to the PRO to research the reference,

Theme

Reader's ticket number

Date

Seat No/Room

Name

Address

Topic	Group Letters	Class No	Piece No	Description	Time Ordered	Time Received	P'Copy No

INF 3/400 would provide you with this portfolio –
from which we have reproduced two posters on page
67.

Preserving the past

The PRO is not only a wonderful quarry for the history
teacher, but also a living example of AT2 and AT3 at
work. The very existence of a national archive – a self-
conscious representation of the nation's past – raises
issues of bias and interpretation.

On the one hand the archive does not only contain
much specific and unashamed propaganda; its contents
also reflect the bias inherent in the attitudes of the
British people in the Era of the Second World War, for
example attitudes towards the role of women, or
towards the twin 'threats' of Fascism and Communism.

On the other hand the creation of a public archive is
itself an exercise in interpretation. Countless public
servants during the past 50 years have been deciding
daily what documents to preserve for posterity and
what to destroy. In this sense the archive was evolving
out of the civil servants' intuitive or self-conscious
interpretation of the past. Investigation 48 suggests a
lighthearted way of looking at this process.

These levels of interpretation add to the fascination
of working with these archives and provide plentiful
opportunities for tackling ATs 2 and 3. However,
discussions on such matters can become repetitive for
pupils. In the investigations, therefore, we have
avoided constantly asking these questions, preferring to
indicate such opportunities in the Teacher's notes.

Local archives

Even if you live a long way from the PRO, you may still
be within a reasonable distance of a local archive office.
It is worth booking a visit for a departmental meeting.
Archive offices are often happy to arrange meetings
with teachers where original sources can be shown and
when information about the services on offer can be
explained. Some offices have staff responsible for
education who are only too pleased to make contact
with teachers. Their concern is often to ensure that their
services are used and that pupils and teachers know
how to make the most of the facilities on offer. If you
want to know about the archive offices in your area
write to the Society of Archivists, Information House,
20–24 Old Street, London EC1V 9AP.

Other resources

The following books have been found useful by the
authors in introducing pupils to source-based work.
They have all been published over the past fifteen years
and should any not be still in print they will probably
be available through local resource centres.

Fines, I,	*Reading Historical Documents* (1988)
Hinton, C,	*What is Evidence?* (1990)
Marwick, A,	*Introduction to History* (1977)
Portal, C (ed.),	*Sources in History* (1987)
Shuter, P,	*Using Historical Sources* (1989)
Wolfson, R, and Aylett, J.F.,	*Examining the Evidence* (1988)

USING THIS MATERIAL IN THE CLASSROOM

Before you start

Read the Teacher's notes thoroughly – both this
introduction and the detailed notes on page 108.

Select your investigations carefully. Think about the
abilities of your pupils and how suitable the
investigation will be for them.

Go through the questions in the investigation
carefully as well. Think about likely answers, and the
best way of using each question. Is it most useful for
group work, whole class discussion or individual work?
Think also about how the pupils' likely answers can be
developed.

Think about whether you should rewrite any
questions or develop new ones of your own. If you like
the sources but not the questions, cut and paste to make
your own worksheet. There is more advice on question
design and differentiation generally on page 8.

Read through the documents and sources yourself.
Spot difficult words and phrases (**NB** we have provided
annotations for each document where there are words
that we expect many pupils will need explaining).
Decide whether our annotations are adequate or will
need supplementing for some pupils. You can add extra
annotation before photocopying.

We have added line numbering to some long
documents. You might wish to do the same for some
shorter ones.

Consider the context in which each investigation is
best used. How much contextual background will need
to be provided and therefore whereabouts in your
course will you use it? Do you need to add to the
introductory background material which we have
provided? This book in no way replaces your narrative
of the causes, experiences and consequences of the
Second World War. It is intended to be integrated into
your course – to complement it and build from it. It
helps to clarify and emphasise key elements in the story.
Above all it introduces pupils to a range of people –
ordinary and extraordinary – so that pupils can begin to
see the war through their eyes.

The investigations

Each investigation has the same basic elements.

Introductory text provides a concise summary of context and background to the investigation. This can be extended by the teacher according to requirements.

The sourceline provides essential information about the documents. This aims to be factual rather than interpretative.

Key questions (in a tinted box) challenge pupils to bring together their understanding of the different documents and their wider knowledge of the period or subject. These questions may be stepped or open-ended. Either way we feel that the key questions give plentiful opportunities for differentiation by outcome.

The documents carefully selected and reproduced so that they are as easy as possible to read and use in class. Many documents have been resized, but not altered or edited. They are faithful reproductions of the originals.

Process questions guide pupils through the investigations step-by-step. These questions lead pupils into the documents, help pupils to make sense of them in a methodical way and give pupils the confidence to find out more from the sources.

Annotation inevitably certain abbreviations, difficult or archaic words, and unfamiliar ideas will need explaining to pupils. This is done through subtle annotation which can be supplemented by the teacher if necessary.

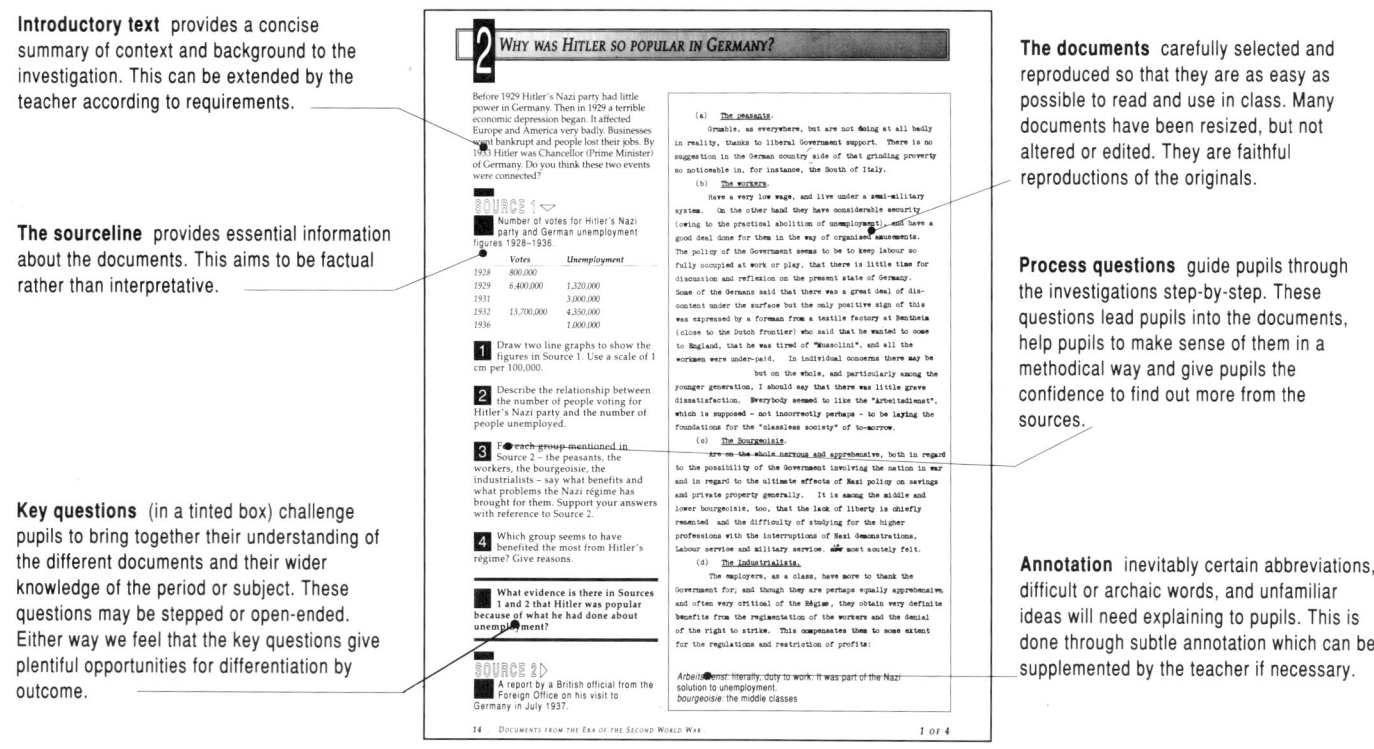

Sources are numbered consecutively through an investigation for ease of reference in class.

Questions are usually numbered consecutively on each page.

Using the investigations

- One-page investigations and even single documents can be used as stimulus material to raise pupils' interest in a subject.
- Longer investigations can be used for detailed work over a number of periods, for both classroom work and homework.
- The investigations provide opportunities for group work, IT work and cross-curricular work.
- The worksheets can be adapted to incorporate your own questions and activities. Look at the sample page above. Some differentiation can be achieved by adjusting the questions given – in this case by deleting questions 1 and 2 before photocopying. Detailed advice on such matters is provided in the Teacher's notes throughout.
- Documents can be remixed to illustrate specific points. For example, investigation 13 (September 1939) uses extracts from various documents to create a decision-making activity for pupils on Home Front priorities.
- Finally, and probably most important, it is possible to ask much broader questions where a number of investigations are used over a period of time. For example, if you used a few of investigations 1, 2, 4, 5, 6 and 11, it would then be possible to ask pupils to explain how British opinions of Hitler changed.

Photocopying

The investigations in this book vary in length from one to four pages.

Four-page investigations should ideally be photocopied as double sided A3 sheets which can then be folded into a four-page 'booklet'. However, to make such a photocopy page 1 needs to be on the right-hand side of page 4. Clearly we cannot lay our book out that way – it would look nonsensical. So probably the most practical way of making such photocopies is for you to take off the binding and file the pages in a ring binder. You could of course photocopy page 1 of the investigation twice, but please be aware that a second generation photocopy loses much of the definition of the original document and you run the risk that the text may be less legible. Furthermore, the better the reprographics the more likely it is that the worksheets will survive more than one use.

By buying this book you have automatically acquired permission to photocopy these investigations for use in your own school or institution. Any further photocopying or electrocopying without written permission from the publishers is expressly forbidden and is an infringement of copyright.

You might wish to photocopy some documents on to OHP acetate, thus allowing pupils to work together as a class on a particularly difficult piece of text.

Some of the documents have been considerably reduced in size. This is unavoidable when producing a book in this A4 format. To overcome the difficulty of handling small print it can be useful to double the size of the photocopy from A4 to A3. We have indicated this with a symbol in the teacher's notes.

Templates

It can be very effective on occasions to make a template for pupils' answers. For example, when writing a reply from a member of the Foreign Office to the Duke of Kent, a template can be made with a 'Foreign Office' heading and photocopied on to the back of the one-page worksheet.

The documents

Because the documents are faithful reproductions of the originals, it follows that not all of them are easy to read or use. This is a point that needs to be discussed with pupils. They may have been given the impression from the edited sources which most textbooks provide that reading original documents is simple. This is clearly not the case. However, this is not a disadvantage. The challenge of reading sources in near to the original form is an important part of pupil motivation. Research into history teaching over the past decade has shown that where children have a choice between working with:

    a) a paraphrase of an original source
    b) a simplified and edited version
    c) the document itself (or a facsimile),

they will prefer the latter, as long as the content is interesting and the task stimulating. We have aimed therefore always to provide documents in which the content itself is interesting and to provide tasks which will fully engage the pupils. This should help them to overcome any difficulty inherent in some of the sources.

The experience of many teachers who use archive material regularly is that pupils are not as self-conscious about the problem as teachers tend to be. Pupils often view reading a document as a game as long as they understand the purpose of the activity and have their interest kindled. They are rarely worried about being seen to be unable to understand some words or phrases. Practice and co-operation bring confidence as well as greater efficiency as pupils learn to read and decipher a document more quickly.

If in doubt, have a go! There is little to lose in the first place as one important lesson for pupils to learn from this book is that history is not actually to be found in neatly packaged and pre-digested source extracts. Real history is a good deal more messy than textbook writers (and many pupils) would like it to be.

Using fascimile documents in class requires certain skills. The prerequisites are persistence and confidence. One leads to the other!

Group work

One important way of developing both attributes – persistence and confidence – is through group work. Group work has many advantages.
1 Group work and class discussion before any individual work is attempted will often prepare the way for pupils to read and understand a difficult document. It will increase their commitment to the task.
2 In group work different groups often come up with their own interpretations of the past using exactly the same source material.
3 In small groups less confident pupils will often venture contributions which they would not risk in whole class discussion or in written work.

Homework

All the investigations have been designed to stand alone. They refer to no textbook and can therefore be used easily for homework.

IT work

Some of the documents (investigation 19 for example) provide a selection of statistics which can be used as raw material for a data base.

IT is a means of working. It allows pupils to manipulate data that would otherwise be time-consuming or impossible. The first test for using any form of IT is: can it be done more quickly or better on the desk with a paper and pencil?

If you decide to use IT, it is always worth consulting a school specialist who will suggest appropriate software. Pupils need wherever possible to be able to use the programmes quickly, so it is a good idea to use whatever data base is regarded as standard in your school. As a historian you are more interested in the historical questions that can be more easily answered by using IT than in the basic principles of data manipulation.

Using the sources as a 'lead-in'

Any of the sources can be selected as a 'lead in' to a particular topic or theme. The majority of those found in this book on a single page can be used as a stimulus. This quick use of sources is both appropriate and practical because it is not always possible to spend a great deal of time reading, cross-referencing and analysing. Stimulating interest through original source material is a useful way of starting a topic. The same materials can be used to explain, illustrate or exemplify points of importance during the teaching of a topic. For example, when discussing the Munich agreement Source 1 in investigation 8 can be introduced to highlight British fears for the outcome of the Sudetenland crisis, and to stimulate class discussion about it.

Using the sources for investigations

The great difference between the work of a professional historian and the activities of pupils in class is that the professional historian knows the subject inside out. He or she is well briefed in recent literature on the subject and knows intimately the whole range of original sources that are available. The professional historian knows the context of the sources and what questions need to be asked. Pupils in class cannot be expected to do the same, nor can they be expected to produce comparable analyses of issues. What they can do by using several sources in an investigation is not only to build up their wider knowledge of a subject, but also to begin to understand that conclusions cannot be drawn from a single document. They can be guided through the techniques of the professional historian according to their own level of ability and intellectual sophistication.

Using the questions

The questions are the driving force behind the investigations and it is crucial that you are happy with them. It is also important to remember the reasons why the questions are being asked in the first place. The rationale is not to produce professional historians, but to replicate on a small scale some of the techniques which professional historians use. Young pupils cannot make startling new discoveries by reading and interpreting a few documents. They cannot be expected to grasp the full context of a period nor to discover new angles on a subject if they do not know what they are looking for. They need *guided access* to the sources. Thus we have provided a set of structured questions for each document: process questions that lead into a document and key questions which allow pupils to reach some broader historical conclusion. When answering all questions, encourage pupils to explain their answers by specific reference to the sources.

NB It is assumed that pupils will usually complete their answers to questions in a separate book or on a separate sheet. These will be a useful part of monitoring their achievement.

You will have to decide whether you want pupils to mark the documents themselves. It is much easier for the pupils if they can, and some questions suggest it. But if you want to reuse the photocopies you can obviously change the questions accordingly.

Setting your own questions

If you like the documents of a particular investigation, but not the questions, the photocopiable format allows you to substitute or add your own questions.

Writing questions which are right for your class is difficult. It is best to write a few, then leave them for a while. On your return try to assess them critically using the following 'question shredder' which can help you to improve and more effectively direct your questions.

The question shredder

1 Will my pupils understand the question? Can it be phrased more simply?
2 Is the purpose of the question clear? Is it a 'process' question or a 'key' question?
3 Has the question got one target or many?
4 What range of answers will my class produce?
5 Will the answers show one level of understanding or several?
6 What might these levels be?

The 'A' teams

Trying to get pupils to say what they mean and to do it succinctly is one of the many objectives of schools history.

Accuracy in the use of language is very important, especially when it involves the interpretation of sources. Historians need to be precise about what they are or are not saying. The use of adverbs and adjectives, which we have characterised as the 'A' teams, can be highlighted whenever pupils are using source material. Making a point of using a variety of words can extend pupils' vocabulary and improve the precision of their statements. For example:

Adjectives	Adverbs
hypothetical	almost
likely	apparently
misleading	arguably
plausible	possibly
reasonable	probably
questionable	presumably
unproven	partly

However, these are not magic words. Pupils should not think that using them will automatically result in good marks. Like a professional historian, any pupil must convince the reader that they have a full understanding. The use of appropriate terminology is a tool. The use of key words does not automatically qualify pupils for high levels of attainment.

'Where do I start?' Advice from the experts

Using documents is all to do with asking questions. Several historians have thought about the processes of using original sources and have bravely put their approaches on paper for others to consider. There is no magic all-embracing scheme. The right questions are determined by the nature of the document. Nevertheless, four of these approaches have been prepared as cue cards that could be used to interrogate sources in this book. Choose a card that you think best suits your pupils or take elements from each to produce your own cue card more suited to the needs of your own class.

'A' was produced by John Fines for use by A level students; 'B' by Arthur Marwick for the use of Open University students; 'C' by the series editor of this book for use with pupils in Key Stages 3 and 4; 'D' by Ian Mason in the context of Key Stage 2 work.

A

Step 1 Describe your document

Step 2 Collect information from the document about people, time, places and ideas

Step 3 Underline everything that you do not understand

Step 4 Read the document again. What is there in the document that marks its period?

Step 5 How reliable is the document?

Step 6 What questions does the document get you thinking about?

Step 7 How useful and significant is the document?

Step 8 Record your findings

B

QUESTIONS ABOUT THE VALUE AND RELIABILITY OF THE SOURCE

1 What type of source is it?

2 What person, or group of persons, created the source in the first place?

3 How and for what purpose did the document come into existence?

4 How far does it provide good first-hand information?

5 Try to understand the document as people at the time would have understood it.

QUESTIONS ABOUT INTERPRETATION

6 What is the main international testimony of the document?

7 Is there any unwitting testimony?

C

READING THE DOCUMENT

1 Read the document through. If you cannot read certain words leave them out and go back to them later.

SORTING THE DETAILS

2 Who wrote it?

3 When was it written?

4 Why was it written?

QUESTIONING THE DOCUMENT

5 Is it a first hand or second hand account?

6 Does this source back up what you already know or is it different?

7 How reliable is this document?

COLLECTING THE EVIDENCE

8 How does this help you with the key question you are asking?

DRAWING CONCLUSIONS

9 What did the original writer intend?

10 What other information can we extract from the document?

11 Is the document connected to other sources or information that you know about?

D

WHAT DOES THE DOCUMENT LOOK LIKE?

1 What size is it?

2 What colour is it?

3 What kind of cover has it?

4 Is it printed or handwritten? Say if it is a letter, book, roll, map, newspaper, drawing, poster, photocopy, or other.

5 Does it have a reference mark?

THE DOCUMENT DESCRIBED

6 Note the title (if none make up a suitable one)

7 Record the date of your document

WHERE THE DOCUMENT COMES FROM

8 Who wrote the document?

9 What kind of person was the writer?

10 Do you think the author was free to write, or paid to write it, or forced to write it?

11 Is the document personal or private, or about a business and commercial, or from government and official?

BACKGROUND

12 What events led to the making of your document?

CONTENT

13 If your document is a short one, briefly say what it is about and copy the important words exactly

14 If your document is a long one, choose the important pieces and describe them

TRUTHFULNESS

15 Did the writer of your document see things at firsthand?

16 Does the writer's point of view affect what is written?

17 How can the information in your document be checked?

18 How true do you think the information in your document is?

CONCLUSIONS

19 What new things does your document tell you?

20 What things do you find interesting or odd about your document?

Assessment and the Attainment Targets

Much has already been said and written in previous publications about the nature of the Attainment Targets and the need to see them as a bank of historical ideas which pupils need to understand and skills they need to acquire. We would particularly recommend the advice given in *Peace and War* (The Schools History Project's core text for Y9). We do not intend to reiterate such advice at this stage, particularly in view of the recasting of the Attainment Targets under the 1994 review of the National Curriculum.

National Curriculum History provides a useful although imperfect framework that should be dominated by the nature of historical enquiry – sensible, adult questions about the past that are appropriate to the issues in hand.

Under the original orders history could be seen as a process in which historical enquiry (AT3) leads to pupils creating their own historical narrative (AT1a and AT1c) and their own historical explanations (AT1b) while also studying the interpretations of others. Each of these broad concepts will remain embodied in the Key Elements for the revised Programme of Study, and they are basic to the assumptions about the nature of historical enquiry taken by the authors of this volume.

It is also worth explaining in some detail how these investigations reflect our assumptions about assessment.

1 Assessment is part of a process – a cycle of planning, teaching, assessing, recording, reporting and finally evaluating teaching strategies to see how they should be adjusted. The purpose of assessment is to move the pupils on to the next level of knowing about, understanding and studying history.
2 Assessment is much more than testing. It is certainly much more than a memory test.
3 Assessment needs to give pupils the opportunity to show what they can do, not what they cannot do.
4 Assessment needs to look at as broad a picture of pupils' work and attainment as possible – including their written work, oral work, class work, homework, group work and individual work; their historical enquiry, their historical investigation and their historical explanation.

Setting appropriate work for an individual pupil begins in knowing the pupil and his/her previous achievements. Only the teacher who knows the pupil well can decide what is appropriate. What the authors of this text have done is to attempt to provide pupils with open-ended opportunities to demonstrate what they know, understand and are able to do.

The matrix opposite illustrates the way that the investigations may give access to the Attainment Targets, although, as we hope you will quickly realise, it shows only a small part of the range of historical work that is possible from the investigations in this book. We hope that you and your pupils will enjoy them.

ATTAINMENT TARGET FOCUS MATRIX

	AT1									AT2			AT3			
	a			b			c									
Investigation	1 2	3 4 5	6 7	1 2	3 4 5	6 7 8 9	2	3 4 5	6 7 8 9	1 2 3	4 5 6	7 8 9 10	1 2 3 4	5 6	7 8 9 10	
1	■				■								■			1
2					■	■			■					■		2
3					■								■			3
4								■	■							4
5								■	■							5
6				■	■											6
7								■	■	■	■			■		7
8					■	■				■						8
9						■			■			■				9
10								■								10
11													■			11
12				■	■											12
13								■								13
14													■	■	■	14
15								■	■							15
16										■				■		16
17		■							■							17
18								■	■							18
19								■	■							19
20								■					■			20
21		■														21
22								■								22
23					■	■										23
24								■	■				■			24
25								■	■							25
26													■	■		26
27								■					■	■		27
28								■								28
29								■	■							29
30											■			■	■	30
31					■											31
32										■	■				■	32
33													■			33
34					■											34
35													■	■		35
36													■			36
37										■	■					37
38				■				■								38
39								■					■			39
40													■			40
41									■				■	■		41
42								■	■							42
43								■	■	■						43
44					■	■										44
45					■											45
46													■	■	■	46
47					■			■	■							47
48											■	■				48

Each year during the late 1930s the Foreign Office prepared biographies of the leading political personalities in Germany. Source 1 is two extracts from the biography for Adolf Hitler.

SOURCE 1

A biography of Adolf Hitler written in 1937.

1 Draw a timeline to cover the period 1889–1945. Use a scale of 5cm per decade.

2 Underline any dates mentioned in Source 1. Use this information to mark the details of Hitler's life on to your timeline.

3 Choose one moment in his life when he was lucky; one where he showed great ability; and one where circumstances helped him to succeed.

4 Choose two moments which were turning points in his career. Explain your choice.

68. *Hitler, Adolf.*—Born the 20th April, 1889, in Braunau in the Valley of the Inn, where his father, Alois Hitler, was a local customs official on the Bavarian frontier. On retiring in 1896 Alois Hitler took to farming at Lambach, but failing in health, retired a year later to a little cottage in Leonding, where the boy, Adolf, age 8, attended the village school. Here he showed no talent. His favourite game was "soldiers," his only sister, Paula, and a few comrades taking part. Although frail, Hitler took the lead in these local games and delivered speeches to the troops. A copiously illustrated history on the Franco-Prussian War, showing
10 French soldiers in retreat and Prussian soldiers triumphant, was his most treasured possession. The boy was given to day-dreaming, and his bad record in class exasperated his father, who punished him from time to time. His mother, on the other hand, was very lenient to the boy, who remains to this day a teetotaller at her behest. In 1903, when Hitler's father died, he suffered a little from lung trouble, and four years later, when his mother also died, he was forced to seek his fortune in Vienna.

After considerable privation he obtained work as a builder's labourer, only to lose it when a Jewish trade-union official discovered that he was not a member of the union. Politically, he was impressed by the anti-semitic pamphlets of
20 Karl Lüger, the Burgomaster of Vienna and by the Austrian pan-Germanist writers. In 1912 he went to Munich, and earned a precarious living as an assistant house painter and draughtsman. When the war broke out he enlisted in a Bavarian infantry regiment. In 1917 he was appointed battalion runner, and eventually the colonel of his regiment entrusted him with the task of counter-ing enemy propaganda, which was thrown into the trenches in the form of pamphlets from aeroplanes. Hitler had already attracted attention by his gift of speech, and he observed that the methods of propagandists like Mr. Lloyd George were extremely easy to copy. This lesson served him subsequently when he took to politics. Transferred to the north of France Hitler
30 was badly gassed in an attack by the Canadian forces, and the revolution found him half blind in hospital at Pasewalk.

He returned to Munich fiercely resentful of the revolution and determined to join the first available counter-movement. Accordingly, he became the seventh member of a little coterie, the "Deutsche Arbeiter-Partei," founded by one Dexler. In May 1919 the Munich Soviet Republic was overthrown and a *bourgeois* coalition under the military assumed control. Bavaria was at that time overrun by irregular military formations, many of whose members at Hitler's instigation joined the Deutsche Arbeiter-Partei. The 60th recruit was Captain Röhm. Hitler was given charge of propaganda, and he was henceforth
40 employed by the local Reichswehr as political teacher for their evening classes. His party, which soon altered its name to "Nationalsocialistische Deutsche Arbeiter-Partei," drew up a programme of twenty-five points in February 1920. In the following month the Munich Government was overthrown and replaced by a Government still more to the Right under von Kahr, and national socialism began to make headway in Bavaria. Composed largely of ex-service men, it introduced a new element—that of violence in speech and behaviour. They made a point of breaking-up Social Democratic and Communist meetings by main force, and most meetings in those days ended in a free fight with beer mugs. In December 1920 the party purchased the *Völkischer Beobachter*. It then numbered
50 3,000 members, and Hitler's personality gradually began to dominate the move-ment. In November 1922 the Bavarian Minister of the Interior, Dr. Schweyer, deemed it necessary to summon Hitler and warn him against subversive plans, whereupon Hitler tendered his word of honour that he would never, during his life, attempt a "Putsch." This was one of the instances of a broken pledge in his career.

In 1921 the party founded the S.A. to protect speakers at its meetings, and in 1923 Hitler entered into close relations with Ludendorff, in conjunction with whom he undertook the notorious but abortive attempt to seize Munich and usurp the Government of Bavaria in November 1923. Hitler had, in the meantime,
60 quarrelled with the Reichswehr. The troops now obeyed the instructions of the Munich Government and checked the "revolution." Hitler, owing to Ludendorff's participation, got off with the mild sentence of one year's imprisonment. For a moment he seriously contemplated suicide in view of the ruin of his plans. During his incarceration in the fortress at Landsberg he wrote *Mein Kampf*, which was printed in the following year soon after his liberation and return to Munich.

continued ▷

anti-semitic: hostile to or against the Jews
Völkischer Beobachter: a pro-Nazi German newspaper
SA: the army of the Nazi party

5 Which of the following phrases best describes the attitude of the writers of Source 1 to Hitler?
a) they admire him
b) they distrust him
c) they are confused by him
d) they hate him.
Support your answer by reference to the source.

6 Work in pairs. You are both journalists and have received a leaked copy of this paper.
One of you works for a pro-Nazi paper; the other for an anti-Nazi paper.
a) Write a short article for your paper describing Hitler's rise to power.
b) From other books on the Second World War, choose one portrait of Hitler to illustrate your article.

deprived him of his passport and he was now devoid of nationality. His movement died down during the prosperous years 1925–28, and by March 1927 most
70 of the orders against him were rescinded. By 1929 he had again, however, established himself rather firmly in Bavaria and Thuringia, though he had lost heavily at the 1928 election. The youth of the country this time was rallying to his banner, especially the university students of both sexes who could find no commercial opening after taking their degrees. In 1930 Dr. Brüning, by a pardonable miscalculation, gave Hitler his first big opportunity. He dissolved the Reichstag in order to get a mandate for the Young plan. Hitler, to his own great surprise, scored a triumph and found himself at the head of a new great political party which sent 107 Deputies to the Reichstag. In 1928 his small party of twenty-five had dwindled to twelve, and the prospects seemed gloomy. In two
80 years the whole situation had completely changed. In October 1931 Hitler was received for the first time by the President as a notable political leader. He refused to join the Brüning coalition, and in 1932 stood against Hindenburg himself for the presidency of the Reich, having acquired German citizenship by obtaining a sinecure at the Brunswick Legation in Berlin. The country was then treated to an exhibition of electioneering of a new kind, in the course of which Hitler's inexhaustible energy and talent as a stump orator was displayed to the full. He polled 36·8 per cent. of the electorate, and though defeated, had electrified German politics and compelled his political opponents to exert every ounce of energy to defeat him. President von Hindenburg fought his campaign
90 with the help of a powerful political syndicate, which included all the moderate parties and the Social Democrats.

The remainder of Hitler's career is identical with the internal political development of Germany since the presidential election of 1932. Disaster again threatened him in the winter of 1932. After gaining 230 seats at the general election in July of that year, he lost thirty-four seats in November. Through the intrigues of Herr von Papen he was, nevertheless, offered the Chancellorship, and his appointment as Chancellor on the 31st January, 1933, so encouraged his followers that they seized the occasion to stage a revolution, which ended in the complete seizure of Germany and the identification of the State with national
100 socialism.

The death of Hindenburg in August 1934 came at a convenient time for Hitler, who was able, at a moment when he badly needed an accession of moral authority, to assume the title of Führer und Reichskanzler and become the Commander-in-chief of the armed forces of the Reich.

Hitler is a man of simple tastes, a vegetarian for health reasons, a non-smoker and teetotaller. Possessed of extraordinary vitality, four hours' sleep and twenty hours' work make up his normal working day. He is constantly on the move, usually by aeroplane or fast car. He manages to spend most week-ends at a little châlet in the Bavarian hills, the property of his sister. The profit on the
110 enormous sales of *Mein Kampf* alone has made Hitler a rich man. He dislikes ceremony, and is only at his ease among his intimates, Hess, Brückner, &c.

As a speaker, Hitler exercises astonishing sway over a German audience, presumably because public speaking is an unknown art in Germany. His speeches are practically repetitions of a few simple main theses, in the course of which platitudes are uttered with such extraordinary emphasis that an unsophisticated audience mistakes them for newly minted political aphorisms. He has sized up the German audience during his fifteen years of apprenticeship with astonishing accuracy. This and an undeniable political instinct have brought him to the top of the tree.

In appearance Hitler is unprepossessing, but is said to possess a certain
120 charm of manner. Beyond an unfortunate love affair, in the course of which the object of his choice, a Munich lady of good social standing, rejected his suit, Hitler seems to have had little to do with the fair sex.

The Young plan: the plan to reduce German reparations for the Great War. In many Germans' eyes it did not reduce them enough

2 WHY WAS HITLER SO POPULAR IN GERMANY?

Before 1929 Hitler's Nazi party had little power in Germany. Then in 1929 a terrible economic depression began. It affected Europe and America very badly. Businesses went bankrupt and people lost their jobs. By 1933 Hitler was Chancellor (Prime Minister) of Germany. Do you think these two events were connected?

SOURCE 1 ▽

Number of votes for Hitler's Nazi party and German unemployment figures 1928–1936.

	Votes	Unemployment
1928	800,000	
1929	6,400,000	1,320,000
1931		3,000,000
1932	13,700,000	4,350,000
1936		1,000,000

1 Draw two line graphs to show the figures in Source 1. Use a scale of 1 cm per 100,000.

2 Describe the relationship between the number of people voting for Hitler's Nazi party and the number of people unemployed.

3 For each group mentioned in Source 2 – the peasants, the workers, the bourgeoisie, the industrialists – say what benefits and what problems the Nazi régime has brought for them. Support your answers with reference to Source 2.

4 Which group seems to have benefited the most from Hitler's régime? Give reasons.

5 What evidence is there in Sources 1 and 2 that Hitler was popular because of what he had done about unemployment?

SOURCE 2 ▷

A report by a British official from the Foreign Office on his visit to Germany in July 1937.

(a) The peasants.

Grumble, as everywhere, but are not doing at all badly in reality, thanks to liberal Government support. There is no suggestion in the German country side of that grinding proverty so noticeable in, for instance, the South of Italy.

(b) The workers.

Have a very low wage, and live under a semi-military system. On the other hand they have considerable security (owing to the practical abolition of unemployment), and have a good deal done for them in the way of organised amusements. The policy of the Government seems to be to keep labour so fully occupied at work or play, that there is little time for discussion and reflexion on the present state of Germany. Some of the Germans said that there was a great deal of dis-content under the surface but the only positive sign of this was expressed by a foreman from a textile factory at Bentheim (close to the Dutch frontier) who said that he wanted to come to England, that he was tired of "Mussolini", and all the workmen were under-paid. In individual concerns there may be but on the whole, and particularly among the younger generation, I should say that there was little grave dissatisfaction. Everybody seemed to like the "Arbeitsdienst", which is supposed - not incorrectly perhaps - to be laying the foundations for the "classless society" of to-morrow.

(c) The Bourgeoisie.

Are on the whole nervous and apprehensive, both in regard to the possibility of the Government involving the nation in war and in regard to the ultimate effects of Nazi policy on savings and private property generally. It is among the middle and lower bourgeoisie, too, that the lack of liberty is chiefly resented and the difficulty of studying for the higher professions with the interruptions of Nazi demonstrations, Labour service and military service, are most acutely felt.

(d) The Industrialists.

The employers, as a class, have more to thank the Government for; and though they are perhaps equally apprehensive, and often very critical of the Régime, they obtain very definite benefits from the regimentation of the workers and the denial of the right to strike. This compensates them to some extent for the regulations and restriction of profits:

Arbeitsdienst: literally, duty to work. It was part of the Nazi solution to unemployment.
bourgeoisie: the middle classes

SOURCE 3 ▷

A report by Miss Rinder, a British visitor to Germany in December 1937. She was a private visitor, but she passed on her impressions of Germany to an official in the Foreign Office.

1 What similarities does Miss Rinder see between Germany and Russia?

2 How has the Hitler Youth organization helped Hitler's popularity?

3 Why was Miss Rinder depressed?

4 This indeed, struck her as one of the chief features of the regime.   Every German was now taught to believe – and often did genuinely believe – that conditions in foreign countries, including this country, were immeasurably worse than in Germany;   and any evidence to the contrary was immediately suppressed, if possible.   (There is here, of course, a close parallel with Russia).   The general, state of ignorance and muddled thinking, indeed, among even the educated classes filled her with dismay and alarm;   and she found young men trained in the special "Schools for Leaders" attached to the Hitler Youth, who told her seriously that when they left the Hitler Youth at the age of thirty they would be fit to occupy any position, however responsible, in any branch of life.

In general, Miss Rinder came away depressed over the future prospects for the peace of Europe.   She found the whole younger generation of Germans being taught that they were a chosen people with a sacred right to expand at the expense of others; and, to judge from some of the school and university textbooks which she saw at Frau Gärtner's, no limit seemed to be placed to this expansion, even Alsace-Lorraine, which Hitler is supposed to have definitely renounced being marked as a German irredenta, which must be recovered in the future.   I quoted to her the poem from "Punch" in 1870, cited in one of Sir Robert Vansittart's memoranda:

"What is the German Fatherland?
"Come children, take your maps in hand,
"And see if you can tell me what
"The German Fatherland is not"—

and She said that this expressed only too well her own feeling about present Nazi aims.

L. Colker
December 16th.

P.S. I hope Frau Gärtner will not be allowed to come back to this country.

Frau Gärtner: Miss Rinder's (pro-Nazi) host in Germany
irredenta: former territory to be recovered

SOURCE 4

Notes attached to Miss Rinder's report by two Foreign Office officials.

1 Do the comments in Source 4 suggest that Miss Rinder is a reliable or unreliable witness of conditions in Germany?

A

Visitors' impressions of Germany seem to be entirely subjective. Either they see everything through rose-coloured spectacles, e.g. Lord Londonderry & the others quoted by Miss Rinder or, like Miss Rinder herself, they are suspicious & naturally find grounds to justify their suspicions. In her case Frau Görtner has wasted her time & Nazi money.

B

Personally I shd. say that Miss Rinder's impressions were pretty accurate. They coincide to a large extent with those which I recorded after my own visit to Germany in July

(C8138/165/18 - 1937)

I spent yesterday evening in a bierstube in HOF with a stonemason from Breslau and a commercial traveller from Leipzig. They were both ardent supporters of the Party, and the stonemason had been a S.A. man in the early days and had lost most of his teeth in a fracas with communists. He had secured a good job in Hof where he had arrived only a few days ago, but he had just had orders to go to Nuremberg for work in connection with the next Parteitag. This did not suit him at all, but he was quite resigned about it as it was for the good of the Party.

The men were complete strangers to each other. They were very communicative, and as they agreed on almost every subject that we discussed their views probably represent the feelings of the rank and file of the Party in Silesia and Saxony.

Both of them were very National and very Socialist. They were enthusiastic about the Anschluss and were quite convinced that the Sudeten would be absorbed by the end of this year. They agreed that life in Germany at the moment was far from ideal and that RM 45 per month was too much to ask the stonemason to pay in taxes out of a salary of only RM 260. On the other hand they were prepared to put up with this sort of thing and a great deal more besides for the following reasons. Firstly, the fact that now there was work for everyone. Secondly, because capitalism was disappearing in Germany. Thirdly, on account of the Winterhilfe which they regarded as a marvellous insitution. And fourthly, for the reason that the Jews were at last getting their deserts. They both considered that the greatest and most important role of National Socialism was its fight against the Jewish race.

Their hopes that Germany and England would ever come to a satisfactory understanding so long as England had a democratic Government were very faint. They argued that England must inevitably be governed by the Left, who were friendly with France and Moscow, or by the Right, who were under the influence of the old aristocracy. As the English aristocracy were some 90% Jew there was no hope in this direction.

Between them they could only produce one point in England's favour. They had both had experience of foreign troops in Germany after the war. They were most eulogistic about the British troops with whom they had come into contact, and said their behaviour had always been very correct, friendly and gentlemanly. Their remarks about the French troops were unprintable.

Bierstube: bar
SA man: a member of the Nazi party army
Parteitag: Nazi party day

RM: Reichsmark, the German currency
Winterhilfe: system of government payments made to relieve suffering in winter
eulogistic: full of praise for

◁SOURCE 5
A report by Colonel F.R. MacFarlane on a conversation he had in a bar in Germany in April 1938. The conversation took place shortly after the *Anschluss* (the union of Germany with Austria).

1 Source 5 gives various reasons for Hitler's popularity. Underline any that you can find.

2 Choose the two most important reasons and explain your choice.

3 What do the men not like about Germany under Hitler?

4 Does this conversation support or contradict Miss Rinder's view (Source 3) that people in Germany are badly informed about life in other countries? Explain your answer.

5 Using Sources 1–5 and your wider knowledge about life in Hitler's Germany, write an essay entitled 'Why was Hitler popular in Germany in the 1930s'?

3 GERMAN REARMAMENT

The Treaty of Versailles which followed the First World War limited the German army to 100,000 soldiers and the German navy to 36 ships. The Treaty also forbade the Germans to have an air force. Within three days of coming to power in 1933, Hitler told his military commanders that he was going to rearm Germany.

Between 1933 and 1935 rearmament was secret. Then early in 1935 Hitler held a 'Proclamation of Freedom to Rearm' rally. In March army conscription was reintroduced, and in June Germany signed a Naval Agreement with Britain which allowed Germany to expand its navy.

SOURCE 1 ▽

A telegram from the British embassy in Berlin on 16 March 1935, the day Hitler announced the start of conscription. An Italian official, Signor Suvich, had put forward proposals for how to respond to the German announcement.

From GERMANY.   1

Decypher.   Sir E. Phipps (Berlin).   **150**

Signor Suvich's proposal arouses my misgivings.
If we threaten Hitler and he continues to flout us
his position will become stronger than ever and he may
openly denounce the entire Treaty.   Again it seems
unwise to form a "military bloc" unless we be all
agreed in advance as to our demands in case he yields
or alternatively we be all prepared to go to war if he
does not yield.

He practically says that he will be content with 500,000
men if Russia stands pat with 1,000,000 and France has
two years service.   He also agrees to what amounts to
a 2 to 1 margin of superiority for France and ourselves
in the air and he claims a third of our naval tonnage or
parity with France at sea.   Moreover control has not
been ruled out.

---

1 Read Source 1. With a partner, try to work out what Signor Suvich's proposal might have been.

2 Which Treaty is being talked about in line 4?

3 What size does Hitler claim he intends the new German army to be?

4 Does the writer seem more worried about the German announcement or the proposals of Signor Suvich? Explain your answers.

MARCH 17, **Sunday Dispatch** 1935.

HITLER TELLS WHY HE HAS STARTED CONSCRIPTION

SOURCE 2 ▽

From an article in *The Times*, 1 July 1935, reporting a speech by the British Prime Minister.

To many of us, who remember it too well—to those of us who remember the race in naval armaments before the War between this country and Germany, and who remember how the whole atmosphere was poisoned by this naval rivalry, the news that, as the result of Herr Hitler's offer, a permanent and fixed relationship between the German and British Fleets at 35 to 100 had been established must come as a great relief and a great gratification. And the announcement made by the German representatives during the recent naval discussions that Germany independently of the action of other Powers would never again resort to what we call unrestricted submarine warfare must be a matter of genuine satisfaction.

GERMANY'S HONOURABLE MOTIVES

I regret profoundly observations from one or two members in the House of Commons that you cannot trust the Germans to keep their word. When you are trying to negotiate limitation of armaments or disarmament, what can you do if you do not trust? You revert straight to the law of the jungle and no progress is possible. The Germans and ourselves entered into this, in my belief, with equally honourable motives, and I rejoice to think that they as well as ourselves are in favour of the complete abolition of the submarine.

---

5 Read Source 2. What has happened since Source 1 was written?

6 Under the Naval Agreement, what restrictions were placed on the German navy?

7 The British Prime Minister wants to avoid an 'arms race'. Explain what an arms race is, and draw up a list of reasons why Europe might want to avoid one.

By the Treaty of Versailles Germany could not have any soldiers or armaments in the border area with France – the Rhineland. This was known as the 'demilitarisation' of the Rhineland.

On 7 March 1936 Hitler sent his troops into the Rhineland. On 14 March officials from France, Italy, Belgium and Britain met to discuss what to do.

SOURCE 1 ▷ A telegram written by a British representative on 14 March 1936 reporting on discussions between the four 'Locarno Powers' (France, Italy, Belgium, Britain). It begins with the view of Monsieur Paul Boncour, a French spokesman.

1 Work in groups. Draw up a list of arguments for and against the following options:
a) to invade the Rhineland and force out the German troops
b) to threaten invasion if the German troops do not withdraw
c) to introduce economic sanctions if the German troopsdo not withdraw
d) to let the German troops stay, but draw up a new agreement to keep peace on the French border.

2 Read Source 1. Underline in three different colours sentences which describe the opinions of the French, the British and the Belgian representatives. Which of the options discussed in question 1 do
a) France
b) Britain
c) Belgium
seem to favour?

In his view it was quite indispensable that the German troops should be withdrawn from the Rhineland as a preliminary to negotiations. We told Monsieur Paul-Boncour that in our view the policy which he put forward might well result in war. We believed that the German Chancellor could not withdraw from the Rhineland all the troops which he had put into it. To ask him to do so was to court refusal with all the consequences; more particularly since Monsieur Boncour himself had visualised successive stages of economic, financial and military sanctions. We added that we were convinced that British public opinion was not prepared to go to war in order that the Germans should be compelled to go out of the Rhineland one week and be allowed to come into it the next. In the view of the British public it would not be worth the number of British lives.

Monsieur Flandin explained that even if military sanctions were reached it was not necessarily intended to attack the Rhineland if effective economic and financial sanctions together with a blockade might suffice for the purpose in the present depressed condition that exists in German industry and finance. We, however, maintained our attitude that to demand the complete evacuation of the Rhineland was to ask for refusal. This view was supported by Belgian Prime Minister, whose attitude was that it was essential to put before the Germans an offer which was moderate in their eyes and in the eyes of the world. If the German Government refused to accept that offer it would be essential that the Locarno Powers should see the matter through to the end whatever the consequences. Belgian Prime Minister laid emphasis upon there being agreement to do this among the Locarno Powers before the process was begun.

3 In both 1871 and 1914 German troops had invaded France. Use your knowledge of what happened after 1914 to argue the case that the French are putting forward.

4 The reoccupation of the Rhineland is seen by many historians as the first step in a process that led to the Second World War three years later. What evidence is there in this report to suggest that in 1936 people:
a) feared this event would lead to a war
b) wanted to avoid another war at all costs?

It is February 1936. Britain is anxious about German rearmament. Might Hitler use his army to invade neighbouring countries?

SOURCE 1 ▽

Extracts from a report by Arnold Toynbee on an interview he had with Hitler on 28 February 1936.

A

Herr Hitler gave me an interview the Friday before last(28th February 1936). He spoke for an hour and three-quarters.

B

In talking to me, Hitler covered the whole field of German foreign policy, leading off with his relations with Soviet Russia and then passing over to his relations with England. The points that most struck me in what he said were these:-

(a) His personal mission is to be the saviour from Communism, not only for Germany, but for the whole of Europe.

(b) He feels himself bound to think and act in European terms, and not merely in German terms, because, if the European Powers fall into conflict with one another again, then, in his view, Communism will swamp them all - including his own National-Socialist Germany. Germany, he said, cannot hold out against Communism by herself.

C

And if the English, with their many commitments all over the world, found themselves in need of help, he would then be eager to give it to us, because England's cause would be Europe's cause, and therefore Germany's. (N.B. He meant military help, and he was thinking in very concrete terms. He mentioned "six divisions and some warships!)

D

He disclaimed any ambition to conquer a great empire for Germany in Eastern Europe. This came out very explicitly, because the one word that I got in edge-wise was a question on this point.

He regarded these East-European populations as inferior (minderwertig) and he did not want to have them inside his system. Even if he could conquer them, it would take a permanent garrison of 600,000 German troops to hold them down. The fundamental principle of National-Socialism was to build up a Reich on an exclusively national basis - reuniting the whole German nation, but not including anybody else.

In spite of Mein Kampf and in spite of "the Rosenberg Plan" I have a very strong conviction that, on this rather vital point, Hitler was quite sincere in what he said to me.

He went even further. "I want England's friendship", he said; "And, if you English will make friends with us, you may name your conditions - including, if you like, conditions about Eastern Europe."

E

About Austria he said: "I am not bothering myself, because Austria is bound to fall to us sooner or later." (He produced some figures about the decline in the Austrian birthrate as evidence that Austria was being ruined, socially and morally, by the present regime).

F

He mentioned Japan quite early in the interview, a propos of Russia. He knew, he said, that one of the things that was making the English take a more friendly line towards Russia was our anxiety over the present imperialistic policy of Japan. But if we wanted a friend in need against Japan, why should that friend be Russia? Why should it not be Germany?

G

The weakness of Hitler's position is that he has always to be playing a dramatic part in the sight of his own German audience. Up to now, his role has been that of the champion against Bolshevism. This role is dangerous internationally, because it compels Hitler to go on saying and doing things which antagonise the Russians, and frighten them more and more.

H

My impression is that he has begun to realise the danger, here, of a disastrous smash, and that he is eager now to change his role and to appear as "the good European" and "the associate of England" - allowing his anti-Russian role to fall into the background. This would be an alternative way, for him, of getting the prestige and justification, on his home front, that he simply must have, in some form or other. If he can get it in a way that might lead to peace instead of to war, I believe he would be vastly relieved.

I therefore believe that any response from the English side to his overtures for our friendship would produce an enormous counter-response to us from Hitler.

A

(Minutes.) ... *and* 28/7 Knowing Mr Toynbee personally, I have great respect for his learning ~~Crawford~~. AR. 26/3

L.C.C. but none for his judgment. 16/3

March 25

B

Both Mr Toynbee and Mr Howard Price suggest that much can be achieved by treating Herr Hitler with courtesy and be "response from the English side to his overtures".

Twice in the last 15 months he have made two separate series of the most obvious advances to him, that of February 1935 produced the conscription decree. That of this autumn & winter ended in the reoccupation of the Rhineland.

R.F.Wigram c.20/3
16/3

Copy Berlin

11648

Sargent March 18

March 18

We do our best. I fear + think we are always courteous.

SOURCE 2

The reaction of Ministers in the British government to Mr Toynbee's report.

1 Work in groups of five. Each member of the group should take one of the following subjects. Decide, using the evidence in Source 1, what Hitler's attitude is towards your subject.
  a) Communism
  b) Austria
  c) Japan
  d) Britain
  e) Eastern Europe.

2 In Mr Toynbee's opinion, how should Britain treat Hitler?

3 Write one paragraph of advice for the British government about whether or not they should be worried about Germany's plans.

4 Just a few days after the interview in Source 1 Hitler sent his troops into the Rhineland area of Germany – breaking one of the basic agreements of the Treaty of Versailles

You are a minister in the British goverment and have just received this report. Write a note to go with it to the Prime Minister stating what you now think of its proposals.

5 What does the handwritten note initialled 'LC' (Source 2A) say about Mr Toynbee?

6 What does R.F. Wigram (Source 2B) think is the result of treating Hitler with courtesy?

During the 1930s many people in Europe were more afraid of Communism than they were of Fascism. In 1936 an 'Anti-Comintern' pact had been signed between Germany and Japan. In 1937 Italy signed it too. They promised to help each other in the fight against Communism around the world.

I think it desirable that the various

Governments which ~~might~~ *may* be contemplating joining

the anti-Comintern <u>bloc</u> or ~~to whom it~~ *who* may be

to receive

expected an invitation to join ~~might be ex-~~

~~tended~~ should be ~~be~~ discreetly reminded of

H.M.G.'s dislike of ideological <u>blocs</u>.

While you should not go out of your way

to raise the subject, I shall be glad therefore

if you will take advantage of any suitable

opening to make clear to the Government to

which you are accredited how much H.M.G. in the

United Kingdom dislike and distrust the

formation of such <u>blocs</u>, which only tend to

divide the world into hostile camps and obstruct

the promotion of peace and *international* co-operation.

Addressed to Vienna No. 10 , to Prague No 15

to Belgrade No. 20 , to Bucharest No. 17 , to

Sofia No. 6 , to Durazzo No. 2 , to Budapest

No. 11 , to Berne No. 7 , to Athens No. 22

to ~~Lisbon~~ *Warsaw* No. 12

HMG: His Majesty's Government (ie the British government)
Durazzo: former name for Durrës

SOURCE 1

A memorandum from the British Foreign Office to its representatives around Europe.

1 This telegram was sent to 10 countries in Europe. The capital cities of these countries are listed in the last paragraph. Find out from an atlas which the countries were. On the blank map of Europe below shade:
  a) members of the 'Anti-Comintern' pact in one colour
  b) Russia (a Communist country) in another colour
  c) other countries mentioned in Source 1 in a third colour.

2 Why do you think the British government approached these countries in particular?

3 Why do you think the British government was opposed to 'the formation of such blocs'? Think about:
  a) events that led to the First World War
  b) the state of Europe in 1937.

A report by Mr Law, a British businessman about the state of Germany in July 1937.

1 Look at the following statements and read Source 1 carefully.
- Germany is ready for a revolution against Hitler
- The German economy is thriving
- Food is in short supply
- Germans blame their problems on other countries
- Germans have no free time
- German rearmament is increasing in speed
- Unemployment is widespread
- The Jews are suffering badly.

a) Tick the statements which seem to be correct, and indicate what line of Source 1 supports this.

b) Cross out those statements that seem to be incorrect. Write an alternative statement and indicate the evidence in Source 1 that supports your view.

I have just looked up the letter I wrote to you on November 18th.
last year on my return from a somewhat similar journey undertaken for
the same purpose.   Once more I do not propose to give you statistics
or definite facts.   All I can do is to describe the general impression

5 which the country made on me.   Shortly I found very little change.
If the people did not look quite so depressed one can, I think,
attribute the fact to the difference of season.   When I was there
before it was dark and wet.   This time it was fine and very hot.
Last time too I was mainly in the distressed industrial area of

10 Chemnitz.   This time I drove through the smiling orchards and corn-
fields of Southern Germany where it is more difficult to realise that
the Nazi poison has pentrated.   Nevertheless I heard that there is as
much discontent as ever, only that it is a more passive, hopeless
discontent.   There is no thought of changing the régime.   Only an

15 unsuccessful war or a revolution could do that, and there is no nucleus
round which hostile forces could concentrate.   Moreover the thought
of a revolution is to most people even more repugnant than the
continuance of the present régime.   For the vast majority of the
population all their ills are due to the foreign exchange crisis and

20 to the fact that they lost the war.   It is not without significance
that there is no leisure in Germany.   If you are not working you are
marching or singing or attending meetings of your particular "front" -
arbeiter-front or whatnot.   There is no time even to fish; for the
sale of fishing apparatus in the shops has fallen almost to zero.

25 Therefore community grumbling has been abolished.

It seems fairly certain that
there has been a certain slackening in the pace of rearmament and
that this is due to the need of imports of food and of raw material
for goods destined for the export market.   Butter and fats are still

30 rationed and other foodstuffs tend to deteriorate in quality because
the workers cannot afford to buy the same quality as formerly.

The pressure on the Jews goes on unrelentingly although the
Nuremberg laws are supposed to have regulated their position.   It
is difficult for a Jew to keep his job.   Virtually impossible to

35 get a new one.   To an unknown number of unemployed Jews must be
added 970,000 men and women over 40 years of age who are workless.
Of these it is proposed to force 140,000 into industry and commerce
by telling each firm how many extra employees over 40 must be taken
on.   Theoretically young workers may be displaced to make room for

40 old ones, but as the older workers are usually married and have
therefore to be paid higher wages the extra expense often turns a
profit into a loss.

arbeiter-front: workers' group

SOURCE 2 ▷

Further extracts from Mr Law's report, July 1937.

1 Read Source 2. Why in Mr Law's opinion is Hitler dangerous?

2 In lines 60–61 of the report, someone has changed the wording of Mr Law's report before the Cabinet read it.
a) What does the original wording suggest was Mr Law's opinion of appeasement?
b) How has the new wording changed the opinion?
c) Why do you think this change was made?

3 The report in Sources 1 and 2 is going to be circulated to the Cabinet with some notes indicating where it came from and why the Cabinet should take note of it. Write these notes. You might also include your own advice on whether the government should follow:
a) a policy of rearmament
b) a policy of appeasing Hitler.

I am told, on what I believe to be very good German authority, that really the most dangerous man of all is the Führer
45 himself. He falls into fits of passion and will listen to no advice. It was on his orders and against the advice of the Foreign Office and the army that recently an American was beheaded. It was again on his direct orders and before he could receive any advice that the bombardment of Almeria took place.
50 If this is true - as I believe it to be - the picture is not a cheerful one. Noone wants war, certainly, but when you have a passionate lunatic at the top who still commands the devotion of the populace and who is evidently prepared to run great risks, then already the situation is dangerous. But when, besides that, the
55 Russian army appears not exactly at the height of its efficiency, when (as it is believed in Germany) France is tottering on the edge of communism and Franco is at the gates of Bilbao, then we ought to be on our guard.
I was told in Berlin that another publicity campaign was
60 contemplated in England by ~~the usual~~ those English people who are ~~make-some-concessions-shake-the-~~ advocating close relations with Germany. ~~hand-of-our-German-cousins group.)~~ This I am informed both by Englishmen in Berlin and by patriotic Germans who do not like Nazism would be at this juncture a most disastrous mistake. No further advances should be made to Germany at the present time. Germany
65 is beginning to be impressed by our rearmament. There is a hope that when she finds the pace too hot she may be prepared to change her ways, but any advance towards her now will be taken as a sign of weakness and will nullify all the restraining effect of the steps we are now taking at such great financial cost. My friends were
70 most insistent on the capital importance of preventing the launching of any friendly campaign accompanied by vague talk of concessions. England has stated her terms, they say, let her abide by them, remaining polite but firm. This attitude and this attitude alone will be understood by the present rulers of Germany.

bombardment of Almeria: a bomb attack in the Spanish Civil War

3 Count Bernstorff said that Herr Hitler has lately been more frequently subject to fits, in the course of which he foams at the mouth and becomes very violent. One such fit occurred a short time ago when he drove through Munich and saw that the rebuilding which he had planned was not progressing as fast as he had expected. On being told that the reason was the lack of iron and steel, he developed a fit and became so violent that he had to be restrained by his A.D.C's till a doctor could be sent for to give him a sedative injection. Herr Hitler's main occupation nowadays is town-planning and he plays about all day long with models of Berlin, Nuremburg and Munich. He takes practically no interest in anything else. None of his Ministers, except Goebbels and Goering, can be certain of access to him.

A.D.C's: aides-de-camp, i.e. assistants

◁ SOURCE 3

Report on a conversation with Count Bernstorff, a German opposed to the Nazi régime.

4 Read Source 3. Do Sources 2 and 3 give a similar view of Hitler?

5 Does this make them reliable sources?

6 Why might Sources 2 or 3 be unreliable in telling us what Hitler was really like?

Comments of officials from the British Foreign Office on the reports in Sources 1–3.

A

If Mr. Law's story of the increasing irresponsibility of Hitler is true - and it is largely borne out by what Count Bernstorff recently told Mr. Stevenson (that paper has been submitted separately) - then the general view he expresses at the end of his letter that this is not the moment to make advances to Germany is a justified one; if a man cannot be trusted in his sane moments, he should be trusted even less when he develops into what Mr. Law calls a "passionate lunatic".

We know, moreover, that the Germans are impressed by our rearmament, and what Mr. Law writes at the top of page 2 about the slackening of German rearmament because of the need for food-imports is the same as what Mr. Gainer has reported (in C 4002).   These two factors together represent a decline in Germany's military position vis-à-vis us, as seen from the German side.   Since Hitler is already "prepared to run great risks", any appearance that this decline is being averted or reversed would be just the thing to encourage him to dangerous courses, given his present lunatic state.

An earlier letter from Mr. Law (C 8176 - 1936) was shown to certain members of the Cabinet. It may be held desirable to do the same with this one or with a part of it, and to draw attention to the fact that the view expressed by Mr. Law at the end of it is shared by Englishmen in Berlin and by patriotic anti-Nazi Germans.

A. Rumbold
18/6

B

I don't quite know what Mr. Law's friends mean when they say "England has stated her terms ... let her abide by them".

It is always a difficult question to decide how to deal with a "passionate lunatic". If he is really past humouring, a strait jacket is the best thing, but I don't know that we are in a position to resort to this remedy.

O.S.
June 23, 1937

1 According to the typed note (A) in Source 4, how is British rearmament progressing?

2 You have been asked by the British government to prepare notes for them on whether Hitler can be trusted. They have Sources 1–4 but they want you to give a longer term view. Your report should indicate your views on the following:
   a) Does Hitler tell the truth?
   b) Does Hitler keep his promises?

Anschluss is a German word meaning 'union'. On 12 March 1938 Hitler sent German troops into Austria and united Austria with Germany.

> I have therefore decided to place the help of the Reich at the disposal of the millions of Germans in Austria. Since this morning the soldiers of the German armed forces have been marching across all the German-Austrian frontiers! Mechanised troops, infantry divisions and S.S. troops on the ground and squadrons of German aeroplanes in the blue heavens—summoned by the new National Socialist régime itself in Vienna—will be a guarantee that the Austrian people will at last in the near future have the opportunity, by means of a real plebiscite, to decide for itself its future destiny. Behind these troops stand the will and the determination of the whole German nation.
>
> I myself, as leader and Chancellor of the German people, will be happy once more as a German and free citizen to visit again that country, which is also my home. But the world may rest assured that the German people in Austria in these days are living hours of deepest joy and exultation.
>
> They see in the brothers hastening to their help the saviours from their deepest need. Long live the National Socialist German Reich! Long live National Socialist Austria!
>
> *March* 12, 1938.

◁ SOURCE 1

Hitler's proclamation, broadcast at 12.00 midday on 12 March on all German and Austrian radio stations.

1 Read Source 1. Why does Hitler say he has sent troops into Austria?

2 Does he think he has the support of the Austrians?

SOURCE 2 ▷

A report written by an official of the British Embassy in Berlin about the attitude of German people to the *Anschluss*.

3 According to Source 2, what was the most obvious result of the *Anschluss*?

4 Why should the *Anschluss* increase Hitler's popularity?

5 In lines 13–21, Source 2 lists a number of consequences for Germany of the *Anschluss* with Austria. Write each one on a separate card. Using all that you know about this period in history, put these in an order of importance for:
 a) Hitler
 b) the British government
 c) People in Germany
 d) Germans living in Austria.

British Consulate General,

Munich.

24th March 1938.

Sir,

So far as Germany herself is concerned the most obvious result of the Anschluss has been to increase Herr Hitler's personal prestige and popularity, which were already approaching perilously near to a
5 worship, religious in its fervour.

2. The plebiscite which will take place on the 10th April cannot but show an overwhelming majority in favour of Herr Hitler's action. The issue upon which this plebiscite is to be taken is in fact already decided and
10 the plebiscite will merely endorse the decision and can change nothing. The great majority of Germans in all walks of life and of all shades of political opinion approve of the Anschluss. Greater Germany has become a fact; six and a half million people have been added to
15 Germany's population; the area of Germany is now greater than before the war; stocks of gold and foreign currency have fallen into Germany's hands, as also raw materials, minerals, and agricultural products; the military strength of Germany has received a valuable addition; German
20 influence in Eastern and South Eastern Europe, both political and economic, cannot but enormously increase. What people when asked to approve of this could respond otherwise than with 'Yes', even were the plebiscite to be held under conditions which would satisfy democratic ideas ?

plebiscite: referendum

5.   One factor is perhaps more disquieting
than the German peoples' approval of the end and that is
its approval of the means used to attain that end. From
the very day that action against Austria was inaugurated a
5 campaign was started in the press and wireless in order to
educate the people to approve also of the methods. No
people is today more ignorant of the views of the outside
world than is the German people; no people can more easily
be made to believe what its Government wishes to believe.

10 6.   The sinister aspect of the case is,
however, that the more forward spirits of the N.S.D.A.P.
have been proved to be right. Cautious and moderate
influences have suffered eclipse. The forward policy
has been vindicated and doubters have been won over. If
15 another moment comes when Germany claims that the
interests of the German race are involved she may be
tempted and will be strongly urged to repeat the
experiment. Rearmament, the denunciation of the Treaty
of Locarno, and the Anschluss are major instances of the
20 piecemeal destruction of the Treaty of Versailles. None
of these changes in the status quo has been negotiated
though the possibility and the machinery for so doing
have always existed. All these questions have been
solved by unilateral action on Germany's part and the
25 last by a definite show of armed force. The temptation
to tear up the remaining paragraphs of the Treaty of
Versailles in the same way must be overwhelming.
7.   It is,however,unlikely that the danger
is immediate unless a sudden emergency arise. None of the
30 blows above mentioned has been struck without careful
preparation although in the case of Austria the moment
came sooner than had been expected and planned. Austria
has first to be fully absorbed. There are grave problems
to be solved there, problems of an economic, financial,
35 political and administrative nature, before the time can
become ripe for another move. Europe should be able to
obtain a breathing space in which to prepare – for what ?
For war or to set in train negotiations designed to solve
by more civilised means those European questions which
40 Germany intends shall be solved in one way or another ?
8.   A doubt must, however, arise as to the
ability of modern Germany to negotiate – undue exercise
of strength in the past may have brought impotence in that
respect in its train, and other methods have been shown
45 to be highly efficacious and incomparably speedier.
                I have the honour to be,
                        Sir,
        Your Excellency's most obedient servant,
                (Sd) D. St. Clair Gainer

◁ SOURCE 3

A further extract from the report to the British government about German attitudes to the *Anschluss*.

1 Highlight in one colour all the opinions expressed in Sources 2 and 3. Highlight any facts in Sources 2 and 3 in another colour.

2 Study the statement in lines 6–9 of Source 3. Do you think this is a fact or an opinion? Explain your choice.

3 What other evidence might you look for to find out whether this statement was fact or opinion?

4 List the examples given of Hitler's breaking of the Treaty of Versailles (lines 18–20).

5 Does the writer expect that Hitler will break the remaining elements of the Treaty of Versailles?

6 After the *Anschluss* Hitler held a plebiscite (a referendum) so that all Germans and Austrians could vote on whether they approved of it. Write a speech for Hitler to give on the morning of the plebiscite telling German people why they should vote 'Yes'.

THE SUMMER AND AUTUMN OF '38: ARP AND MUNICH

It is July 1938. Over the past six months, international tension has risen sharply. In March Austria was united with Germany. Germany and Britain are rearming fast. Now Hitler is making no secret of his plans to incorporate the German-speaking part of Czechoslovakia (the *Sudetenland*) into Germany.

You and your family live in London, in a house like the one in Source 1. You have just received your weekly copy of the *Illustrated London News* for 16 July 1938. It contains a special feature on air raid precautions, including the drawings and adverts in Sources 1 and 2. Study the information carefully. How do you react?

SOURCE 1 ▷

Extracts from the *Illustrated London News*, 16 July 1938.

1 Source 1B is a drawing of a 'refuge room'. With a partner, see how many of the numbered items you can identify.

2 Why would each item be needed if an air raid came?

3 What else might you need?

HORRIBLE but Possible !

that your windows may one day be shattered by a bomb explosion . . . Vicious fragments will fly about the room . . . poison gas will have ready entry through the gap.

IT IS WISE TO FIT ONE ROOM WITH **INDESTRUCTO** LAMINATED GLASS

which will keep the room entirely gas-proof

A REAL PROTECTION FOR ANY BUILDING

Write for full particulars to the Advisory Dept. of

BRITISH INDESTRUCTO GLASS, Ltd., Park Royal Rd., Willesden, N.W.10

◁ SOURCE 2

Advertisements from the *Illustrated London News*, 16 July 1938.

4 Write a page of dialogue between members of the family who have read the special feature. Include their views on:

a) why the magazine is running this air raid feature

b) why war is possible

c) what, if any, air-raid precautions they will take.

EVERYTHING FOR SAFETY EVERYWHERE
AIR RAID PRECAUTIONS EQUIPMENT

GENERAL CIVILIAN RESPIRATORS

CIVILIAN DUTY RESPIRATORS

GENERAL SERVICE RESPIRATORS

PROTECTIVE CLOTHING

STEEL HELMETS

FIRST AID OUTFITS

OXYGEN ADMINISTRATION APPARATUS

GAS SMELLING SAMPLES

STEEL STRETCHERS

REDHILL CONTAINERS

STIRRUP PUMPS

All materials for Gas-Proofing Rooms, etc., etc.

Manufacturers of breathing apparatus of every description

Established 1819

It is October 1938. You have just received your copy of the *Illustrated London News* for 8 October 1938. It carries the pictures and document in Source 3. The Prime Minister, Neville Chamberlain, has just returned from Munich having signed an agreement with Germany. This agreement stated that Germany was allowed to take over the *Sudetenland*, but that their 'territorial ambitions' must stop there. Chamberlain said that the agreement he had reached with Hitler promised 'peace for our time'.

We, the German Führer and Chancellor and the British Prime Minister, have had a further meeting today and are agreed in recognising that the question of Anglo-German relations is of the first importance for the two countries and for Europe.

We regard the agreement signed last night and the Anglo-German Naval Agreement as symbolic of the desire of our two peoples never to go to war with one another again.

We are resolved that the method of consultation shall be the method adopted to deal with any other questions that may concern our two countries, and we are determined to continue our efforts to remove possible sources of difference and thus to contribute to assure the peace of Europe.

Neville Chamberlain

September 30. 1938.

"I RECOMMEND YOU TO GO HOME AND SLEEP QUIETLY IN YOUR BEDS": MR. CHAMBERLAIN, LOOKING OUT FROM AN UPPER WINDOW OF NO. 10, WITH HIS WIFE, SPEAKING TO AN EXCITED CROWD IN DOWNING STREET. *(Topical.)*

"I HAD ANOTHER TALK WITH HERR HITLER, AND HERE IS A PAPER WHICH BEARS HIS NAME AS WELL AS MINE": THE DOCUMENT MR. CHAMBERLAIN READ AT HESTON. *(Topical.)*

SOURCE 3

From the *Illustrated London News*, 8 October 1938 (the actual caption of the top picture has been removed).

1 Read the document in Source 3. What is Hitler promising?

2 Why do you think British people responded so enthusiastically to the Munich agreement?

3 The photograph at the top of Source 3 has become one of the most famous of this period. Write two captions for it. One caption should be for possible use in this issue of the *Illustrated London News*. The other should be a caption for use in a school history textbook today. Explain the differences between the two captions.

SOURCE 4 ▽
A chart from the *Illustrated London News*, 8 October 1938.

1 Study Source 4 carefully. Below the chart, the *Illustrated London News* had written 'A diary of the crisis'. Working in groups, take one of the following dates from the chart:

a) 12 September 1938
b) 14 September 1938
c) 22 September 1938
d) 26 September 1938
e) 30 September 1938.

Using information from reference books, write a few sentences to explain the political events of this date.

2 Choose one moment in the 'crisis' that you think was a turning point. Explain your choice.

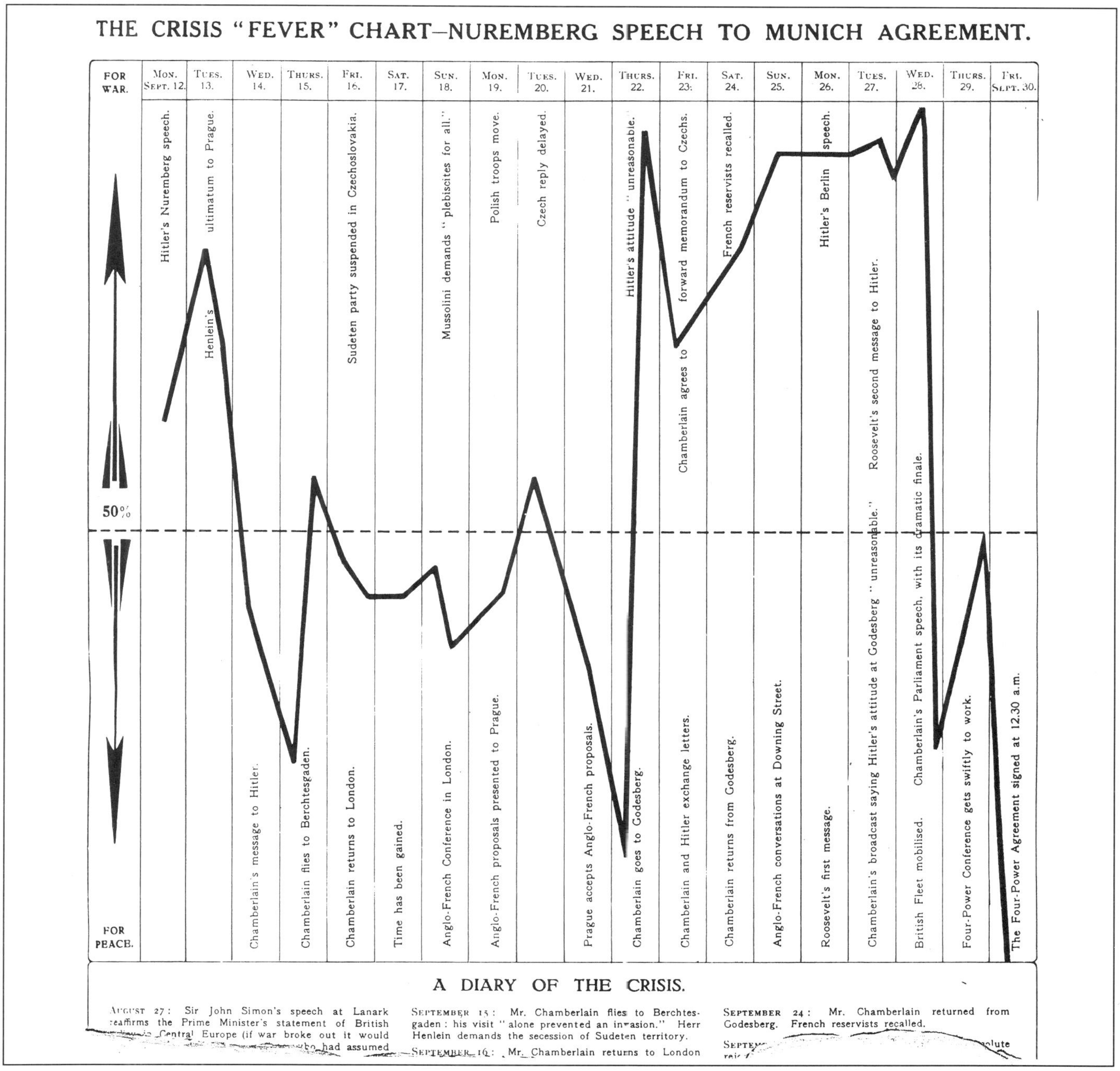

THE CRISIS "FEVER" CHART—NUREMBERG SPEECH TO MUNICH AGREEMENT.

FOR WAR.

| MON. SEPT. 12. | TUES. 13. | WED. 14. | THURS. 15. | FRI. 16. | SAT. 17. | SUN. 18. | MON. 19. | TUES. 20. | WED. 21. | THURS. 22. | FRI. 23. | SAT. 24. | SUN. 25. | MON. 26. | TUES. 27. | WED. 28. | THURS. 29. | FRI. SEPT. 30. |

Hitler's Nuremberg speech.

Henlein's ultimatum to Prague.

Sudeten party suspended in Czechoslovakia.

Mussolini demands "plebiscites for all."

Polish troops move.

Czech reply delayed.

Hitler's attitude "unreasonable."

Chamberlain agrees to forward memorandum to Czechs.

French reservists recalled.

Hitler's Berlin speech.

Roosevelt's second message to Hitler.

Chamberlain's Parliament speech, with its dramatic finale.

50%

Chamberlain's message to Hitler.

Chamberlain flies to Berchtesgaden.

Chamberlain returns to London.

Time has been gained.

Anglo-French Conference in London.

Anglo-French proposals presented to Prague.

Prague accepts Anglo-French proposals.

Chamberlain goes to Godesberg.

Chamberlain and Hitler exchange letters.

Chamberlain returns from Godesberg.

Anglo-French conversations at Downing Street.

Roosevelt's first message.

Chamberlain's broadcast saying Hitler's attitude at Godesberg "unreasonable."

British Fleet mobilised.

Four-Power Conference gets swiftly to work.

The Four-Power Agreement signed at 12.30 a.m.

FOR PEACE.

A DIARY OF THE CRISIS.

AUGUST 27: Sir John Simon's speech at Lanark reaffirms the Prime Minister's statement of British ... Central Europe (if war broke out it would ... had assumed

SEPTEMBER 15: Mr. Chamberlain flies to Berchtesgaden; his visit "alone prevented an invasion." Herr Henlein demands the secession of Sudeten territory.
SEPTEMBER 16: Mr. Chamberlain returns to London

SEPTEMBER 24: Mr. Chamberlain returned from Godesberg. French reservists recalled.
SEPTE... ...olute ...

---

3 Write another page of dialogue between the members of a family living in 1938. Include their views on whether they agree or disagree with Mr Chamberlain that this settlement will bring lasting peace.

SOURCE 1 ▷

A letter from the Duke of Kent's assistant to the Foreign Office, 6 July 1939.

H/xiv/213   Duke of Kent°
7

9. MOTCOMB STREET, S.W.1.

6th July, 1939. 19

Dear Mallet,

The Duke of Kent has asked me to enquire about the question of a summer holiday on the Continent.

His Royal Highness would like to leave London about the 24th or 25th of this month, and wants to stay away for three weeks, or possibly a month. His Royal Highness would like to go to Munich to see his sister-in-law, and then on to Yugoslavia to stay with the Prince Regent. The Duke of Kent might also like to spend a short time in Italy.

I should be most grateful if you would speak to the Secretary of State and find out whether it would be possible for His Royal Highness to take a holiday on these lines.

Yours Sincerely,

John Fowler

Mallet, Esq.,
Foreign Office,
Whitehall, S.W.1.

SOURCE 2 ▽

The government's notes on the Duke of Kent's plans.

I think it would certainly look better if the Duke could omit this year his visit to Munich. Quite apart from the political uncertainty of the international situation, we clearly do not wish to encourage British subjects to spend money in Germany this year and I fear that once it became known that the Duke of Kent was going to Germany it might encourage a great many hesitating British tourists to go to Germany who otherwise would not have done so. The daily German advertisements in the Times calling on British tourists to come to Germany show what great importance the German Government attach to obtaining foreign currency by the process of attracting British tourists to Germany. This in itself is a reason for discouraging British subjects from visiting Germany in the present circumstances.

O.V. Sargent

1 Read Source 1. What do the Duke's holiday plans suggest about the state of affairs in Europe in July 1939?

2 Does this letter surprise you? Give reasons.

3 Read Source 2. What is the Foreign Office most afraid of if the Duke does go to Germany?

4 Write the reply from the Foreign Office to Mr Fowler.

'HE MAY CHANGE HIS MIND TOMORROW': *Poland*

Under the Treaty of Versailles of 1919:
• Germany's army was limited to 100,000 soldiers
• Germany could not have an air force
• Germany could not have troops in the Rhineland
• Germany was forbidden to unite with Austria
• German land was handed over to Poland (Danzig and the 'Polish Corridor')

1 On a map or a timeline, make a summary of the ways that Hitler had broken the terms of the Treaty of Versailles by July 1938.

2 Were any of these terms still unbroken in 1938?

3 Write down the meaning of the following words used in Source 1: *coup; contiguous; equitable*. Use a dictionary if you wish.

4 In your own words, write the meaning of the following phrases: 'He is not prepared to risk his life's work on a single throw' (line 8); 'Danzig cannot be left as a running sore' (line 16); 'In Germany it has become a stalking-horse for the Corridor' (line 25).

SOURCE 1

Extracts from a letter from the British Embassy in Berlin, 17 July 1939.

BRITISH EMBASSY,
BERLIN.
July 17th, 1939.

Dear Secretary of State,

In my telegram No. 406 I endeavoured to sum up, in accordance with the impressions which I derive from the best authorities here, the position as Hitler regards it for the moment. It is an unfortunate fact that he may change his mind tomorrow. Personally however I believe that he realises quite well today that he cannot make another coup without the grave risk of finding half the world in arms against him. He is not prepared to risk his life's work on a single throw. He will consequently move cautiously.

At the same time he is quite determined that in one form or another Danzig shall be reincorporated in Germany. He will never abandon that determination. Nor will anything, I fear, ever convince me that the Poles are not supremely foolish, if they fail to make the best bargain now with Hitler himself that they can. Danzig cannot be

- 2 -

left as a running sore, otherwise, in the end, the Poles will lose the Corridor itself which is a much bigger question than Danzig and one in which the Germans are far more interested than Danzig itself. The last word in Germany is always with the army and no war office could view the separation between its main country and one of its provinces without wishing to remove that hindrance. 20

I feel most strongly that, if we are to have peace, we must put Danzig back into its proper perspective. In 25 Germany it has become the stalking-horse for the Corridor: in England people believe that the incorporation of Danzig in Germany means taking it away from Poland. It is not even isolated in the middle of the Corridor, it is actually contiguous to East Prussia. It should not really be diff- 30 icult to find an equitable solution, whereby every economic and strategic necessity would be reserved to Poland, while permitting the re-inclusion of the city as a Free City in East Prussia.

5 Do you think that this letter is suggesting that Britain should continue to appease Hitler – ie give him what he wants – or that Britain should go to war with Hitler? Explain your answer.

In August 1939 Hitler invaded Poland. Twenty-four hours later, Britain and France were at war with Germany.

It took Hitler less than three weeks to conquer half of Poland. He then tabled peace proposals. Source 1 is a draft for the Prime Minister's speech reacting to these proposals.

SOURCE 1 ▷

Extracts from the Prime Minister Neville Chamberlain's speech, 3 September 1939.

> This repeated disregard of his word and these sudden reversals of policy bring me to the fundamental difficulty in dealing with the wider proposals in the German Chancellor's speech. The plain truth is that,
> 5 after our past experience, it is no longer possible to rely upon the unsupported word of the present German Government.
>
> It was not therefore with any vindictive purpose that we embarked on war. It is not alone the freedom
> 10 of the small nations that is at stake: there is also in jeopardy the peaceful existence of Great Britain, the Dominions, France, and indeed of all freedom-loving countries. Whatever may be the issue of the present struggle, and in whatever way it may be brought to a
> 15 conclusion, the world will not be the same world that we have known before. Deep changes will inevitably leave their mark on every field of men's thought and action, and if humanity is to guide aright the new forces that will be in operation all nations will have their part to play.
> 20 His Majesty's Government know all too well that in modern war between great Powers victor and vanquished must alike suffer cruel loss. But surrender to wrong-doing would spell the extinction of all hope, and the annihilation of all those values of life which have
> 25 through centuries been at once the mark and the inspiration of human progress.
>
> I am certain that all the peoples of Europe, including the people of Germany, long for peace, a peace which will enable them to live their lives without fear,
> 30 and to devote their energies and their gifts to the development of their culture, the pursuit of their ideals and the improvement of their material prosperity. The peace which we are determined to secure, however, must be a real and settled peace, not an uneasy truce interrupted
> 35 by constant alarms and repeated threats. What stands

vindictive: revengeful

continued ▷

1 Read Source 1 carefully. Are the British government going to accept the German peace proposals?

2 Find three reasons for their decision.

3 Which of these reasons do you think is the most important? Explain your answer.

in the way of such a peace? It is the German **Government**, and the German Government alone, for it is **they who by** repeated acts of aggression have robbed all **Europe of** tranquillity and implanted in the hearts of all **their**

40 **neighbours** an ever-present sense of insecurity and **fear.**

Herr Hitler rejected all suggestions for **peace** until he had overwhelmed Poland, as he had previously overthrown Czechoslovakia. Peace conditions cannot be acceptable which begin by condoning aggression.

45 The proposals in the German Chancellor's speech are vague and uncertain and contain no suggestion for righting the wrongs done to Czechoslovakia and to Poland.

Even if Herr Hitler's proposals were more closely defined and contained suggestions to right these wrongs,

50 it would still be necessary to ask by what practical means the German Government intend to convince the world that aggression will cease and that pledges will be kept. Past experience has shown that no reliance can be placed upon the **promises** of the present German Government. Accordingly,

55 acts - not words alone - must be forthcoming before <u>we and France, our gallant and trusted ally</u>, would be justified in ceasing to wage war to the utmost of <u>our</u> strength. Only when world confidence is restored will it be possible to find solutions of those vital questions of disarmament and

60 restoration of trade which are essential to the well-being of the peoples.

There is thus a primary condition to be satisfied. Only the German Government can fulfil it. If they will not, there can as yet be no new or better world order of

65 the kind for which all nations yearn.

The issue is therefore plain. Either the German Government must give convincing proof of the sincerity of their desire for peace by definite acts and by the provision of effective guarantees of their intention to fulfil their

70 undertakings or we must persevere in our duty to the end. It is for Germany to make her choice.

4 What do you think the Prime Minister means by 'a better world order' (line 64)?

5 Rewrite lines 66–71 in your own words so that it is clear what choice the Prime Minister is giving Germany.

6 Work in groups. Your teacher will play you a tape recording of Prime Minister's Question Time in the House of Commons. It is 1939.
a) Your group must prepare a set of questions that you wish to ask the Prime Minister about the outbreak of war.
b) Write out each of your questions on a separate piece of paper.
c) Swap your cards with another group and draft replies to the other group's questions.

It is September 1939. Britain is now at war with Germany. Bomb and gas attacks are expected.

You are a member of the government. Which of the measures shown in Source 1 are you going to take? Are there any that do not seem a good idea?

SOURCE 1

1 For each measure list its advantages and disadvantages.

2 Cut out the cards.

3 Put them in an order of priority - which should be done first? Explain your choice.

A Evacuate women and children from areas that might be bombed

EVACUATION!
the most effective **A.R.P**

ARP: air raid precautions

B Ration food

ON HIS MAJESTY'S SERVICE

OFFICIAL PAID

Your Ration Book

Issued to safeguard your food supply

C Put in prison any German citizens who are living in Britain

ALIENS INTERNED

aliens: citizens of enemy countries

D Issue gas masks to every person

EVERYTHING FOR SAFETY EVERYWHERE

AIR RAID PRECAUTIONS EQUIPMENT

GENERAL CIVILIAN RESPIRATORS
CIVILIAN DUTY RESPIRATORS
GENERAL SERVICE RESPIRATORS
PROTECTIVE CLOTHING
STEEL HELMETS
FIRST AID OUTFITS
OXYGEN ADMINISTRATION APPARATUS
GAS SMELLING SAMPLES
STEEL STRETCHERS
REDHILL CONTAINERS
STIRRUP PUMPS

E Distribute air raid shelters to every household

F Censor newspapers

14 PROPAGANDA: *believe it or not*

When war broke out the British government knew it was important for them to control what the public read or saw about the conflict. They set up the Ministry of Information to distribute 'official' information and news about the war. The Ministry of Information produced propaganda in the form of posters, leaflets, films and broadcasts.

We are going to see from Sources 1–4 what the purpose of such propaganda was and how it helped the country to keep up the fight against Germany.

SOURCE 1 ▷
A Ministry of Information poster, 1940.

1 Why are there two German soldiers on the poster?

2 What are the two German soldiers doing?

3 Who do you think is holding the guns with the bayonets?

4 What were:
a) the advantages
b) the disadvantages of reminding people in 1940 about the First World War?

◁ SOURCE 2
A Ministry of Information poster, 1943.

5 Who does the outline figure represent?

6 To what jobs do you think the poster is referring?

7 Source 2 was produced in 1943. What does the poster tell you about the government's concerns at this stage in the war?

SOURCE 3 ▷

A Ministry of Information poster, 1941.

1 Write down the message of this poster in your own words.

2 Why is the paper and metal kept separate from the other rubbish?

3 What other items were people encouraged to save?

4 Whose is the hand putting the lid on Hitler?

5 What might be put in the bucket labelled 'pig's feed' and how could an ordinary family use pig's feed?

Help put the lid on Hitler
BY SAVING YOUR
OLD METAL AND PAPER

SOURCE 4 ▷

A cartoon intended for a poster produced by the Ministry of Information.

6 Who is the person in the front of the cartoon?

7 Why is he shown as such a large figure?

8 Who do the figures climbing over the wall represent?

9 Why might these people be climbing over the wall?

10 When do you think this poster was produced?

11 Decide who this cartoon will most appeal to and write a caption to go with it on a poster.

12 For each of these posters say whether you think it is aimed at:
a) women or men
b) younger people or older people?

13 From all that you know about the Second World War, explain how each of the posters might help the British government during the war.

14 Choose one of the posters which you think is particularly effective propaganda and explain your choice.

15 You have to brief the artists who are designing propaganda posters for the government. Write down five points that the government might want artists to think about in future poster designs.

SOURCE 1 ▷

A letter written by an army captain to the British government. He wrote this on his own initiative and is expressing his own opinions.

T-alat Dali   Probably new full moon
week ends June 7/8 – 15".   21st May, 1940

From the various Government announcements, it appears that the Government consider that there will be time to evacuate London for themselves, the Departments and children when the bombs begin to fall. If this is so, then experience in other countries shows that they may be greatly mistaken, and if they escape at all, will find themselves fleeing for their lives and certainly not as a coherent body. There will be no time.

So we may imagine that at or about 3 a.m. on the given day, the selected areas, without much warning, will be heavily bombed followed, in the dust and confusion, by parachutists and troop carriers. From experience abroad, there seems little doubt that for a time at least they might well be successful.

London would be wholly or partially isolated, rail, road, telephone and telegraph communications cut, and chaos reign. We cannot imagine that the enemy would be content with this. On the contrary, it may be expected that bombers flying high will appear over London and drop bombs quite indiscriminately, followed by shooting down balloons and diving attacks on Government Offices (They will...) drop parachutists in the parks and horse-guard parades in an endeavour to seize the King, Government and Departmental Chiefs, destroy the War Office, Admiralty, and so on.

All the heads are now isolated from their bodies, the members of the Government may be prisoners or fleeing, fighting will be going on continuously all round London, the coast ports and finally London will be under bombing attack hour after hour, until it surrenders like Rotterdam. That may be the enemy's plan. It would admittedly be a costly and desperate effort by the enemy, but does anyone suggest that he is not desperate.

Only one man may know the day and the hour, but it is not difficult to anticipate. The action to take is clear, before it is

TOO LATE

WE HAVE BEEN WARNED

balloons: barrage balloons (large balloons held in place by wires which stopped German bombers flying low)

1 Read Source 1 carefully. Use the information it contains to put the following events in order.
- Parachutists land on London parks
- Heavy bombing all over London
- Attacks on important buildings and people
- Careful bombing of selected areas of London
- Roads, railways and telephones cut.

2 Why did the writer expect Hitler's attack at the time of the 'full moon' and at the weekend?

3 Why might the Germans want to seize the King?

4 The writer says 'The action to take is clear'.
a) What action do you think he wanted the government to take?
b) What action do you think the government should take to deal with the threat described in this letter?

16 FEAR OF INVASION: 'they may land anywhere'

In July 1940 the army estimated that there were more than 500 miles of vulnerable beaches which were unprotected against invasion. They ordered extra mines to be laid around the eastern and southern coasts of Britain.

A summary of a telephone conversation between Captain Denaro, a mine-laying specialist, and Mr Cleave, who lived on the sea front on the Sussex coast, September 1940.

        Digest of conversation that took place over the 'phone when Captain Denaro rang me up on Sunday the 22nd of September 1940 at 9.45 a.m.

        Hullo. Is that Mr Cleave. Yes, who is that speaking? I am Captain Denaro of the Royal Engineers. Oh yes. About your letter. He said he would not remove the mines. I replied, surely they could be removed to a safer position? He said, he would have the position surveyed. I told him the matter was most urgent, and had counted 13 strewn over the foreshore immediately opposite my house, laying loose and washed about by the tide, and further said, when his men were laying the mines, I pointed out the position in which they were being set would prove a menace, as the battering they would receive from a high tide, and a strong wind, coupled with the further risk of any flotsam and jetsam striking them, would explode them. He said I did not understand the position, and he intended to guard the whole coast. I replied I quite agreed and understood about taking every precaution against an enemy, but he surely did not seriously anticipate, out of the hundreds of miles surrounding the British Isles, the enemy would pick on my 200 feet of foreshore for his invasion plan, and even if he did, the mines would be no deterrent, as they would have already exploded and have done their damage, not to Jerry, but to me. He laughed, and said, they may land anywhere. I replied, yes, but surely the end you are endeavouring to attain, could be so attained without having my property periodically damaged. He asked if I was nervous. I said no, and had yet to learn that objecting to one's house and home being blown up was a symptom of nervousness, but was apprehensive of having my home blown to blazes. I told him, on two separate occasions mines had exploded, and it was not altogether enjoyable expecting at every high tide for more to go off, and I did most strongly object to being blown up by my own people. He suggested I should let the matter drop, and say no more about it, to which I replied, I most certainly did not intend to let the matter drop. He said my letter had threatened him, and although he did not like turning people out of their homes, if I persisted, he would ask for a compulsory evacuation. I replied we had been asked to stick it, and we were going to stick it, and the leaving of the premises would in no way prevent more damage as the matter was at present. I again urged that the mines be removed from the immediate vicinity, and failing this, could they not be properly secured to prevent accidental explosion, but because I lodged a legitimate complaint, to threaten me with expulsion, was only burking the question, and to adopt such an attitude was quite untenable. He again said he would have the position surveyed.

1 Why do you think that mines were placed on certain beaches during the war?

2 What is Mr Cleave's main complaint?

3 Why might his views on the usefulness of mining beaches be biased?

4 In what ways is Source 1 a useful piece of evidence about life in the Second World War?

In the summer and autumn of 1939, the British government evacuated around 650,000 children and 25,000 civil servants from dangerous areas to 'safe' parts of the country. Many other families arranged their own evacuation. But by Christmas 1939 there had been very few attacks on British cities and many parents had taken their children home.

SOURCE 1 ▽
Extracts from a government report into evacuation, April 1940.

1 Read Source 1 carefully. What is the total number of British children who returned home between December 1939 and March 1940?

2 Does Source 1 suggest that evacuation had been successful or unsuccessful up to that date? Explain your answer.

> The rate of return has in fact slowed down since Christmas. 700,000 children were evacuated in September. The numbers remaining in the reception areas were:-
>
> December 434,000
> January............... 393,000
> February 365,000
> March 347,000
>
> In Scotland the number of children evacuated in September was about 100,000: the number now remaining is about 30,000.
>
> 5. In recent months, however, the situation in the receiving districts has been difficult. It is very hard for billeting officers to find any new billets. Large numbers of householders desire to be relieved of the children for whom they are caring on the ground of the labour, responsibilities and interference with their domestic life, and there are continuous representations that the amount of the billeting allowances is inadequate.
>
> The appeal to other householders to enrol for service has met with a very limited response and is not likely to provide an effective solution.
>
> It is not considered that the existing scheme can be maintained much longer on its present basis.
>
> 6. On the other hand it is still considered that the Government will not wish to direct the termination of the scheme and the return of the children to the large towns. Such a direction would of course have a great significance in relation to the general conduct of the war.

billeting officer: person in charge of finding homes (billets) for evacuees in a particular area

domestic life: home life

representations: complaints

SOURCE 2
An extract from a report by a women's deputation to the Ministry of Health, December 1939.

> The speakers urged that the Government should make greater use of publicity of all kinds to bring home to parents the reasons why evacuation had been undertaken, and why those who had been transferred to the relatively safer parts of the country should remain in their billets. It was suggested that people thought of the possibility of a child being actually hit and killed by a bomb but they did not appreciate or take into account the very serious effects on a child's mind and health of warnings and gunfire, and the other distractions of aerial warfare. The speakers agreed that in present circumstances evacuation could not be made compulsory. But they thought that by propaganda parents could be convinced of the need for parting from their children, especially if steps could be taken to bring the social and educational services in the reception areas up to the standard of those in the evacuable areas.

3 Read Source 2. According to this document, what measures might persuade people to part with their children?

SOURCE 3 ▷

An extract from one of the government's daily reports on evacuation, November 1940.

Evacuation.

People were becoming more and more unwilling to be evacuated to any other part of London and preferred if they went at all to go to country districts. Evacuation of school-children was proceeding at the rate of 2,000 a day some having been sent out during the last ten days. Parents were, however, unwilling to be parted from their children, and arrangements had therefore been made to evacuate mothers with children of any age. Homeless mothers and children numbering 2,400 had been sent first. The evacuation of this class would be carried on continuously. They would be followed by mothers and children from eight London Boroughs where conditions, particularly in regard to shelter, were at least good. It was thought best not to make too great a demand on reception areas at first, but the movement would be extended as soon as possible to other boroughs. All those evacuated were being sent first for 48 hours to emergency hospitals in reception areas, where they could, if necessary, be cleansed, before being sent to billets or to hostels provided for the difficult cases. The aged and infirm in emergency centres and in shelters had been registered and were being taken to hospitals in London. It was hoped to move them to hospitals in the country as soon as possible. Damage and casualties in hospitals had been small in proportion to the number of hits scored, but the moral effect was such that it might be necessary to evacuate many London hospitals. In addition to organised moves, there was a considerable amount of voluntary evacuation which included both rich and poor. There was also some return movement.

1 Compare Sources 1 and 3. How do people's attitudes to evacuation seem to have changed between April and November 1940?

2 Is there any evidence that people's attitudes had stayed the same?

3 The government said at the start of the war that mothers could not be evacuated with their children. Suggest why they had changed their minds.

4 Do you think Source 4 was issued
a) in September 1939 (when evacuation started)
b) in April 1940 (when many evacuees were returning to London)
c) in 1941 (after the bombing of London had started)?
Explain your choice.

5 'Leaflets and posters didn't persuade people to evacuate their children: only the bombs could do that.' Do you agree with this statement? Give your reasons.

6 Christmas 1940 was a difficult time for Britain, particularly in the big cities where most of the bombing had been. Despite this, many people still wanted their children to come home for Christmas.

In groups, produce a short piece of drama which could be filmed and shown in cinemas before the main film. It should aim to persuade parents to leave their children in the country for Christmas. You could take the roles of different people in a family discussing evacuation, or you may have your own ideas.

SOURCE 4

A government evacuation poster.

LEAVE THIS TO US SONNY — <u>YOU</u> OUGHT TO BE OUT OF LONDON

MINISTRY OF HEALTH EVACUATION SCHEME

While most children were evacuated to 'safe' areas of Britain, over 70,000 were sent abroad. They either went privately (if their parents could afford it), or through a government scheme. Most of these children went to countries in the British Empire. The most popular countries were Australia, Canada, South Africa and New Zealand. There was no risk of air raids in these countries, but the voyage to them was very dangerous.

A voyage to New Zealand took six weeks. The first part was across the dangerous Atlantic towards the Panama Canal.

All ships in the Atlantic Ocean were threatened by German submarines, which were trying to cut off Britain's trade. Ships had to travel in convoys, with warships to guard them.

To keep the children occupied during their journey, a daily programme of lessons and other activities was arranged. Once they arrived, the evacuees were looked after by local families, as they would have been in England. The difference was that visits, phone-calls, and at times even letters were impossible.

SOURCE 1

An extract from a report of the Chief Escort on board RMS *Rangitata* sailing to New Zealand, August 1940.

> MEDICAL.
>
> The Medical Inspection proved that the childrens' home School Doctors had only passed suitably fit children, but the Dentist's work was much heavier than should have been necessary. In the course of his visit to Z.2. Party he found it necessary to make extractions from more than 60 childrens mouths. In one case he even found it necessary to make nine extractions. The teeth in this case were only milk teeth and easily removed, nevertheless the shock to the child's system must have been considerable. Several other children had to have three or four teeth extracted, and this could not possibly have been in the best interest of the health of any of the children, when one remembers that they were about to embark upon a journey which was not only new to the children but extremely hazardous.

'Z.2. Party': a code name for the group of children on board RMS *Rangitata*

SOURCE 2

An extract from a report of the Chaplain on board RMS *Rangitata*.

> We embarked on the R.M.S. Rangitata on Wednesday 28th August, and left Liverpool early the following morning. We were in convoy, and next to the Dutch ship Volundam which was conveying a large number of children to Canada.
>
> On the night of Friday (30th) the convoy was attacked by U boats. A torpedo narrowly missed us and struck the Volundam. We were ordered to take all our children to their boat stations, were we remained all that night. Our ship was manouvered out of the convoy. Next morning there was not a ship to be seen and we crossed the Atlantic alone. For several nights the children slept on the floor of their boat station, (the 1st class longe). The children behaved splendidly during this critical time. There was no sign of alarm or panic. I took prayers with them each evening.
>
> When things had settled down, we organised a regular daily routine programme of lessons, physical training, etc. I took prayers each morning at 9.15 for the whole company, followed by a short Bible reading and religious instruction. At 11.30 I took the under 12 for 20 minutes and told them a Bible story. In the afternoon from 2 - 2.30 I took the over 12 and gave them an instruction on the lines of a Confirmation class. I usually had short evening prayers with my group each night before going to bed.

boat stations: areas from which passengers could board life boats in an emergency

1 Read Source 1. Why do you think the dentist took such drastic action before the ship sailed?

2 Read Source 2. The *Rangitata* left Liverpool in a convoy. What were the advantages of this?

3 Why do you think the RMS *Rangitata* ended up travelling alone?

SOURCE 3 ▷
Children on board the RMS *Rangitata*.

A

After Embarkation it was discovered that the promised parcel of handicraft materials and the goods for use in connection with 'School' lessons had not been placed aboard. This was a great loss, and could not be replaced. The task of getting a School routine working was a difficult one, which would not have been felt on the short voyage to Canada, but on a trip which extended to a matter of five or six weeks it was disticly disadvantageous, and a serious handicap to the teachers.

The Chief Escort provided, from her own personal funds, materials for the making of over twenty dresses for girls who were not too well supplied with cotton frocks, and the children have had immense pleasure in making up their own frocks and have worn them with real pride.

In the matter of arranging for school work we were greatly helped by the fact that amongst our Escorts we had four extremely capable teachers whose methods were modern and very acceptable to the children.

The lesson period for each day lasts for two hours daily, nine thirty to eleven thirty each morning. The period is divided into four sections of twenty five minutes each, five minutes being allowed between classes for the journey between 'classrooms'. The children were divided into four groups.

    Class 1. Children 5,6,a d 7 years. also 8 years.
    "   2.   "   9,10 " 11
    "   3. Girls 12 years and over.
    "   4. Boys 12 "   "   "

This grouping worked very satisfactorily, and the children were happy in their work.

Classes were formed for the study of sewing, drawing, dancing, diction, history and geography, which last included some New Zealand history and information about Panama and Pitcairn Island.

It was not possible to form the classes until the seventh day of the voyage, but by the time classes were commenced the children were ready to fall into their regular routine and settled down immediately to work. Their pleasure in their work was enhanced by the fact that part of their lesson time was devoted to rehearsals for a Concert which they gave to the passengers during the last week of the . The passengers have been greatly interested in the progress of the children, and after the Concert we were the recipients of numerous congratulations on the work which they displayed.

B

We arrived at Wellington on Friday October 4th, and were given a warm reception by the Prime Minister and other representative New Zealanders. The children had a very happy voyage. There was no sickness and no accidents.

The following day I took a party of 50 children to Auckland. We were accompanied by several local officials. About 30 of the children were going to relatives in various parts of the island. Most of the children were collected in Auckland, but I took several to places further North. The remaining 20 were allocated to homes in Auckland. There were 1,000 applications for them, so the local committee had some difficulty in deciding to whom they should go. Great care was taken to place children in homes with a congenial environment, e.g the son of a policeman was, if possible, placed in a policeman's home, and so on. I saw some of the homes, and have returned to England quite convinced that the children are well and happily placed.

◁ SOURCE 4
Further extracts from a report of the Chief Escort on board RMS *Rangitata*.

1 Study Source 3. Do you think this shows the children leaving Liverpool, in mid-Atlantic, or arriving in Wellington? Explain your choice.

2 Use Sources 2 and 4 to design a typical morning's timetable for children on the *Rangitata*. Start the timetable at 9:30 am and finish it at 2:30pm.

3 Sources 2 and 4 were written by the Chief Escort and Chaplain to their employers *after* he voyage had taken place. What sort of impression would they want their employers to have of the voyage?

4 How might this affect the details they included?

5 Are their reports reliable evidence about life on board the *Rangitata?*

6 Read Source 4B. How did the host families in New Zealand react to the evacuees?

7 Compare their reaction to what you know about the reactions of host families in Britain.Explain the reasons for differences and similarities.

8 You are one of the children on board RMS *Rangitata*. Using Sources 1–4 to help you, write diary entries for four days in the voyage. Include your thoughts and feelings at each stage and illustrate your diary.

Throughout the war some of the fiercest battles took place at sea. Allied and German warships and submarines fought the Battle of the Atlantic in the north of the Atlantic Ocean.

For the Germans one of the main objectives was to sink Allied merchant ships. For the Allies the aim was to seek out and destroy the German submarines. Between 1939 and 1945 German ships and submarines sunk more than 5000 merchant ships. Some of them were carrying food, some were carrying weapons. Others were carrying children – evacuees from the bombing in Britain.

Sources 1–3 tell the story of the *City of Benares*. This passenger ship was on its way to Canada when it was torpedoed in September 1940. Of the 96 children on board, 77 were killed.

SOURCE 1 ▷

A report by the Chief Escort on the sinking of the *City of Benares*.

1 On the original of Source 1 lines 20–33 have been damaged, and the right-hand side torn off. Working with a partner, try to complete each line.

2 Do you think that the children were well prepared for the dangers of the voyage?

3 What do you think of the proposals made by the Chief Escort? Can you add any other proposals of your own?

I feel that the members of the Board would like a detailed report of the torpedoing of the City of Benares (D11). That ship, carrying 90 children and 9 adults in charge of the party, sailed from Liverpool on Friday September 13th at 6.15 p.m.
Before sailing there had been many hours of boat drill in which the crew had practised getting the children into the boats. This was done over and over again. 42 of
10 the crew were white and 166 were Laskars and there were white officers and crew supervising the lowering of each boat.

They had an uneventful voyage until Tuesday September 17th when at 10 o'clock at night a torpedo struck the ship on the port side abaft, below where the children were quartered. It was a moonlight night. The visibility was
20 good but there was a heavy Atlantic swell. There is some doubt about the strength of the wind. The Admiralty record it as 60 or 70 miles an hour in the Channel. The Destroyer, ... hurricane, that went to the rescue, reported the sea as being so rough that it could not proceed at more than 15 knotts most of the night. Apparently the wind increased in force during the night after the boats were launched and ... and rain added to the miseries of the night.

When the torpedoe struck the ship at least one ... killed and a number wounded. The force of the expl...
30 blocked the gangway but should not have prevented ... children from proceeding to the boat deck. The Chi... searched all the cabins and lavatories before leavi... the children mustered at their boat stations. Th... slight list, which increased as the minutes went ... must have added to the difficulty of launching the boats. The conditions were such that there was very little chance of launching boats without there being water-logged. I think, 12 boats were launched, nearly all full of water and only one of them was dry.

Many of the passengers were critical of the behaviour
40 of the Laskars. On the other hand one or two of the children praised them. The Chief Officer thought that they had behaved very well and were good seamen. He and the purser and the other white crew all agreed that the conditions were such that no crew could have lowered the boats and kept them dry. This opinion was confirmed by the Marine Superintendent of the Royal Mail Line who has had 30 years experience. I interviewed the Managing Director and the Marine Superintendent of the City Line, who said that although they had had 5 ships sunk, there had been no complaints against the Laskars before.
50 Indeed on one occasion, the sinking of the Birmingham, they had been commanded. Similarily in the Great War they had behaved with bravery in circumstances like this. Some passengers complained that the Laskars wrapped themselves in the sails, when in the Life Boats, and took no further interest. It is clear that Laskars have no great vitality. They gave up the struggle and died after a few hours and therefore were of no use in the boats, of no comfort to the children, and only added to the scenes of horror.

One further question arises as to whether, in view of this
60 recent record of casualties, we are justified in continuing our policy of sending children overseas. It is a difficult decision to take. On the one hand there is the delightful welcome and home life awaiting our children, free from the war atmosphere and particularly the nervous effects and discomforts of air-raids. On the other hand the risks of achieving it seem latterly to be increasing. My own view is that even if a ship is proceeding in slow convoy, the conditions in the North Atlantic are such that there must be a high rate of casualties if a ship is torpedoed. It will
70 not be possible to launch safely boats in conditions of gale and Atlantic swell common to the winter months. An exception, I think, can be made in the case of first liners which are escorted in respect of which experience shows a remarkable record of safety. There is no reason why the traffic to the other Dominions should not proceed. Statistics show a much lower rate of sinkings on these routes and if a disaster should occur, the chances of survival are much greater. In the early stages the boats are near land or near the other ships in the convoy and, as the voyage proceeds, it is towards calmer waters and with a rising temperature.

I therefore suggest that the Board should:-
  (1) Only send children in ships with white crews.
80   (2) Announce the suspension of evacuation on the North Atlantic route during the winter months, except in the case of fast escorted liners.
  (3) Continue sending children to the other 3 Dominions, provided convoys are available.

22.9.40.   G.N.S.

the other 3 Dominions:
South Africa, Australia and New Zealand

SINKING OF CHILD REFUGEE SHIP - FIRST GERMAN COMMENT.

THE REUTER LIE AGENCY REPORTS WITH A LOUD EXCLAMATION OF PAIN THE
TORPEDOING OF AN ARMED BRITISH AUXILIARY STEAMER, WHICH DESCRIBED
AS HEADING TOWARDS CANADA.   TWO HUNDRED AND NINETY THREE PERSONS,
AMONG THEM EIGHTY THREE CHILDREN ARE SAID TO HAVE BEEN KILLED.
REUTER MAINTAINS THAT THE SHIP WAS TORPEDOED ON SEPTEMBER 17TH
BUT CHURCHILL GRANTED HIMSELF THE SURPRISINGLY LONG PERIOD OF
SIX DAYS IN ORDER TO REPORT THIS INCIDENT, WHERE EVEN THE NAME OF
THE SHIP CANNOT BE GIVEN.   ACCORDING TO A TIME TESTED PATTERN
OF HORROR, THE CASE IS BEING ADORNED DRAMATICALLY.   THE CAPTAIN
IT IS SAID SANK WITH HIS SHIP AMID THE WAVES AND HIS LAST WORDS
WERE ACCORDING TO REETER: QUOTE TAKE CARE AND GET THE CHILDREN
INTO THE LIFEBOATS UNQUOTE.   NOBODY SEEMS TO NOTICE IN THE
BRITISH MINISTRY OF INFORMATION THAT IT MUST HAVE BEEN TOO LATE
FOR THAT, SINCE THE CAPTAIN HAD ALREADY SUNK WITH BIS SHIP.
IN ANY CASE, THIS CASE IS AGAIN A QUOTE CHURCHILL CASE UNQUOTE,
QUITE INDEPENDENTLY OF THE QUESTIONS WHETHER IT TOOK PLACE,
IN WHAT FORM IT TOOK PLACE AND WHAT SUCCESS IT HAD ON THE PART
OF THE GERMANS, REPEATED AND EMPHATIC WARNINGS HAD BEEN GIVEN
AGAINST SENDING TRANSPORTS OF CHILDREN ACROSS THE DANGER ZONE.
CONSEQUENTLY, IF THERE IS ANY TRUTH IN THIS SRRPRISING AND
FRESH SINKING OF A HIP, SUCH AS BRITISH PROPAGANDA CAUSES TO
HAPPEN EVERY FOUR OR FIVE WEEKS, AS EVERYBODY KNOWS - THEN THE
BRITISH GOVERNMENT OF CRIMINALS IS ITSELF RESPONSIBLE FOR IT.
IT APPEARS, MOREOVER, THAT THE SCOUNDRELS OF THE THAMES,
DELIBERATELY SEND SOME CHILDREN ON EVERY BOAT SAILING FOR AMERICA
IN ORDER TO PIN THE BLAME OF THE TRAGIC HAPPENING N XX ON THE
GERMANS SHOULD ANYTHING BEFALL THE SHIP. THUS IT IS EASY TO
DECLARE EVERY SINGLE ARMED AUXILIARY STEAMER TO BE A TRANSPORT
OF CHILDREN, ALTHOUGH THE SHIP WHICH IS NOW ALLEGED TO HAVE BEEN
TORPEDOED WAS CARRYING FOR EXAMPLE THE ILLFAMED WARMONGER WEBB,
A BRITISH COLONEL, WHO WANTED TO TRAVEL TO THE U.S.A. AND IT IS
PIQUANT THAT HE WAS IN THE COMPANY OF THE WIDELY REPUTED
REFUGEE RUDOLF OLDEN.
+++++++14.25++++23.9.40++

A telegram giving the German reaction to the sinking of the *City of Benares*.

1 What excuses do the Germans make for sinking the *City of Benares?*

2 Who do they blame for the tragedy?

3 Thirteen children were saved. Write an account of the attack described in Source 1 from the point of view of a child who survived.

4 Look at Source 3. How did Barbara Fairhead die?

5 What consolation is offered to her mother?

6 Why would Mrs Fairhead's friends have to judge what information to pass on?

SOURCE 3 ▽

A letter sent by Government officials to the Red Cross, who were dealing with enquiries about children on the *City of Benares.*

25th January, 1941.

Dear Madam,

Re Barbara Fairhead.

You will remember that I spoke to you on the telephone about the sad case of this little girl who was lost on the "City of Benares".   I mentioned that we were trying to obtain further particulars about her from our escort. I have now ascertained that Barbara was in a boat which was capsized when being launched from the ship.   The Chief Escort tells us that all the children in the section to which Barbara belonged were on deck with their escort before the launching of the boats, so that there could have been no possibility of this little girl having been trapped on the boat or injured by the explosion.   As neither their escort or any of her section survived, it is impossible to say actually what happened.   Barbara must have either been drowned when the boat capsized, or have been picked up by another boat and have died from exposure.   The only consolation that can be offered to the mother is that if she were drowned when the boat capsized this must have been a speedy death, and if she dies from exposure we are told by survivors that the children who died in this way did not greatly suffer "It was like a gradual falling asleep from which nothing could rouse them".

Mrs Fairhead's friend will be able to judge how much of this information should be passed on to the mother.

Yours faithfully,
E. M. DAVIES

7 From all that you know about:
a) evacuation in Britain
b) evacuation abroad
c) the Battle of the Atlantic,
explain whether you would have wanted to be evacuated overseas in September 1939, September 1940 or September 1941.

The threat

Before the Second World War, Britain had never faced the threat of large-scale bombing. But by 1939 experts in the air force warned of disaster if Hitler chose to bomb British cities. They said that new planes and new weapons threatened terrible destruction in British cities. Gas bombs, for example, had been used by both sides in the First World War. What if Hitler chose to drop gas bombs on British cities? The government was deeply concerned about these new threats.

CONFIDENTIAL

31 May, 1939.

My dear Trenchard

    I am replying to your letter of the 22nd May, 1939, on the subject of bombing accuracy.

    As regards high level bombing, I am afraid we have to admit that bombing accuracy has fallen off recently with the introduction of high speed monoplane aircraft. The reasons, apart from the obvious one of training difficulties during expansion, are simple. The high speed means that the bomb must be dropped at a greater horizontal distance from the target than formerly, which in anything but very good weather conditions allows the crew very much less time for last-minute corrections. (Like all other weapons, the accuracy of the bomb decreases as the range increases). Modern aircraft, moreover, do not "flat turn" easily and so the necessary small corrections during the run-up are upset by banking the aircraft and, consequently, the bomb sight.

Marshal of the Royal Air Force
  The Rt.Hon. Viscount Trenchard, G.C. ., G.C.V.O., D.S.C.,
      Dancers Hill House,
        Barnet,
          Herts.

◁ **SOURCE 1**

The reply of an expert to questions from a government enquiry, 31 May 1939.

1 Read Source 1. The writer thinks that the speed of monoplane aircraft makes them less accurate as bombers. Draw a diagram to illustrate what the writer means.

2 What other reasons does the writer give for the inaccuracy of monoplane bombers?

3 What would be the best forms of protection against the methods of attack mentioned in Sources 1 and 2?

monoplane: an aircraft with one set of wings (like modern planes)

banking: turning the aircraft with one wing higher than the other

SOURCE 2 ▷

One of a series of 20 weekly 'quizzes' which appeared in British newspapers in 1941.

Gas Raid Quiz... No. 18

ISSUED BY THE MINISTRY OF HOME SECURITY

WILL HITLER USE GAS THIS WINTER?

ANSWER: NO ONE, FROM THE PRIME MINISTER DOWN, KNOWS THIS. THE ENEMY MAY USE GAS AS A DESPERATE EFFORT, AND WHEN HE DOES USE IT HE WON'T SPARE US! — YOU RISK YOUR LIFE EVERY TIME YOU GO OUT WITHOUT A GAS MASK!

This space is presented by Whitbread and Co. Ltd.

Anderson shelters

In preparation for the bombing of British cities, the government distributed 'Anderson' air raid shelters to houses in high risk areas. These shelters were designed to be put together in the garden of your home.

SOURCE 3
Instructions for assembling an Anderson shelter from the *Illustrated London News*, July 1940.

SOURCE 4 ▷
Minutes of a meeting of the War Cabinet, 25 May 1940.

1 Read Source 4. What is the Prime Minister worried about?

2 Can you think of any reasons why people might not have erected or used their shelter properly? Source 3 may help you.

3 Why do you think the government were worried about this problem in May and June 1940?

4 Work in pairs. It is June 1940. Using Sources 2–4, design a poster to encourage people:
a) to build their Anderson shelter
b) to use it.

> 5. In connection with the discussion recorded in Minute 2, THE PRIME MINISTER said that the bombing by the enemy of targets in this country should give a welcome stimulus to air raid precautions activities. He had noticed several reports in the Press that Anderson shelters were not being properly used by the public.
>
> THE MINISTER OF HOME SECURITY said that the number of such cases was almost negligible, and the Press reports were much exaggerated. Some cases had occurred of the materials for shelters being left lying about while awaiting missing components. In other cases, there had been no able-bodied person in the household who could erect the shelter. Local authorities had been given stringent instructions to remove shelters which were not erected, and to give them to other householders who were in need of them.
>
> THE PRIME MINISTER urged that this was not enough; the persons responsible should be punished in some way. The Government had the necessary powers under the new Act.

The Blitz begins

The Blitz began in September 1940 with a ferocious raid on London. Over the next twelve months, the nerve of the population and the quality of air raid shelters were put to a most severe test.

Shelter

SOURCE 5▷
A back garden of a house in Croydon after an air raid in 1940. The family using the shelter survived.

1 You are a government ARP inspector. You have been called to see the damage shown in Source 5 on the morning after the raid. Write a detailed description of what you see, including an assessment of how effective the Anderson shelter has been.

Anderson shelters were only one type of shelter. In 1940 the government introduced Morrison shelters for houses without gardens. These were steel cages which people put inside a suitable room in their house.

Many people in London took to sleeping on the platforms of Underground stations, although early in the war the government tried to stop them. People also sheltered under railway arches, in deep trenches which had been dug in public parks, or in basements.

SOURCE 6▷
Children sheltering from flying bombs in a trench in Kent in 1944.

IMPORTANT NOTICE

AIR RAIDS

Please note that immediately an AIR RAID WARNING is given this house will be closed.

Customers living or working within easy distance should at once leave for their homes or places of business.

For those remaining, limited cellar accommodation will be available as shelter, at customers' own risk.

Issued by the Licensed Victuallers' Central Protection Society of London, Ltd., 27, Russell Square, W.C.1

SOURCE 7

A notice posted in pubs in 1942.

SOURCE 8

From a government report into Air Raid precautions, written in 1942.

1 Make a list of all types of shelter mentioned in the last four pages. Using Sources 1–8 and your own research, make a chart to show the advantages and disadvantages of each one as a wartime shelter.

2 Which type of shelter do you think would have been
   a) the most popular
   b) the safest
   c) the most comfortable?

LARGE LICENSED HOUSES

Name of House	Old or New	Type of business, local or visiting	No. of customers at peak hour	Approx. No. of persons for whom shelter accommodation available in cellar	Availability of Public Shelter in the vicinity	Construction of roof above cellar	Condition of roof	(1) Entrance and (2) Emergency Exit	Whether Designated	Suitability for a shelter
Railway Tavern Liverpool Street	Old	Local at peak hour	230	75 – 100	Public shelter about 200 yards away	Wooden floor and joists	Probably sound	(1) Narrow steep steps additional entrance from street possible (2) Barrel chute	No	Yes
Cock Tavern Old Street	do	Local	200	nil	Arrangements made for accommodation in private shelter close at hand	do.	doubtful	(1) narrow steps (2) Barrel chute	No	No

SOURCE 1 ▷

A press release from the government in 1944.

1 Study Source 1 carefully and mark the following events on the graph. You will need to use your own research in textbooks to find out when they happened.
  a) The Battle of Britain
  b) Hitler's invasion of Russia
  c) The appointment of 'Bomber' Harris to Bomber command.

2 Describe the relationship between these events and changes in the pattern of bombing.

3 Look at Source 2. How did London's population change over this period?

4 Can you give reasons for this change?

5 How did the number of people sheltering change over this period?

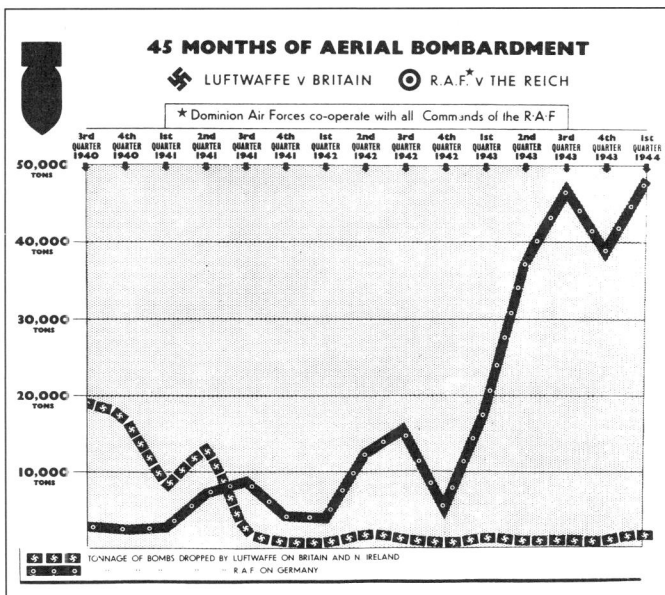

45 MONTHS OF AERIAL BOMBARDMENT
LUFTWAFFE v BRITAIN ● R.A.F.* v THE REICH
* Dominion Air Forces co-operate with all Commands of the R·A·F
TONNAGE OF BOMBS DROPPED BY LUFTWAFFE ON BRITAIN AND N. IRELAND / R.A.F. ON GERMANY

6 Use information given in Source 1 to help you explain this change.

7 Study the statistics for November 1940 and August 1941 in Source 2. Draw a graph (such as a pie chart or a divided bar graph) to show what percentage of those sheltering (the Grand Total) used each type of shelter.

8 Describe the changes in the use of shelters which took place between November 1940 and August 1941. What did not change?

SOURCE 2

A government census into the use made of air raid shelters in London between November 1940 ▽ and August 1941.

LONDON REGION (TOTALS)	ESTIMATED POPULATION	PUBLIC SHELTERS				DOMESTIC SHELTERS		GRAND TOTAL PUBLIC AND DOMESTIC
		BASEMENTS No. of occupants	TRENCHES No. of occupants	SURFACE SHELTERS No. of occupants	RAILWAY ARCHES, TUNNELS, etc. No. of occupants	ANDERSONS No. of occupants	OTHERS (SURFACE AND STRUTTED BASEMENTS, etc.) No. of occupants	
1940	–	–	–	–	–	–	–	–
November	7,832,235	192,105	119,985	74,970	82,943	1,860,844	273,144	2,603,991
December	7,746,852	160,632	71,995	51,407	84,145	1,271,453	208,730	1,848,362
1941	–	–	–	–	–	–	–	–
January	7,372,361	117,195	50,449	35,247	67,426	883,335	160,526	1,314,178
February	7,256,741	93,854	32,709	19,539	56,674	No census taken during this month		
March	6,701,066	85,271	30,112	17,144	48,814	No census taken during this month		
April	6,550,263	79,509	26,552	19,178	54,640	740,921	101,816	1,022,616
May	6,667,514	87,709	31,883	21,788	58,850	768,199	112,735	1,081,164
June	6,490,121	73,984	25,327	17,431	54,676	683,497	104,971	959,886
July	6,302,895	44,004	15,351	11,326	34,172	475,300	73,218	661,171
August	6,251,043	39,666	13,578	9,715	30,206	419,243	76,963	599,069

The London Underground stations were favourite places of shelter for ordinary people. However, it was not only individuals that had to be protected against air raids. Whole organisations 'went underground' as well.

1 On a map of London which your teacher will give you, mark each of the most popular stations in Source 1.

2 Think of three reasons why they might be the most popular stations.

3 On the same map, mark the approximate site of Down Street station (Source 2).

4 Study Source 2 carefully. What arrangements have been made for:
a) comfort
b) communications
c) safety?

5 Design a suitable underground shelter for one of the following:
a) the War Cabinet
b) a hospital
c) a school.

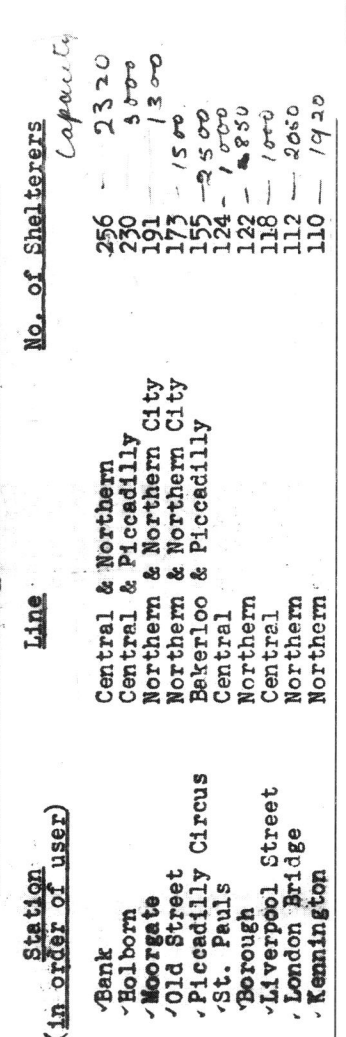

TUBE SHELTERS
NO. OF PERSONS SHELTERING AT TUBE STATIONS ON FRIDAY, 16TH JANUARY, 1942

Station (in order of user)	Line	No. of Shelterers	Capacity
Bank	Central & Northern	256	2320
Holborn	Central & Piccadilly	230	3000
Moorgate	Northern & Northern City	191	1300
Old Street	Northern & Northern City	173	1500
Piccadilly Circus	Bakerloo & Piccadilly	155	2500
St. Pauls	Central	124	1850
Borough	Northern	122	1000
Liverpool Street	Central	118	1000
London Bridge	Northern	112	2060
Kennington	Northern	110	1920

SOURCE 1 The ten most popular station shelters in the census taken on 16 January 1942.

SOURCE 2 The plan for the headquarters of the Railway Executive Committee, which controlled the movement of trains around Britain. Down Street Station was a disused station between Hyde Park Corner and Green Park on the Piccadilly line.

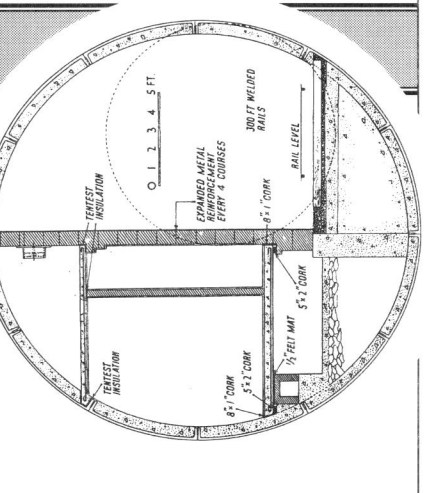

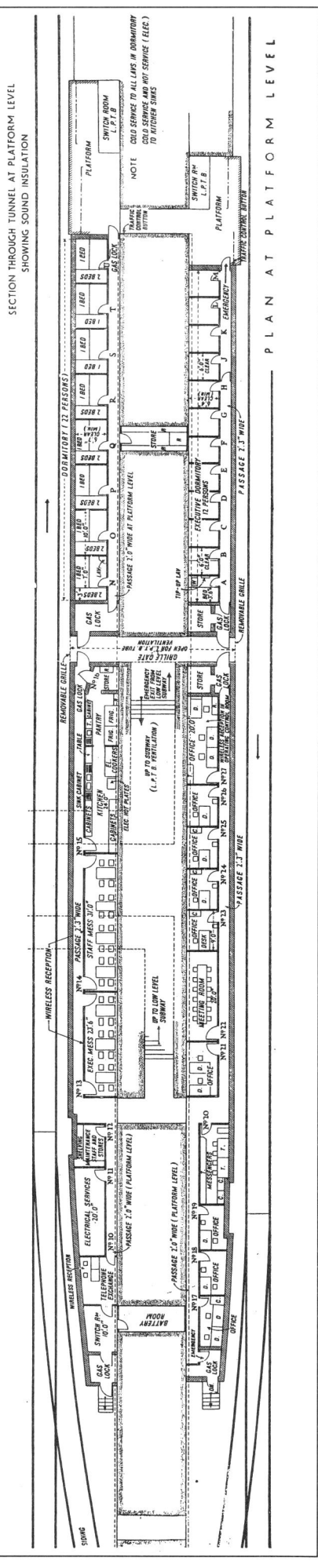

SECTION THROUGH TUNNEL AT PLATFORM LEVEL
SHOWING SOUND INSULATION

PLAN AT PLATFORM LEVEL

Many civilians were killed in the Blitz by explosions, fires, flying glass, or falling masonry. However, the single incident which caused the most deaths came not from a bomb, but from a single tragic slip, as you will see from Source 1, which tells the story of the disaster at Bethnal Green Tube station on 3 March 1943, when 173 people were crushed to death.

SOURCE 1 ▷

An extract from the government enquiry into the Bethnal Green accident. This is a transcript of the original.

1 Read the account of the disaster in Source 1. Make a list of all the different causes of the disaster.

2 Choose the three most important causes.

3 If any one of these causes had been absent, would the disaster still have happened? Explain your answer.

4 What does this incident tell you about people's fears of German air raids in 1943?

5 Why do you think the government did not want the press to publish details of this accident?

The shelter in question was adapted from a tube station in course of construction together with the adjoining sections of tunnel, and was opened early in October 1940. It has a total bunked accommodation of something over 5,000, with additional shelter for another 5,000. It has only one entrance, though there is an emergency exit some half a mile away in another borough. It was and is the largest single unit of deep shelter in the whole area, and provides a greater proportion of deep shelter per head of population than there is in any of the adjoining boroughs. The shelter population is drawn from the whole surrounding area and people come to it from considerable distances. From its opening it was used by large numbers nightly during the period of intensive bombing, 1940/1941. The use of the shelter became a regular routine and night after night the bulk of the inmates arrived before black out and stayed until the morning. Since the summer of 1941 the regular users have dwindled from some thousands nightly to a mere 200–300. The largest recorded attendance was about 7,000.

On the 16th January, 1943, the papers published an account of a British raid in Berlin., The shelter was used by a fair number of people on the nights succeeding and particularly during the light German reprisal raid on 17th January. On the 28th February 500 people were checked out of the shelter and on the 1st March, 587. News was received on the 2nd March of our heavy raid on Berlin on the 1st, and on that night 850 people actually used the shelter. Again many people were seen in the neighbourhood of the shelter in the streets, obviously up to a late hour prepared to use the shelter if an alert was sounded. The general expectation, however, seems from my inquiries to have been that a reprisal attack was far more likely to be launched on the 3rd.

The state of mind of the people of the area appeared most clearly during my inquiry. They take a most intelligent interest in the accounts of our bombing of the enemy, particularly remembering what they themselves experienced. They did not miss the optimistic accounts in our Press of the results achieved on this occasion, and had noted the changed nature of bombing tactics and the accounts of the results of the ultra-heavy bombs coming into use. The result was that people had made up their minds that in case of an alert it was necessary, or at any rate, wise to get into deep shelter with as little delay as possible. They were a little nervous and apprehensive, though not more so I think than is natural under the circumstances.

On the night of 3rd March the alert sounded at 8.17 p.m precisely. By this time it was estimated that about 500–600 people were already in the shelter. The gates had all been opened some time prior to the alert. The chances of a raid were freely discussed but the people were perfectly orderly and normal in the manner of their entry up to the time of the

continued ▷

sounding of the alert. Immediately the alert was sounded and a large number of people left their homes in the utmost haste for the shelter. A great many were running. Two cinemas at least in the near vicinity disgorged a large number of people and at least 3 omnibuses set down their passengers outside the shelter. From 8.17 and for the next ten minutes there was a hurried convergence of hundreds of people towards, and at, the gates of the shelter. The people were nervous and anxious to get under cover. The entrance of the shelter was densely packed though there was no actual disorder, and the people were able to enter the shelter in a hurried but orderly stream. As fast as they passed down the stairs, numbers were converging at the entrance behind them. In the 10 minutes succeeding the alert it is estimated that some 1,500 people entered the shelter.

At precisely 8.27 p.m. a salvo of rockets was discharged from a battery some third of a mile away. This caused a great deal of alarm. Some people on their way to the shelter lay down in the road and then ran on. There were some cries reported that "they were starting dropping them": that it was a land mine; and other alarming observations. The crowd surged forward towards the entrance carrying in front of it those who were entering the shelter, and placing a severe and sudden pressure upon the backs of those already descending the nearly dark stairway.

Simultaneously with the pressure reaching the people on the stairway, a woman who appears to have been holding or leading a child, fell on the third step from the bottom. This was observed both by a witness on the landing below and by at least 2 people in the crowd on the stairs behind her. As a result or, again, simultaneously, a man fell to her left. This occurred in the right hand half of the stairway. So great was the pressure from behind that those impeded by the bodies were forced down on top of them. In a matter of seconds there built an immovable and interlaced mass of bodies 5 or 6 or more deep against which people above and on the stairs continued to be forced by the pressure from behind.

I have not been able to establish definitely whether the woman's fall was accidental or caused by pressure. I think there is little doubt that it was the latter. The evidence of a Mrs. Barber who witnessed the fall from behind seems to be that she, Mrs. Barber, had lost her foothold, and was being carried down with her feet off the ground, before the woman fell. In any case the point is a small one and a solution would not throw further light on the causes and origin of the accident.

The people immediately in front of this accident seem to have moved on without realising that anything had happened. As I have already stated, there is no doubt that they were hurrying to get in to the shelter proper. After a few seconds the "jam" was complete across the full width of the stairway.

Returning to what was occurring at the top of the stairs, there was at the moment when movement forward and into the shelter was arrested, a crowd of about 150–200 outside the shelter and violently anxious to enter it. This crowd was being augmented from minute to minute by fresh arrivals. The immediate effect of the stoppage was to make them press forward harder, and there was an almost instantaneous transition from nervousness and hurry to disorder. There seems to have been an impression among some of the people that they were either being deliberately held back, or that a floodgate situated at the foot of the escalators had been closed against them. All people on the top steps of the stairs were completely unable to move, as were those in the shelter entrance. There were loud cries of distress coming from the staircase, while a good deal of shouting was coming from those trying to gain an entry. The confusion was confounded by numbers of people who, realizing that something was amiss were endeavouring to gain access to the stairs to make enquiries after or assist relatives and friends who had preceded them.

6 Produce a newspaper account of the disaster, imagining that it is written at the time to be published the day after the disaster. Remember that it will be read by the censor.

As soon as war broke out, Britain had to adjust to a wartime way of life.

Sources 1–5 investigate the attitudes of ordinary people to some of these restrictions.

SOURCE 1 ▷
A government announcement in 1940.

1.—(1) No person shall display or cause or permit to be displayed any sign which furnishes any indication of the name of, or the situation of, or the direction of, or the distance to, any place.

(2) For the purpose of this Article the expression " sign " includes any direction post, place name and map.

2. It shall be the duty of the owner of any such sign and the occupier of any land or premises on or to which any such sign is placed or attached forthwith to remove the sign or to obliterate therefrom or conceal any such indication as is mentioned in Article 1 of this Order.

◁ SOURCE 2
A photograph taken in Surrey in 1940.

1 Study Sources 1 and 2. Why do you think the government ordered the removal of all direction signs?

SOURCE 3 ▷
A letter from the Ministry of War Transport in 1940.

COPY   MINISTRY OF WAR TRANSPORT
                                      ROADS DEPT
                                   EASTERN DIVISION.

                                   Palace Chambers,
                                    Silver Street,
                                    BEDFORD.

R.D.E. 217.II.

Dear Sir,

                    Replacement of Direction Signs.

        The Country Surveyor of Bedfordshire has drawn my attention to the conditions arising from the lack of a direction sign at the crossroads at Crosshall, on the Great North Road, approximately one mile north of Eaton Socon (map reference, 84,626804). There is a house at the corner and the lady residing there complains bitterly of the inconvenience caused to her by drivers of vehicles enquiring the route to various places. The lady making the complaint does not object to answering enquiries during the daylight hours, but she is sometimes knocked up two or three times during the night.

        The County Surveyor is fully sympathetic towards the application she has made that the direction signs should be re-erected at the crossroads, but the difficulty is that the crossroads are not situated within a built-up area, although it is not far removed from Eaton Socon and St.Neots. He is, however, prepared to give a very definite undertaking that in the event of an emergency arising necessitating the removal of the direction signs, this particular one would receive very prompt attention.

        I understand that the Chief Constable raises no objection to the re-erection of the sign, but it becomes necessary for me to refer the matter to you. The assurance that this particular sign would receive prompt attention should the necessity arise, should, I think be a sufficient safeguard and in all the circumstances I shall be glad to hear that you raise no objection to the replacement.

                    Yours faithfully,

                    (sgd) F.G. Richards,
                    for Divisional Road Engineer,
                        Eastern Division.

Chief Engineer,
Eastern Command.
Home Forces.

2 Read Source 3. What problem has the removal of direction signs caused for the woman making the complaint?

3 Make a list of other problems that may have resulted from the removal of direction signs.

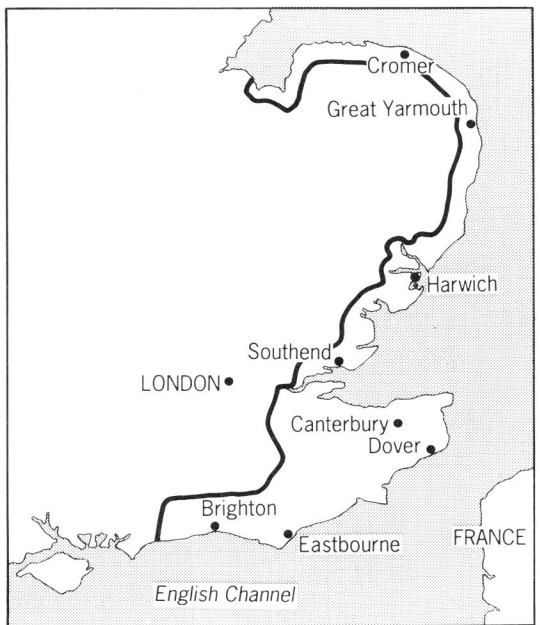

SOURCE 4
A map showing restricted areas in 1939.

1 Look at Source 4. Have you ever visited any of the areas which were restricted in the Second World War? Why did you go there?

2 Make a list of possible reasons why the government might want to restrict access to coastal areas.

SOURCE 5 ▷
A letter written to the commander of the Home Forces in South-east England by an army colleague, April 1943.

People wrote to the government asking for permission to bathe on the restricted beaches. Many people living near the beaches were particularly angry to see soldiers using them for swimming and sunbathing in their free time, although civilians were forbidden to do so. In summer 1942 the government did relax restrictions, but only for a short while.

HEADQUARTERS,
12 CORPS,
HOME FORCES.

DO.646/1 G.

28th April, 1943.

My dear Jack, /15A.

Many thanks for your letter SE.6154/Ops of 23 Apr 43.

I entirely agree with your views on the undesirability of opening bathing facilities to civilians. If once we allow Tom, Dick and Harry, and their wives, families and girl friends to have access to the beaches we shall, sooner or later, land ourselves in trouble owing to people straying into minefields or being shot up by sneak raiders. If once that happens we shall be asked to provide guides through the minefields and AA protection for civilian bathers, besides getting the blame for events which are beyond our control.

As a nation we are still undisciplined after three and a half years of war, and I do not subscribe to the theory that what is sauce for the goose is also sauce for the gander.

I am told that the fullest use was made of the beaches last year to teach troops to swim as part of their training and that some units began the summer with a negligible number of swimmers and finished with a high percentage who could do a hundred yards or more in clothing and equipment.

In view of what we hope lies before us I am strongly in favour of the troops being _made_ to bathe in order that they may have confidence if they find themselves in the water during a landing operation. This should be as much part of their training as anything else and for that reason we must accept certain risks and provide such protective measures as we can, just as we do when any body of soldiers is collected for any type of military exercise.

Our training as a whole will be interfered with if we have to provide protective measures for civilians and without such measures civilians will be liable to unnecessary danger.

I, therefore, urge that the troops should be made to bathe and that civilians should be kept off the beaches.

Yours Ever

Montague Burford

Lt-Gen J.G. des R. Swayne, CB, CBE,
Commander,
South Eastern Command,

AA: anti-aircraft

3 With a partner, decide what the following phrases in Source 5 mean:
a) 'Tom, Dick and Harry'
b) 'sneak raiders'
c) 'what is sauce for the goose is also sauce for the gander'.

4 Why does the writer think the restrictions on beach access are a good idea?

5 Write a reply from someone living in a house near to the sea. Your letter should be understanding and polite, but should also suggest ways in which civilians could be allowed access to the beaches without harming the war effort.

What was rationing?

One of the main aims of the German operations in the Battle of the Atlantic was to cut off supplies of food and other goods coming into Britain. From the experience of the First World War, the British government knew that rationing would be necessary in wartime if food and other essential supplies were not to run out. A rationing system was therefore put into place very early in the war.

1 Study Sources 1, 2 and 3. From these make a list of all the items which were rationed.

2 For each item in your list say:
a) whether it would have to be imported or whether it could be home produced
b) why it was important to control supplies of this item.

3 Not all food was rationed. For example, at the start of the war the government decided against rationing the following foods: bread and flour, vegetables, fish, cheese, milk, coffee. Why do you think these foods were not rationed?

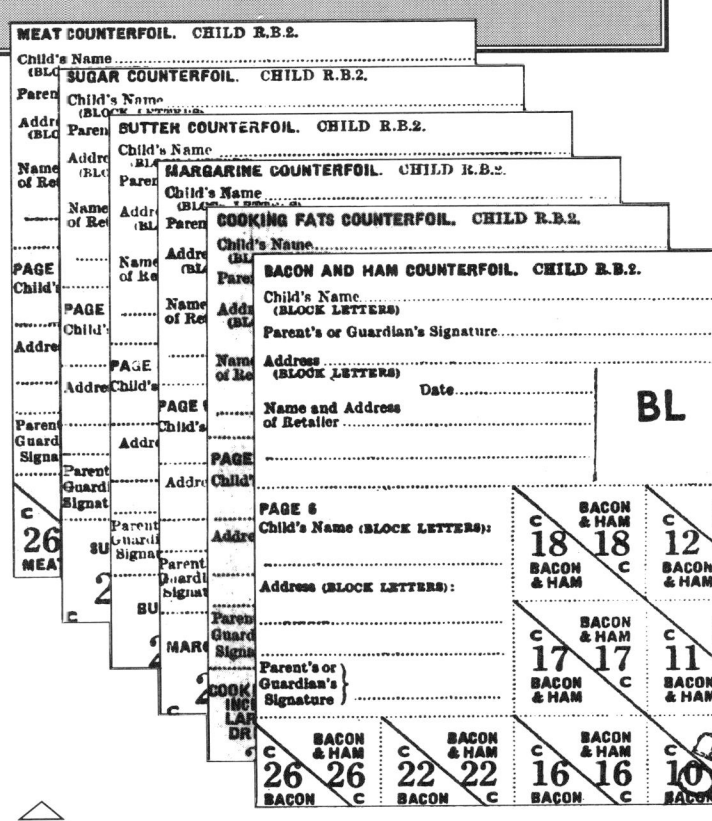

SOURCE 1

Pages from a child's ration book.

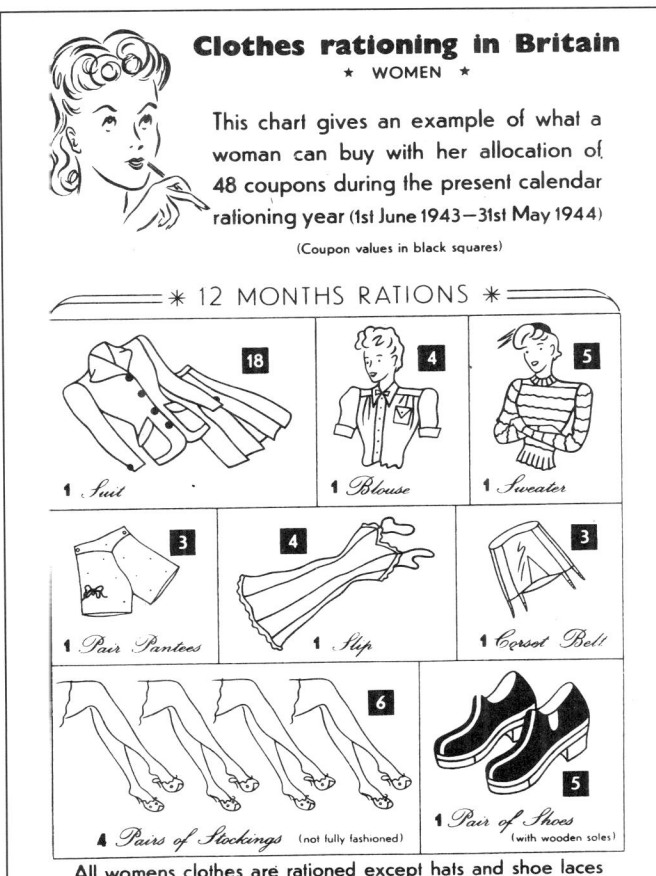

Clothes rationing in Britain
★ WOMEN ★

This chart gives an example of what a woman can buy with her allocation of 48 coupons during the present calendar rationing year (1st June 1943—31st May 1944)

(Coupon values in black squares)

═ ✳ 12 MONTHS RATIONS ✳ ═

18 — 1 Suit
4 — 1 Blouse
5 — 1 Sweater
3 — 1 Pair Panties
4 — 1 Slip
3 — 1 Corset Belt
6 — 4 Pairs of Stockings (not fully fashioned)
5 — 1 Pair of Shoes (with wooden soles)

All womens clothes are rationed except hats and shoe laces

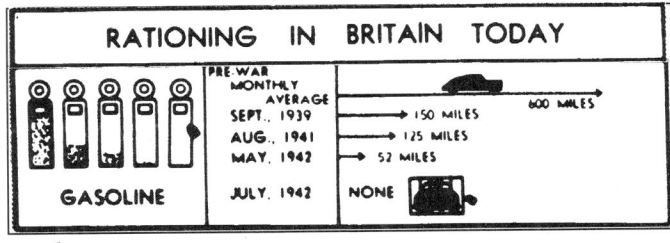

RATIONING IN BRITAIN TODAY

	PRE-WAR MONTHLY AVERAGE	
	SEPT., 1939	150 MILES
	AUG., 1941	125 MILES
	MAY, 1942	52 MILES
GASOLINE	JULY, 1942	NONE

600 MILES

SOURCE 2

From the *Illustrated London News*, December 1942.

◁ SOURCE 3

A government leaflet from 1944.

MINISTRY OF FOOD

YOUR NEW RATION BOOK

HOW TO REGISTER WITH THE SHOPS

The new Ration Books are now being distributed. As soon as you receive your new Book you must fill in the particulars as explained below, and then take the Book to the shops for fresh Registration. It has been found possible to allow *immediate* Registration, and the sooner you register the better. This is what to do:—

1 On the pages of coupons for Rationed Foods (Meat, Bacon, Butter and Sugar) you must fill in your name and address (BLOCK LETTERS) in the space provided in the centre of each page.

2 At the foot of these pages are spaces marked 'Counterfoil'. Here you must write your name and address, the date, and the name and address of the shop where you wish to buy the particular food during the six months' period beginning July 8th.

3 Inside the front cover of your Ration Book you must write the names and addresses of the shops.

4 As soon as you have done this, take the Book to each of the shops with whom you intend to register, so that they may cut out their counterfoils.

EVERYONE MUST REGISTER FOR THE NEW PERIOD

The Ministry of Food is responsible both for the supply and quality of rationed foods. No retailer is, therefore, in a better position than another to secure supplies of rationed foods, nor can one retailer promise to provide a better quality than another.

SOURCE 4
Government instructions about rationing, June 1940.

How rationing worked
Each person in Britain received a ration book. There were different ration books for children and adults.

SOURCE 5 ▷
Pages from a child's ration book.

1 Using Sources 4 and 5, explain how somebody obtained their rations.

2 Do you think the system of rationing described in Sources 4 and 5 could have been improved? Give reasons for your answer.

3 How might people have been able to supplement their rations?

How to use this Ration Book

INSTRUCTIONS TO PARENT OR GUARDIAN

1. Write the child's name in BLOCK letters in the space provided on the reference leaf (page 16).

2. To buy any food that is rationed you must register the child with a shop which sells that food.

3. How to register with a shop. Write the names and addresses of the shopkeepers with whom you intend to register the child in the spaces inside the front cover.

4. Write your name and the child's name and address (in BLOCK letters) and the date on the counterfoil at the top of the pages of coupons numbered 5, 6, 7, 8 and (if margarine and cooking fats are rationed) 9 and 10.

5. Then take this book to the shops from which you mean to buy the child's butchers' meat, bacon and ham, sugar, butter and any other foods which may be rationed. The shopkeeper with whom you are registered for each of these foods will write his name and address on the counterfoil, which he will cut off and keep.

6. Every time you buy rationed food for the child you must hand this ration book in at the shop, and the shopkeeper will cut off the correct coupons. (You cannot use coupons which you yourself have taken off).

7. To save trouble you may tell the shopkeeper to take a whole page of coupons. If you do so you must first write the child's name and address and sign your name in the space provided on the page, and the shopkeeper must write the words "Page deposited", the number of the page and the date, below his name and address inside the cover.

8. BUT do not have a whole page taken out if you expect the child to go away from home to a boarding school or on holiday.

9. COUPONS **NOT** USED IN THE WEEK FOR WHICH THEY ARE INTENDED CANNOT BE USED LATER. Cut them off and destroy them.

10. If the child lives in a hotel, boarding house, or similar establishment, do not take this book to a shop yourself—hand it to the manager or whoever is responsible for the feeding

PAGE 4

arrangements; he or she will use the coupons and return the book when the child leaves.

11. If the child goes to a boarding school, hand this book to the head of the school for use there during term.

12. Leaving home on holiday or removal.—The procedure for a child who goes away from home on holidays or moves to another district will be the same as that set out in paragraphs 12 and 14 of the instructions in the General Ration Book (R.B.1).

13. If the child leaves home suddenly, because of an air raid or other emergency, the person accompanying the child should take this ration book with him if possible. In any case they should go to the nearest Food Office for an emergency card on arrival.

14. If the child is leaving Great Britain, the procedure is the same as that set out in paragraph 16 of the instructions in the General Ration Book (R.B.1).

15. Spare coupons. Do nothing with the pages numbered 11, 12 and 13 until you are told what to do.

16. Spare counterfoils. Do nothing with the counterfoils on page 15 (marked S.C.1, S.C.2, S.C.3, and S.C.4) until told what to do.

17. Penalties for misuse. Any false statement, misuse of this book or breach of these instructions renders you liable to a penalty.

This book may only be used by or on behalf of the person named on the cover

How did rationing change during the war?

SOURCE 6 ▷
A chart published in the *Illustrated London News*, December 1942.

1 Study Source 6 carefully. Work in groups of six. Take one panel each and summarise the changes described in your panel. (NB the person who takes the rationing panel will need to look back to page one of this investigation.)

2 Which of the changes mentioned in Source 6 would have most effect on:
a) a poor family
b) a rich family living in Britain?

3 Can you see connections in Source 6 between:
a) the numbers registered for national service and the numbers unemployed
b) the restriction of civilian supplies and the increase in war production?
Account for any connections that you see.

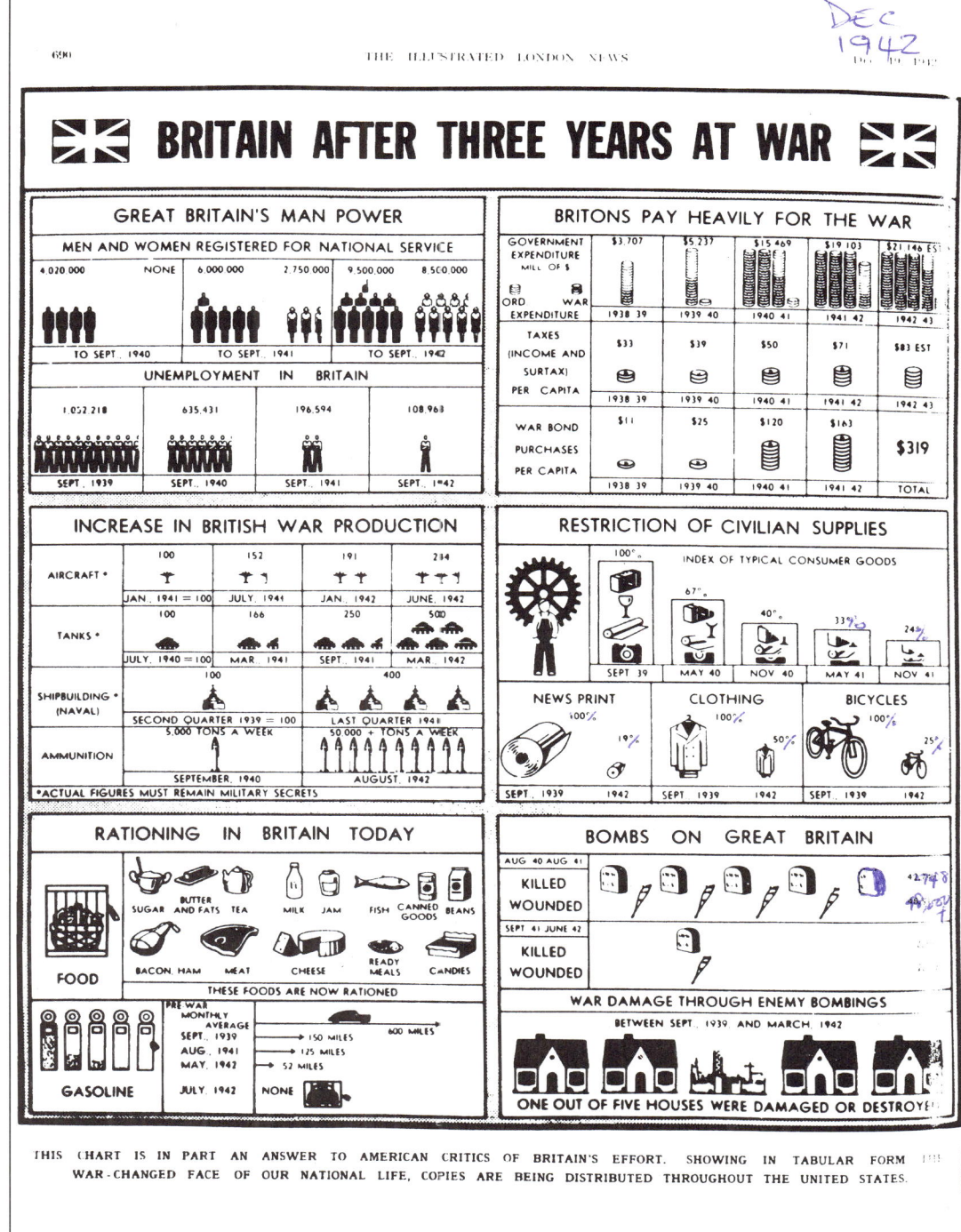

BRITAIN AFTER THREE YEARS AT WAR

THIS CHART IS IN PART AN ANSWER TO AMERICAN CRITICS OF BRITAIN'S EFFORT. SHOWING IN TABULAR FORM WAR-CHANGED FACE OF OUR NATIONAL LIFE, COPIES ARE BEING DISTRIBUTED THROUGHOUT THE UNITED STATES.

II. ATTITUDES TO RATIONING

Immediately the war broke out the main staple foods with the exception of flour and potatoes were rationed and since then a number of other foods have been included in the scheme.

The Survey carried out 5 separate investigations into people's attitudes to rationing. In the beginning of 1942, about one and a half years after rationing had come into force, 4577 people all over England were asked "What do you think about food rationing?" Every one of these 4577 people said that they approved of rationing in principle.

SOURCE 7

A map of Britain showing areas in which the surveys in Sources 8–10 were conducted.

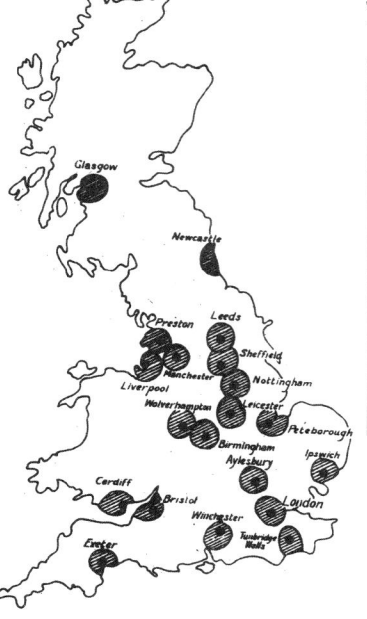

SOURCE 8

An extract from a Ministry of Information Wartime Social Survey entitled 'Attitudes to Rationing', 1942–3.

SOURCE 9

An extract from a Ministry of Information Wartime Social Survey entitled 'Food and Health'.

Interviewing was carried out during the period 30th April – 13th May 1942

The purpose of this inquiry was to discover whether people felt their health had been affected by wartime diet. The replies received are of course, subjective estimates, and the results should be regarded as showing opinions and not facts.

A general sample of the population was interviewed, 2,027 people being selected in representative proportions from different regions and occupations.

Informants were asked: "Do you find that wartime food has affected your general health at all?"

	%
Yes	17.0
Only a little	10.8
No	69.2
Don't know	3.0
Sample:	2,027

IX. WARTIME DIFFICULTIES

An Inquiry made by the Wartime Social Survey for the Ministry of Information, May, 1942

Interviewing was carried out during the period 30th April to 13th May.

"Are you having any personal difficulties as a result of the war?"

The purpose of this question was to find out whether informants felt that they were having difficulties. Only the subjective point of view of the informant was taken into account and no enquiry of a factual sort was made into the difficulties experienced.

Interviewers were instructed not to prompt in any circumstances, and if the informant said "No" they were told to record this answer even though remarks made previously during the interview showed that some difficulties were being experienced.

		%
Yes	753	37.5
No	1258	62.5
Sample	2011	

SOURCE 10 ▷

Extracts from a 1942 Ministry of Information Wartime Social Survey entitled 'Wartime Difficulties'.

How did people feel about rationing and wartime shortages?

1 Study Sources 7–10 carefully. Why do you think every person questioned said that he or she approved of rationing in principle?

2 Does this mean that rationing was popular?

3 According to Source 9, were people affected physically by rationing?

4 What might you like to know about the Government Wartime Social Surveys before you decided whether or not the evidence in Sources 7–9 was reliable?

5 What do the sources in this investigation tell us about the attitude at home to wartime restrictions?

All those who said they were having difficulties were asked what these were.

		% of sample
Food (shortage, rationing, price)	257	12.8
Money (reduced income, increased cost of living)	158	7.9
Work (too much work, not enough rest, inconvenient hours)	66	3.3
Anxiety about family (members in Forces or away from home)	63	3.1
Clothing (coupons)	63	3.1
Transport (bad service, etc.)	59	
Labour shortage (managers and employers)	53	
House bombed or damaged	35	
Evacuated	33	
Tobacco & drinks (shortage, price)	31	
Unsettled feeling (disorganisation of ordinary life or "nerves")	31	
Food regulations (distributive workers)	25	
Petrol shortage	14	
Fuel shortage	11	
Billetees	10	
Blackout	6	
Miscellaneous	73	
Total having difficulties:	(749)	
Sample	2011	

Well before the war started, the British government began to think about the effects of war on the economy and particularly on food production.

As in the First World War, women were expected to be an important resource. Male workers could be released for the armed forces while women helped to maintain production on the land.

Sources 1–3 are all posters issued by the government in the early years of the war.

1 Look carefully at Sources 1–3. Make a list of all the activities you can see women doing.

2 Which of the posters are asking women to join the Land Army?

3 What message do you think the third poster is trying to put across?

4 In what ways do the posters give the impression that life in the Women's Land Army was an enjoyable experience?

5 In what way do you think these posters could be described as propaganda?

SOURCE 1 ▷

SOURCE 2 ▷

SOURCE 3 ◁

GROWTH OF BRITAIN'S Women's Land Army

1940	1942	1943
8,981	59,380	84,463★

★ Of this total, 5,332 women work in the forests and woods of Britain as members of the Women's Timber Corps

The Women's Land Army helped Britain to feed its population during the war years. The work was varied and tough. It included milking and dairy work, care of animals, tractor driving, field work, pest control, fruit and vegetable cultivation and timber production.

To join the Land Army you had to be aged 17–40 and to be strong and healthy. You also had to be able to give full time service anywhere in Britain that you might be sent.

Source 1 shows you the rate at which the Land Army grew. Sources 2–11 give you various impressions of what life was like in the Women's Land Army.

◀ SOURCE 1
A government press release.

SOURCE 2 ▷
A drawing from 'The Land Girl', a magazine for members of the Land Army, December 1940. It was drawn by a member of the Land Army.

1 List the differences and similarities between the two images of a Land Girl in Source 2.

As we hope we look.

As we generally do look.

M. Fedden (Glos.)
W.L.A. No. 22675

Doreen O'Neill, W.L.A. 35597 (W. Sussex).

Her First Attempt

O Daisy, *need* you look so stern?
　I know it's early in the day,
But Land Girls have a lot to learn,
　(That's what I heard the farmer say).

O Daisy, *must* you swish your tail,
　And look at me with eyes of scorn?
For if you overturn the pail—
　I'll get the blame, *you'll* only yawn !

O Daisy dear ! That moo must mean :
　" *You've* never milked a cow before ! "
I know I've not, but still, I'm keen—
　Good-bye, I'm off to milk some more !

　　　DAPHNE J. POOLE,
　　　　　W.L.A. 36759, Herts.

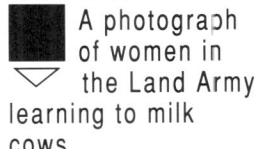

SOURCE 3
A drawing from 'The Land Girl', August 1944. It was drawn by a member of the Land Army.

SOURCE 4
A photograph of women in the Land Army learning to milk cows.

1 Briefly describe what you see happening in the drawing in Source 3.

2 Look at Source 4. Why do you think the women are not practising on 'real' cows?

3 What impressions of women are given by Sources 3 and 4?

4 Which of the images in Sources 2–4 would the government prefer the public to see? Explain your choice.

British Official Photograph.
DISTRIBUTED BY THE MINISTRY OF INFORMATION NO.D.11247........
ARREST THAT RAT.
Amid the lovely Sussex Downs is a training school for Rat
Exterminators. The trainees are girls of the Women's Land
Army, who in times of peace worked in homes shops and factories. They are combating the vast army of 50,000,000
rats which devour the nation's food. The girls are volunteers from all parts of Britain and are trained by Major
M. Phillips, a Ministry of Agriculture expert and one of
the most successful rat exterminators in the country. He
teaches them all he has learnt in years of rat-hunting:
how to recognise rat trails, how to track down their lairs
and how to exterminate them. He shows them the time hon-
oured method of working with dogs, then initiates them into
scientific methods, which are far more effective and account
for rats in thousands instead of tens. When the girls are
trained they are placed in "pools" ready to travel to all
parts of their county and clear rat-infested farms and
fields and in this way assist in the war effort. As rats
not only eat, but destroy enormous stocks, the work of these
volunteers of the W.L.A. is invaluable.

SOURCE 5

A description of the work of the rat-catchers.

1 Read Source 5 carefully. Why was rat-catching important during the War?

2 What methods of killing rats are explained to the women?

3 Is it possible to say anything about the success of the two women in catching rats from one photograph (Source 6)?

4 Why do you think the Ministry of Information might want to see this photograph distributed publicly?

SOURCE 7 ▷

The front page of the 'Land Girl', August 1941.

5 According to Source 7, what problems did the two Land Girls face?

6 Why do you think this article was put on the front page?

7 Why do you think that some farmers needed to be persuaded to employ Land Girls?

SOURCE 6

A photo of two members of the Land Army at work.

THE LAND GIRL

No. 5. Vol. 2.   AUGUST 1941   Price 3d.

TWO GOOD GIRLS

NOT long ago a farmer was persuaded, much against his will, to employ two Land Girls. When they arrived they were given the stiffest and most unpleasant tasks he could find, but, as he was startled to discover, they made a better job of them than any men workers he had ever had.

One of the best things about this perfectly true story is that it was during the *first* month of their employment that these two girls did so well. Probably, like many other new volunteers, they arrived looking forward to farm life, hoping to show what they had learnt in their training, eager to do their best. They met all the usual difficulties, a new place, strange people, an unfamiliar life—in addition, they had the (fortunately much less common) experience of being unwelcome. It must have been sheer determination not to be beaten in the war work they had promised to do which kept them at their posts and brought them finally the respect and admiration of those who had never wanted them to come.

The first month is a difficult time for any new member of the Land Army and it is essential to remember that right judgment takes time. If you are tempted to throw up your job remember that what you think and feel now will probably seem incredible to you a few months hence. Give the Land Army and yourself a fair chance and determine that, having put your hand to the plough, you will not turn back until victory is won.

M. A. P.

2   THE LAND GIRL   JULY, 1940

HELPING THE FARMER

Mr. S. B. Carter has kindly given us permission to print the following extracts from his recent broadcast.

DON'T forget a pair of loose fitting gloves for the first day or two at any rate. And trim those long nails down a bit—otherwise you are likely to break them off short—and whilst you are at it I should leave the nail polish off for a day or two. It doesn't matter a bit, of course, but it does look a bit more workmanlike to turn out all natural for once. I cannot begin to advise you about make-up, but I do know that a bottle of calamine lotion will save the skin on your nose if the sun did happen to be fierce.

One of the curses of work in the open air is the midges and the gnats. Get yourself a bottle of oil of lavender or oil of cloves and rub it well round your neck and behind your ears and round your wrists and ankles before you start out in the day. It is surprising how this helps. That and a tin of zinc ointment should protect you against most of the insects you are likely to come up against.

When you get to the farm remember that, although you are probably a frightfully big noise in your own office, down on the farm you are just an office boy and conduct yourself accordingly. Keep your mouth shut and your eyes and ears open and when the farm workmen show you how to do a certain operation follow them explicitly. It is not a bit of good trying to invent short cuts, because they have proved over hundreds of years the best way to do that particular job. I said a moment ago, keep your mouth shut. Of course, I don't mean that you should be absolutely dumb, but take hay-making, for instance; it is a nerve-racking time for the farmer in our British climate, and when he does get going the amount of staff work necessary to keep the gang in the field and the gang at the rick both working to full capacity would make the average staff officer pass out. That being so, the farmer really has not got time to listen to your experiences on the pier at Brighton last year, or the wonderful time

you had on the top of Snowdon in '37. Remember he is the boss, and treat him as you would like to be treated in similar circumstances.

You will find the regular workmen very helpful. Keep both eyes open and watch the economy of effort by which they carry on the day's work. If you are working alongside them don't try and go at twice their pace. If you do you will be stretched out under a hedge after a couple of hours whilst they are still carrying on. Remember all the time that they know what they are doing, and do your best to imitate them. If you will do what you are told without fuss and bother you are going to earn the respect of the farmer and his workmen, you are going to make no small contribution towards the winning of the war, and, what to my mind is the most important thing of all, you are going to learn something about the countryman and the countryman is going to learn something about you, which will be of the utmost value when we come to adjust ourselves after the war.

SOURCE 8

Part of a radio broadcast reprinted in 'The Land Girl', July 1940.

1 What advice were the Land Girls given by Mr Carter?

2 What is Mr Carter's attitude towards Land Girls?

3 Why do you think that it might be important to put part of Mr Carter's broadcast in print after its broadcast on the radio?

SOURCE 9 ▷

A poem published in 'The Land Girl', July 1940.

4 What impression does the poet give of the Land Girl?

5 What does the last line of the poem mean?

6 In what way might a poem like this boost morale amongst the Land Girls?

To All Land Girls

FROM AN ADMIRER OF THEIR WORK.

I saw a Land Girl working
    Alone in an open field.
Her hard, once elegant, hands
    A stalwart hoe did wield.
Her back was bent as she slew the weeds
    That spoiled the potatoes' growth;
She never wilted, she never paused,
    She had taken her silent oath.

At last the day was nearly done,
    The sun was sinking low;
She gathered up her jacket
    Then slowly cleaned her hoe.
She passed the chair where I sat
    (I am feeble in body and sight).
She smiled at me as she said :
    " Been hot to-day. Good-night."

We hear the valiant deeds of our men in
    " furrin parts,"
Deeds which bring the tears to our eyes, a
    glow of pride to our hearts—
But when the war is over and peace at last
    restored,
I shall always remember the Land Girl, who
made her hoe her sword.

BACK TO THE LAND

Words by
P. ADKINS. W.L.A. 28299
& J. MONCRIEFF

Music by
E. K. LORING. W. L. A. 2068

1

Back to the Land, we must all lend a hand,
To the farms and the fields we must go.
There's a job to be done,
Though we can't fire a gun
We can still do our bit with the hoe.
When your muscles are strong
You will soon get along,
And you'll think that a country life's grand.
We're all needed now,
We must all speed the plough,
So come with us—Back to the Land.

2

Back to the Land, with its clay and its sand,
Its granite and gravel and grit,
You grow barley and wheat
And potatoes to eat
To make sure that the nation keeps fit.
Remember the rest
Are all doing their best,
To achieve the results they have planned
We will tell you once more
You can help win the war
If you come with us— Back to the Land.

The above, which is part of a Land Army opera by two Surrey members, should go with a swing at Land Army parties. Single Copies 1d. each, 2d. post free, or 12 for 1s., post free, can be obtained from the Editor.

◁ **SOURCE 10**

A song written by two Land Girls published in 'The Land Girl', August 1940.

1 How can you tell that the song was written by Land Girls?

2 In what ways is it similar to the poem in Source 9?

3 Why do you think the song-writers describe life as a Land Girl in a glamorous way when Source 2 might support the opposite point of view?

4 Does the contradiction between Sources 9 and 10 mean that one of them is unreliable?

SOURCE 11 ▷

A message to the Women's Land Army from Buckingham Palace, 'The Land Girl', December 1941.

5 Several of the sources you have studied so far have encouraged Land Girls in their work. Why do you think it may have been important to have a message of encouragement for them from the Royal Family?

6 Why might this message have been particularly important in the December issue?

7 Using Sources 1–11:
a) write a paragraph to explain what impression the government wanted to give to the public about the Women's Land Army
b) Write another paragraph to explain why a newly-recruited Land Girl might want to give up and go home rather than stay working on the farm.

8 Look back at all the information in this investigation about the Land Army. Take each of the criteria for selection in turn. Explain why these conditions were necessary to become a Land Girl, using Sources 1–11.

9 Some women joined the Land Army and hated the experience. Even so, they stayed on and worked in the Land Army for the whole of the war. Why do you think they did this?

THE LAND GIRL

No. 9. Vol. 2.   DECEMBER, 1941   Price 3d.

MESSAGE TO THE WOMEN'S LAND ARMY

BUCKINGHAM PALACE.

AS your patron I send a message to all those who are enrolled in the Women's Land Army to-day.

You have indeed earned the right to think of yourselves as an Army, for not only are there more than 20,000 serving in your ranks to-day, but by your skill and devotion you have released great battalions of men who now fight for the land which formerly they tilled.

Their task is now in your hands, and it has in these stern days a far greater importance than ever before; every acre cultivated means more food for our own people; every hour worked means fewer ships hazarded on the high seas, and the release of sailors and tonnage for vital war needs.

Whilst therefore you are sustaining life you are doing what is even more precious—you are saving lives.

I do not wonder, then, that you are proud of the share you have in our fortunes to-day.

Work on the land in winter asks more of you than in summer time : the sun shines less warmly and darkness falls before your tasks are done. The need however is as great, and I know well that you will not weary in the labours to which you have set your hand.

Better days lie ahead of us all, and meanwhile I wish you all a very Happy Christmas, and I send you with all my heart every good wish and my thanks for what you are doing.

ELIZABETH R.

WOMEN'S AUXILIARY FIRE SERVICE: UNIFORM FOR GENERAL WORK, WORN BY BOTH OFFICERS AND FIREWOMEN.

SOURCE 1

A RED CROSS NURSE. THE BRITISH RED CROSS AND ST. JOHN AMBULANCE HAVE COMBINED FOR WAR SERVICE.

SOURCE 2

SOURCE 4 ▷

JUST A GOOD AFTERNOON'S WORK

SOURCE 3

Ceaselessly new vehicles roll off the production lines. Army units await them, the ATS deliver them

SOURCE 5 ▷

SOURCE 6

GRINDING A 6-POUNDER TANK-GUN BARREL: MISS ALLEN, WEARING GOGGLES
AS PROTECTION AGAINST WHITE-HOT PARTICLES OF STEEL, MAKES THE SPARKS FL

She's in the Ranks too !

CARING FOR EVACUEES
IS A NATIONAL SERVICE

ISSUED BY THE MINISTRY OF HEALTH

1 Women had a wide range of roles to play in the war. Sources 1–6 portray a few of them. Use these six sources and your own research to write a short account of the ways in which women contributed to the war effort.

29 WHAT WAS IT LIKE TO BE A FEMALE INTERNEE?

By May 1940, the Germans had almost complete control of Holland, Belgium, and Northern France. It seemed that Hitler's next move might be to invade Britain. On 27 May 1940 the British government announced it was going to intern (put in prison) many German and Italian people who were living in Britain – especially those living in high risk areas of Britain such as the southern and eastern coastlines and London.

These people included approximately 5000 women together with their children under 16 years of age.

The villages of Port Erin and Port St. Mary on the Isle of Man were suggested as suitable places to house such numbers. The area was declared a Prohibited Area and was wired off in order to prevent any escapes.

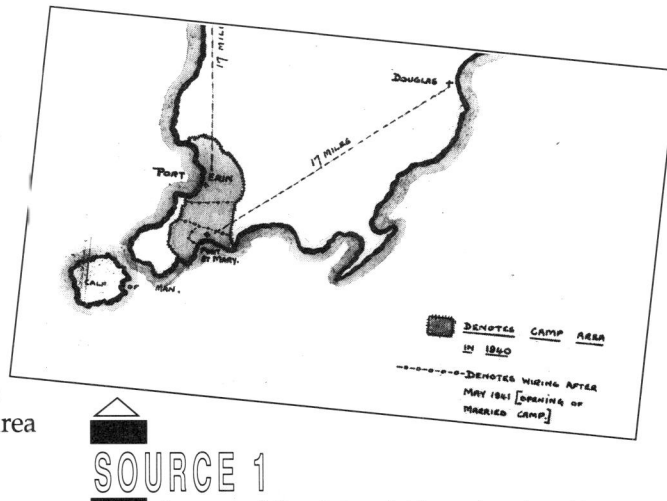

SOURCE 1
A map of the Isle of Man showing the internment camps.

SOURCE 2 ▽
Extracts from an official report into conditions for the internees during the war.

1 Why do you think the government decided to intern German women?

2 Describe in your own words the location of the camp on the Isle of Man.

3 The internees were all kept in one area of the island. Why do you think this was?

A

In order to appreciate the size and ramifications of this so-called Camp one must imagine two small seaside towns situated only 1½ miles apart. The area surrounding both towns was wired with single strand interlaced barb wire to a height of 6 feet, and then with a cross angle wire extending to 7 feet, the enclosed area amounting to 2,120 acres. The main roads to each town were fitted with barriers or gates which were manned throughout the twenty four hours by Auxiliary Constables recruited locally on the Isle of Man. In addition to the manning of the barriers the Auxiliary Constables patrolled the Camp perimeter throughout the day and night. (An advantage in employing local men for this work was that they knew by sight the local residents.

Within the wired area (see map) a community of enemy alien women lived, had access to shops and could walk uninterrupted to any area within the confines of the camp. They could use beaches and foreshore, attend two special matinees at a cinema within the confines of the Camp and, in fact, were able to enjoy the amenities of a seaside resort. They were subject to a strict curfew, that is to say they could only be out of doors from 8a.m. until 9p.m. in summer and 9a.m. to 5.30p.m. in winter. In addition many local defence regulations were made to prevent fraternization between local residents and interned persons. No local residents were permitted to speak to internees or invite them to their homes even though the homes were within the confines of the Camp. This defence regulation had obviously to be interpreted liberally for obvious conversation was necessary between internees and shop-keepers and between landladies and their billetees. To prevent escape by sea the harbour was banned to all shipping.

ramifications: arrangement, organisation
auxiliary constables: extra police
fraternization: making friends

4 Read extracts A–M in source 2 carefully. Make a list of all the restrictions that were imposed on the internees.

B

A Roll Call was made every morning and evening, and householders were made responsible to report any absentees to the Commandant. These Rolls Calls were supervised by Police women. Evening roll call was at 9.30p.m. the lights in bedrooms being allowed on from 9.30p.m. to 10p.m. so that internees were forced to remain in the lounges until roll call if they required a light.

C

The internees were billeted in the hotels, boarding houses, apartment houses and, in fact, in every available house that could offer accommodation. In the early days there was much grumbling through overcrowding, and in some cases there was every justification for such complaints. In the summer of 1940 at least two internees were billeted in each room, and in many cases three or four shared a room.

D

Complaints, however, were rampant, particularly from married women who in the early period were separated from their husbands. The early complaints can be summarized as follows:

   a. Lack of food.

   b. No books for reading or study.

   c. Hold up of mail, and internees only permitted to write two letters per week, and no letter to exceed 24 lines.

   d. Houses and bedrooms were cold with insufficient bed clothing.

   e. No facilities given for education of children.

   f. No religious services.

   g. Many internees had no clothes or money.

   h. Lack of medical attention.

   i. Jews and National Socialists were indiscriminately mixed.

E

The task of segregation was one of the most urgent matters if the camp life was to run smoothly and consequently Nazi houses were set up, as distinct from loyal Germans (Non-Nazis) and further segregation had to be made in the Refugee houses, there being Orthodox or Kosher and Liberal non Kosher houses.

segregation: separation

F

Italian women were billeted in hotels by themselves, as *they did not* get on with German women, and Jehovah's Witnesses were together in another hotel.

G

The laundry problem was solved by the camp securing a number of lock-up garages, fitted with gas boilers, washing baths, mangles, ironing boards and irons. These made ideal centres for washing clothes, with drying grounds provided close by. Each internee had a specified time each week when she could attend the laundry.

H

The greatest hardship in internment were the long winter evenings when internees were forced to occupy a common lounge from 5.30p.m. to 9.30p.m. each evening, seeing the same faces night after night. Over a long period this tried even the most placid persons and I found tempers more frayed from November to March than at any other time of the year.

I

The amount of food was adequate, an allowance of 4 lbs of bread, two-sevenths of an ounce of tea (or coffee) and one pint of milk (exclusive of milk puddings) being allowed per 10 women daily.

swear allegiance: promise loyalty

J

Clothing was provided from Government Funds to those internees who were destitute. In deciding whether an internee was destitute the following rule was applied:- If an internee had over £5 to her credit in the Camp Bank, or if she received money from friends in England to the extent of 10/- per week then she was a non-destitute and was expected to clothe herself. In order to encourage internees to make their own clothes, material was provided instead of ready made articles. This scheme was commendable because it gave women internees something to occupy their time, and gave an added interest in addition to the educational value of learning dressmaking.

K

For those internees who were absolutely penniless the Government provided 1/6d per week pocket money. All internees who were prepared to swear allegiance to the Third Reich and who had signed for Repatriation were, by regulations of the Nazi Government, eligible for pocket money amounting to 5/- per month. This money was received approximately every quarter through the Swiss Government (The Protecting Power).

L

The German Red Cross sent parcels. The German parcels were bulk parcels i.e. parcels addressed and intended for no special individuals but intended for all internees. It was the duty of the Camp Leader to distribute the contents. Every German in the Camp thought she was entitled to a share, but the Nazis maintained that the contents were only for internees who had signed allegiance to the Third Reich. The Camp Administration stood aloof from this argument which raged for the whole of the internment period. The non Nazis complained to the International Red Cross at Geneva and asked for an interpretation of the rule as to who should receive parcels. The International Red Cross were loathe to give any ruling but adopted the attitude that they were purely forwarding agents. The Nazis sought the opinion of the Protecting Power who with admirable diplomacy failed to get any decision.

M

As regards the children. In the early days of the Camp two schools were maintained, one at Port Erin and another at Port St. Mary. The Kindergarten was under the supervision of an English member of the staff but her assistants were all internees who were paid 3/6d per week from Public Funds. There were two Elementary Schools under the direction of fully qualified teachers (members of staff). School equipment, desks, blackboards etc. were kindly loaned by the Isle of Man Educational Authority. Text books were the main problem. We started from scratch and appeals to local residents for school books brought a very mixed collection. The German Red Cross also sent books but as these were mainly highly flavoured with Nazi doctrines they were with-held. The syllabus of the school was set on the lines of an English school with German as the foreign language. This caused complaints from the Nazi parents who, knowing they would be repatriated to Germany pressed for a German curriculum. This was obviously out of the question, for one thing the parents of refugee children asked for an English syllabus even to the exclusion of the teaching of German.

SOURCE 3

A photograph of the kindergarten in the internment camp.

5 List as much information as you can find out from all the sources in this investigation about the following aspects of camp life:
  a) education
  b) relationship between internees
  c) food
  d) clothing.

6 Divide into groups of three and each choose one of the following women:
  a) a pro-Nazi German with a young child
  b) a Jewish woman with a young child
  c) an anti-Nazi German woman with a young child.
Using all of the sources in this investigation write four paragraphs to describe what life in the camp would have been like for the woman you have chosen.

7 Compare your descriptions and discuss any differences.

8 Should these alien women have been interned? Explain your answer.

SOURCE 1 ▽▷

Extracts from two government posters entitled: 'Useful jobs that girls can do to help win the war' and 'Simple jobs boys can do themselves and so help win the war'.

1 Cut up these extracts to make a pile of 16 cards.

2 Sort the cards into two piles: those that you think were part of the 'Jobs for girls . . .' poster and those that you think were part of the 'Jobs for boys . . .' poster.

3 Arrange your extracts into your own posters for girls and boys. There may be some that you would like to put on both posters. Write two more suggestions of your own.

COLLECT WOOD ASH

—the clean white kind—to put in a jar near the sink. It makes a good scouring powder and helps to remove stains from metal and china.

How to Refix HANDLES ON FURNITURE

It's because the holes of the screws which hold them have worked too large that drawer handles, etc., come loose. Take off the fitting and plug these holes by inserting bits of any hard wood—an old wood penholder would do—sharpened to points and snapped off to suitable lengths. These can be hammered in to make a really tight fit. Put the handle back into position and replace screws, which will now hold firmly.

S.O.S. for a SCRUBBING BUCKET

An ordinary pot mender from the ironmonger's will stop a leak in a bucket. The discs should be fixed on each side of the hole and held with a screw and nut, the cork disc being placed inside the bucket under one of the metal discs.

HOW TO OIL DOOR LOCKS

Yale type locks themselves must not be oiled, but a film of oil on the catch bolts is a good thing. Ordinary locks should be oiled by putting just a drop or two of oil. on the catch bolt, turning the handle until the bolt is inside the lock and then blowing sharply, to spread the oil inside the lock.

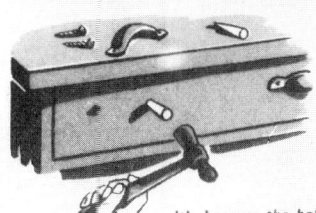

Useful jobs that Girls can do — TO HELP WIN THE WAR

Polishing Pads

for windows and mirrors can be made successfully from worn-out washleather gloves. First rescue any bits good enough for elbow patches or cuff-bindings ; then cut open the fingers, remove fasteners and lay several gloves flat on top of one another. Stitch a small circle in the centre of the pad to hold it together.

HOW TO REPAIR *A Frayed Flex*

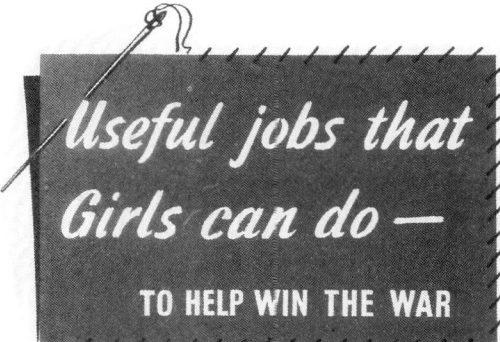

The connecting leads for reading lamps, electric wires, etc., often wear so that the wire itself is exposed where it enters the plug. This is dangerous. Remove the plug from the socket. Get a length of electrician's tape and wind it spiral-wise round the frayed part, wrapping each wire separately first and then binding them together. Pay particular attention to the ends where they join the plug. To prevent fraying in future grip the plug itself when pulling it out, instead of pulling on the wire.

HOW TO MEND A TABLE LEG

Where a table or chair leg has broken, diagonally below the level of the rails connecting the legs, a satisfactory repair can be carried out by warming the broken ends of the leg, well glueing the fracture and pressing the two pieces firmly together. Wipe off the surplus glue with a clean rag soaked in warm water and tightly bind the joint with string. When the glue in the joint has set (allow 24 hours undisturbed) remove the string, soak off if necessary, and clean the joint with a wet rag as before.

In cases where the leg has snapped off across the grain of the wood a temporary repair may be effected as follows :—

Turn the table or chair upside down in a level position, warm and glue the fracture, as previously described, then press the broken leg very firmly downwards until the fractured ends engage closely. Leave the joint undisturbed for 24 hours, then clean off the surplus glue. Prepare two tablets of hardwood or plywood about 4 inches to 5 inches long, ¼ inch thick, and of a width equal to that of the leg. Bore a suitable number of holes in each tablet and screw them on opposite faces of the leg. An equal number of screws should be inserted above and below the fracture and no screws should be inserted within one inch of the joint. The edges of the tablets can be smoothed off and the tablets stained if desired.

WHEN A DRAWER STICKS

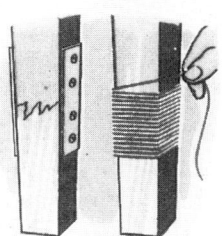

scrape its edges well with a chisel. Then rub the trimmed parts with candle wax.

How to put in a NEW PANE OF GLASS

First take out all remaining fragments of broken glass and every particle of old putty (Fig. 1). Wear old gloves while doing this to guard against cuts. The recess of the wooden frame must be clean or when the new pane is put in position, it may crack.

Now measure the opening of the frame, with the greatest care. Use a wooden rule rather than a tape measure. Find the exact height and width of the recess and then buy a piece of glass that is exactly one-eighth of an inch less both ways than these measurements. (For instance, for a recess 24˝ × 15˝, the glass should be 23⅞˝ × 14⅞˝.) Provide yourself with putty at the same time. Try in the glass, without putty first, to confirm that it really fits.

When you start to fix the new pane, knead the putty well, so that the warmth of your hands will make it soft and pliable. Then, run a very thin line of putty all round the inside of the recess, to make a bed on which the glass may rest (Fig. 2). Next put the pane in position—better get another pair of hands to help you here. When the pane is in place, gently press it back against the wood frame (Fig. 3). If it will not go back, that's because too much putty was used to make the bed—take it out and use less. This is when the pane is apt to crack if any old hard putty

has been left in the frame.

As soon as the glass is in position it should be held by three brads, about 4˝ from corners, with one additional brad at the centre of

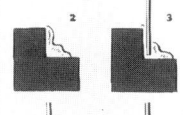

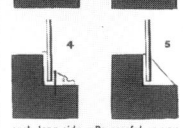

each long side. Be careful as you drive these in—see that they go parallel to the glass but not quite touching it (Fig. 4). If they slant towards the glass, they may crack it.

Now run a fillet of putty all round the edge of the glass and give it a bevelled surface with the blade of an old table knife (Fig. 5). Imitate the surround of one of the existing panes as closely as possible. Finish off by trimming away from the inside any putty squeezed out of the recess.

SNUG SLIPPERS *from* OLD FELT HAT

Make yourself a pair of cosy slippers to save your outdoor shoes *and* your coupons. Besides an old felt hat, you will need several stockings, a little strong canvas and some gay scraps for lining.

First cut paper patterns—two heel pieces, one upper and a sole for each slipper. Use the diagrams as a guide to shape and an old slipper as a guide to size.

Unpick and brush the hat and place the patterns as shown a & b. Cut out and, if you like, cut a simple openwork design on the upper fronts before lining.

Using the same patterns but allowing ¼˝ for turnings, cut out linings. Any soft material will be suitable.

Join felt heel pieces with a flat seam, machined and backstitched. Press turnings outwards and face with tape, for strength. Stitch tape down on each side of seam (c). Do the heel linings the same way. Then join the linings to the felt (uppers and heels) by turning in the lining edges and slip stitching on wrong side.

Cut soles from an old piece of canvas as a foundation for plaiting. Prepare the plaited strands by cutting old stockings spiral-wise (d) and plaiting (e). Sew these strands to the canvas (f) beginning from outer edge and following the arrow.

To join uppers to soles, take the heels first and sew to canvas turnings. Use two needles (see diagram g) each of which should enter the holes made by the other so that the stitches will be even on both sides. Attach uppers in the same way, letting them overlap slightly where they join the heels. Start from centre toe and centre back.

Cut cardboard 'socks' slightly smaller than soles and pad with a layer or two of soft material. Cover with lining material, drawing this together on the underside and stitching firmly. Attach to inside sole with strong adhesive.

How to clear a CHOKED SINK

Place a pail under the screw cap at the bottom of the U bend or trap and undo this cap with the aid of a strong bar —a screwdriver shaft, say. A rush of water will come directly the cap is off and it will bring accumulations of hair, etc., with it. But if the pipe is still stopped up, poke it clear with a stick inserted at the sink end. Be sure to screw cap on again securely.

Sometimes a sink can be cleared if the stoppage is not too stubborn by placing the palm of the hand or a swabbing cloth over the opening and rapidly lifting it up and down, causing suction.

An *EASY* renovation

When the sleeves wear out of a favourite frock and it gets too short for you, turn it into a slipover to wear with a blouse and skirt. The neckline can be cut in square or V shape as suits you best and the armholes rounded deeply. Outline both neck and armholes first with tacking stitches as a guide to cutting. Allow ¼ for turning and face with bias binding. Dart slightly at the waist, shorten to hip length and hem.

TO AVOID 'seating' A SKIRT

Prevention is better than cure—remember not to lounge about in a tailored skirt. Change it directly you come in, always hang it up when it's not being worn and keep it well pressed. For extra precaution, put a rectangle of some strong material—the best part of an old dress or coat lining, for instance, across the back. Cut this a shade narrower than the back breadth and hem it to each side seam. It should be attached to the waistband at the top and come well below the hips.

Simple jobs boys can do themselves— AND SO HELP WIN THE WAR

ISSUED BY THE BOARD OF TRADE

TO REFIX A LOOSE KNIFE HANDLE

is not difficult provided the 'tang' (the bit that goes into the handle) is at least 1½ in. long. First clean out the hole in the handle with a metal skewer. Then powder a little ordinary resin and fill the hole with it; on top put a bit of candle wax the size of a pea. Heat the 'tang' until it will melt the resin and press it into the resin-filled hole. Quickly drop the knife into warm (not hot) water. Leave for a few minutes, take out and trim off any surplus resin.

How to do a DARN

Pass the threads backwards and forwards across the hole, as closely as possible, beginning and ending an inch eash side of the hole, leaving tiny loops at each end. Then re-thread your needle and darn across these threads, ewaving under and over, turning round and coming back so that the needle goes under threads it passed over the time before. Repeat until hole is filled in. The loops at each end allow for stretching and are very important.

HOW TO SEW ON A BUTTON

Mark the exact spot for the button with a pin, and if much pull is likely, cut a small square of extra material to back the button ; or use another small button to take the strain. Start on the inside, having knotted your thread. Pass the needle through the material, the holes in the button, and so through the material again. Go backwards and forwards about ten times, leaving slack enough to form the shank, which should be longer on a thick material than on a thin one. Twist the thread round and round the slack to make a sort of stalk, and take a final stitch or two on the wrong side before cutting it off.

4 Choose two jobs from each poster and say why you think they might help Britain to win the war.

5 Your teacher will tell you which posters the extracts came from. When you have found out, write a paragraph explaining the differences between the roles girls were expected to take and the roles boys were expected to take.

SOURCE 1 ▷

Extracts from an eye-witness report from the Warsaw Ghetto in 1942 (published in Britain and America in 1943).

1 Study the extracts in Source 1 carefully. Explain how the writers are attempting to stir the reader into doing something to help the Polish Jews.

2 There were many letters and reports of this sort circulating around Allied governments during the second half of the war. However, when the full extent of the Nazi atrocities became known after the War, these governments seemed surprised and horrified at what they found. Can you think of any reasons to explain this?

MARCH, 1943   487 15

AN EYE-WITNESS ACCOUNT FROM POLAND

At the end of October 1942 a secret courier of the United Polish Underground Organizations succeeded in getting out of Nazi-invaded Poland. He reached London at the beginning of December, 1942. For over a year "The Courier" had been a disguised member of the police force of Poland that was organized by the Nazi authorities. He brought with him the following personal eye-witness account, which he transmitted to the two Jewish members of the Polish National Council in London:

I WAS in Poland from the month of October, 1941, until the end of October, 1942, on an official mission to the Polish Underground movement. Throughout this period I was in the very midst of Polish underground activities and I have been charged to transmit to you official information and also facts which I saw with my own eyes and which "B" of the Underground General Jewish Workers Union of Poland has requested me to tell you and to all Jews with whom I may come in contact when I get out of Poland.

"B" requested me to inform you of the following: "Tell them 'there' (outside the Nazi-invaded countries) that there are moments when we hate them all; we hate them because they are safe 'there' and do not rescue us . . . Because they don't do enough. We are only too well aware that in the free and civilized world outside, it is not possible to believe *all* that is happening to us. Let the Jewish people, then, do *something* that will force the other world to believe us . . .

"We are all dying here. Let them not retreat until the civilized world will believe us—until it will undertake some action to rescue those of our people who will remain alive. Merely protests or threats are not sufficient."

Long before the orgy of mass murder which commenced in the middle of July, 1942, conditions in the Warsaw Ghetto were desperate. The hunger was so great that the people became crazed. They refused to share their crumbs. Children would permit their old parents to starve to death. There was nothing left to share.

The aged and children, by the hundreds, would drop dead in the streets and no one paid any attention to them. Corpses lying about in the streets no longer made an impression upon the inhabitants of the Ghetto. Every morning in front of practically every gate there would lie naked corpses. They were stripped of their clothes which were badly needed by the living and cast into the street to avoid funeral expenses. All of the dead gathered during the day would be buried in nameless common graves.

There were thousands of children, whose parents were either murdered or dead of hunger, roaming the streets of the Ghetto. The Germans organized actual hunting parties of these children and shot them in the thousands. In general the Germans demonstrate a particular brutality towards Jewish children. One can cite thousands of cases of people, who, upon returning home from a day of forced labor, no longer found their children alive. Like beasts, the Germans comb the Ghetto during the day, drag children out of their homes or off the streets and shoot them before the Ghetto gates or outside of them. The Nazi authorities distributed arms to the Hitler Youths of 15 and 16, who go in hordes through the streets of the Ghetto and kill all whom they meet in their path. They do not choose; children or grown ups. And when the streets are finally deserted they go into the yards and homes or shoot through the windows.

German soldiers and agents of the Gestapo are running the Hitler Youth a close second in this orgy of murder. They come to the Ghetto in an interminable stream. For amusement they run competitions to determine who is the better shot. Some degenerates even mark their corpses with chalk, so as to be able to check the number they have killed. One Gestapo man by the name of Krause is known to enter a home, lock the door and murder an entire family. Then he marks in chalk on the door the number of persons he had shot that day. In the month of October alone, this Krause had marked in chalk on the door of a home the figure 1006—a thousand and six persons he had personally shot.

It was since July 8, however, when the Germans first introduced special "Squads for the Destruction of Jews" (*Juden-Vernichtungskolonnen*), which at once commenced the mass slaughter, that literally an atmosphere of hell began to permeate the Ghetto. On that day, the Nazi authorities demanded of Dr. Czerniakow, head of the Jewish Ghetto Council, that he select 6000 Jews for "deportation". The following day they demanded 10,000 more and again 10,000 a day after and also 10,00 children. Czerniakow's wife was arrested and he was warned that she would be tortured and shot if he would not comply with the demand. When he inquired of the Germans what they intended to do with the Jews marked for "deportation" they laughed to his face and replied that they would do with them what one should do with Jews. On July 25, during one of these sessions with the Nazi authorities, Dr. Czerniakow excused himself, went into another room, and took poison.

In Winston Churchill's words it was the Soviet Union who 'tore the heart out of the German army'. For three years they withstood the onslaught of the German army against Stalingrad and Leningrad. During this period, the Allies in the West built up their forces in preparation for the D-Day landings that began the reconquest of Western Europe. Over 20 million Soviets died in the effort, but they held out and then drove the Germans back.

The Allies did not send troops to help the Soviet army. The British held a rally in the Albert Hall to praise the Soviet war effort, and they created much propaganda to support the Soviet people. Sources 1–5 are some examples: Sources 1–3 were intended for use in Soviet newspapers.

SOURCE 1

A 'picturegraph' prepared in May 1944.

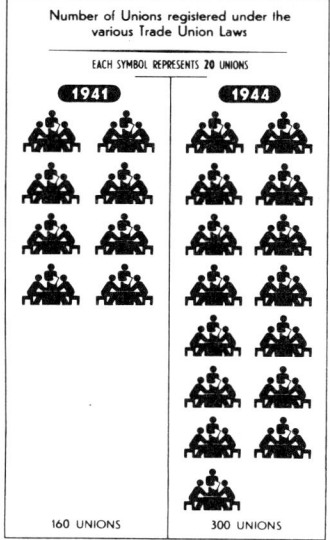

Trade Unions in the British Colonial Empire

DELIBERATELY ENCOURAGED BY GOVERNMENT POLICY

Number of Unions registered under the various Trade Union Laws

EACH SYMBOL REPRESENTS **20** UNIONS

1941 — 160 UNIONS

1944 — 300 UNIONS

SOURCE 2

A 'picturegraph' prepared in October 1944.

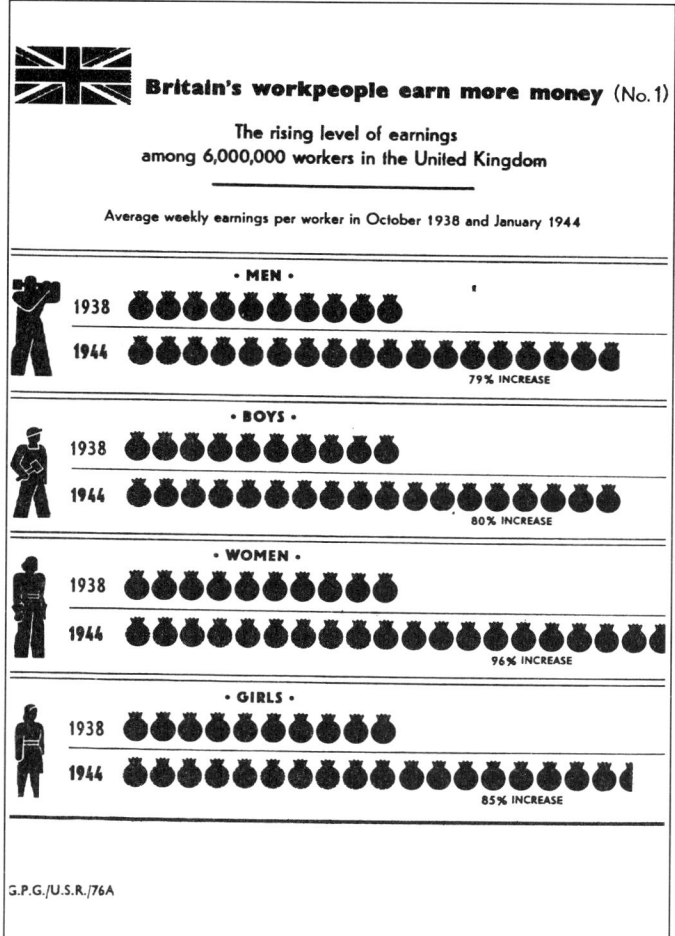

Britain's workpeople earn more money (No. 1)

The rising level of earnings among 6,000,000 workers in the United Kingdom

Average weekly earnings per worker in October 1938 and January 1944

· MEN ·
1938
1944 — 79% INCREASE

· BOYS ·
1938
1944 — 80% INCREASE

· WOMEN ·
1938
1944 — 96% INCREASE

· GIRLS ·
1938
1944 — 85% INCREASE

G.P.G./U.S.R./76A

SOURCE 3 ▷

A 'picturegraph' prepared in January 1944.

R.A.F. smash German supplies bound for the Russian front

Stettin

TO THE RUSSIAN FRONT

Eight times British bombers have flown 1,300 miles to bomb Stettin, the chief Baltic supply port for the German armies in Russia

Stettin was last attacked by the R.A.F. in January 1944. On this and the previous occasion a great force of raiders dropped well over 500 tons of bombs

HEAVY AIR ATTACKS · **A COMPARISON** ·

450 TONS — Luftwaffe's heaviest attack at the height of the London 'blitz'

500 TONS — R.A.F.'s heaviest raids on Stettin

We women of Britain, like our sisters in the Soviet Union, have turned to the most complex tasks of industry. Yesterday we were housekeepers, cooks, we were bringing up our children. Today we handle heavy, man-sized jobs in factories. We work because, like the women of the U.S.S.R., we realise there will be no future for our children or ourselves unless Fascism is destroyed.

One of Britain's women war workers.

TRANSLATION

WE ARE PLEDGED TO SMASH THE FASCIST BARBARIANS

24 HOURS A DAY – UNTIRING, UNRELAXING –

BRITISH WOMEN WORK TO SMASH FASCISM

SOURCE 4
One of a series of eight posters prepared in 1942 for sending to the USSR. (This is a designer's rough; the finished poster had Russian text.)

1 For each of Sources 1–5, say why it is a particularly appropriate message to send to the Soviet Union.

2 Which of these images would be most appropriate in:
a) a newspaper for loyal Communist party officials
b) a newspaper for Soviet soldiers
c) a newspaper for Soviet factory workers
d) a newspaper for the city of Leningrad, which was under siege by the German army from December 1941 until May 1944.

3 Choose one of the newspapers in question 2 above. Write a paragraph of comment to accompany your chosen image on its pages.

SOURCE 5
A cartoon intended for use in Soviet newspapers and posters.

4 Using all the sources in this investigation, list five words or phrases that you think the British government might like the Soviet Union to associate with Britain.

5 Why do you think that the Allies did not send troops to help the Soviet Army to fight the Germans?

All the countries involved in the war produced propaganda. The example produced by Britain on this page was intended to discourage the enemy. British aircraft dropped these leaflets on enemy cities.

SOURCE 1 ▷

A translation of a British propaganda leaflet aimed at the people of Berlin.

BERLINER! Habt Ihr's jetzt begriffen?

Berliner! Habt Ihr den Verstand verloren? Wenn sie Euch erzählen, dass jetzt nur noch England allein den Achsenvölkern gegenübersteht, 47 Millionen gegen 200 Millionen, glaubt Ihr das? Habt Ihr vergessen, dass es ein britisches Weltreich gibt, in dem 492 Millionen gegen Hitler geeinigt sind? Habt Ihr vergessen, dass von den 200 Millionen Sklaven Hitlers mindestens 80 Millionen besiegte Völker sind, die ihre Unterdrücker hassen und auf ihre Stunde warten; und 44 Millionen sind nur Italiener?! Habt Ihr vergessen, dass die ganze industrielle und landwirtschaftliche Produktion Nord- und Südamerikas gegen Euch mobilisiert wird?

Nein, Berliner, Goebbels sagt nicht immer die Wahrheit. Und wenn er Euch sagt, dass England machtlos, ausgehungert, verängstigt ist und in ein paar Tagen erobert werden wird, glaubt Ihr das auch? Habt Ihr vergessen, dass die britische Kriegsflotte mächtiger ist, als alle übrigen europäischen Flotten zusammen? Habt Ihr unsere Luftwaffe vergessen, die in Deutschland herumfliegt, wie es ihr passt und im Juli allein 37 000 Bomben auf militärische Ziele an der Ruhr und im Rheinland abgeworfen hat? Die Bomben, die mit diesen Flugblättern zusammen abgeworfen wurden, sagen Euch —

der Krieg, den Hitler anfing, geht weiter!

Jawohl, Berliner! Erst einmal müsst Ihr nähmlich uns besiegen. Und wenn Ihr hofft, das durch die Luftblockade schaffen zu können, dann überlegt Euch das lieber zweimal; denn die scheint nicht zu funktionieren. Beinahe ein Jahr lang haben sich Goring und Raeder angestrengt, und unsere Kriegsflotte, unsere Handelsflotte, unsere Luftwaffe und unsere Lebensmittelvorräte in England sind alle viel grösser als im letzten September.

Was nun den Versuch eines Einfalles in England angeht, so glauben wir kaum, dass Hitler dazu dumm genug ist. Grossbritannien ist nicht Norwegen. Der Versuch würde das Ende des Krieges — und das Ende von Hitlers Macht bedeuten.

Nein! der Krieg wird anders ausgehen. Dieser lange Krieg — der 1933 anfing, denn Krieg ist die einzige Aufgabe der nationalsozialistischen Diktatur — wird nicht aufhören, wenn Hitler es mag. Wann und wie dieser Krieg aufhört, das bestimmen wir — und mit uns die ganze Welt!

Denn Hitler hat sich verrechnet. Auf seine militärische Macht und die Brutalität der Gestapo gestützt, erwartet er von der Welt, dass sie ihn bewundern soll, den grossen „Eroberer". Aber sie verabscheut ihn. Die nationalsozialistische Diktatur muss untergehen, denn die ganze Aussenwelt ist ihm feindlich, und immer mehr brennt der Hass der Millionen unter seinem Joch.

Volk von Berlin! Früher warst Du einmal als das „hellste" bekannt. Früher wusstest Du, wie Du Deine Meinung durchsetzen konntest. Vielleicht kannst Du nachdenken und herausfinden, wie Du bei Deutschlands Errettung helfen kannst. Im kommenden Kriegswinter aber, und wenn es sein muss noch in vielen Kriegswintern — wirst Du merken, dass wir Recht behalten haben, wenn wir jetzt sagen:

Der Krieg dauert so lange wie Hitlers Regime!

424

1 How does Source 1 encourage Berliners
   a) to doubt their own leaders
   b) to see Britain as a threat?

2 What is the leaflet encouraging Berliners to do?

3 Pick out one fact and one opinion from Source 1. Explain your choices.

4 **Think carefully about what makes good propaganda. Using all that you know about the Second World War, make a leaflet which the Germans might drop on British cities to encourage them to criticise their leaders.**

BERLINERS HAVE YOU GRASPED IT?

Berliners! Have you lost your wits? When you are told that England alone now faces the Axis powers – 47,000,000 people against 200,000,000 – do you believe it? Have you forgotten that there is a British Empire in which 492,000,000 people are united against Hitler? Have you forgotten that of Hitler's 200,000,000 slaves, at least 80,000,000 are conquered nations who hate their conquerors and are awaiting their hour – and 44,000,000 are merely Italians? Have you forgotten that the whole industrial and food productive power of North and South America will be mobilised against you?

No, Berliners, Goebbels does not always tell the truth. And when he tells you that England is powerless, starving, panic-stricken and will be conquered in a few days, do you believe that too? Have you forgotten that the British Navy is more powerful than all other European fleets combined? Have you forgotten our Royal Air Force which flies over Germany at will, and in July alone dropped 37,000 bombs on military targets in the Ruhr and Rhineland? The bombs that fell with these leaflets tell you

THE WAR, WHICH HITLER BEGAN, GOES ON!

Yes, certainly, Berliners! First you have to conquer us. And if you hope to do it by air blockade, then think twice about it, because that doesn't seem to work. For nearly a year Goering and Raeder have exerted themselves and our Navy, our Merchant Marine, our Air Force and our stocks of food in England are all very much larger than last September.

People of Berlin! Once you were known as the "brightest people". Once you knew how to make your opinions felt. Perhaps you can think it over and find out how you can help in Germany's salvation. But in the coming war winter – and if necessary, for many more war winters – you will find that we were right in saying now:

    THE WAR LASTS AS LONG
      AS HITLER'S REGIME!

the Axis powers: Germany and her Allies

34 WHY DID THE ALLIES BOMB GERMAN CITIES?

Having survived the German 'Blitz' on Britain early in the war, the Allies intensified their own bombing of Germany's industries and major cities in 1942. Two years later, with the war moving ever more in the Allies' favour, the Cabinet met to consider what to do now. What role did bombing now have to play?

SOURCE 1

An extract from a report presented to the War Cabinet in August 1944.

1 According to Source 1, what three 'objects' did the Government expect to achieve by intensifying bombing activity?

1ST AUGUST, 1944

WAR CABINET
CHIEFS OF STAFF COMMITTEE

AIR ATTACK ON GERMAN CIVILIAN MORALE
Memorandum by the Chief of Air Staff

At their 222nd (O) Meeting, held on 5th July, the Chiefs of Staff agreed "that the time might well come in the not too distant future when an all-out attack by every means at our disposal on German civilian morale might be decisive" and recommended to the Prime Minister "that the method by which such an attack would be carried out should be examined and all possible preparations made."

2. A preliminary study of this problem has been made by the Air Staff, in consultation with the Foreign Office, the Political Warfare Executive and the Ministry of Economic Warfare; their views are as follows:-

Objects to be achieved

3. It is of great importance that once the issue of the war is clear beyond doubt the German High Command should decide that Germany must accept the necessity of organised surrender. Otherwise the war might be continued into a guerilla phase which would force the Allies to undertake the entire responsibility for the whole administration of Germany. Our object must be to influence the minds of German high political and military authorities in the desired direction to the point where the High Command must either accept the necessity of surrender or be replaced by an alternative Command which does so.

4. These authorities will be influenced mainly by considerations of foreign policy, by the fortunes of the German armed forces and by the condition of the economic and administrative system on which they depend. In the final crisis they may also be affected by certain moral factors. The most important of these are:-

(i) The morale of the political and military leaders themselves. It may be possible to attack this by direct means, such as heavy attacks on the traditional centres of Governmental and military control, as well as by well judged propaganda.

(ii) The morale of the armed forces. This will be affected mainly by conditions in the field and by the extent to which the weapons and essential supplies meet the field army's requirements. It will however also be somewhat influenced by the state of civilian morale.

(iii) The morale of the civilian population, German and foreign.

The Nature of Civilian Morale in Germany

5. The policy of the High Command may be influenced by civilian morale in various ways:-

(a) In an extreme case there might be an outbreak of rioting, strikes or uncontrolled looting or other civil disorder. This is not in any circumstances a probable contingency except among foreign workers.

(b) Bad morale might lead to an increase in voluntary absenteeism, idleness at work and general "unhelpfulness" toward the Government, with very serious effects on administration and production.

(c) Even where morale is not impaired, an attack on it may force the authorities to divert increasing resources to the maintenance of morale at the expense of other vital commitments.

8. In this situation it is unlikely that fluctuations in civilian morale will have any decisive influence upon the High Command until its authority has already been weakened by other causes and the machinery of repression has begun to break down. The occasion for an attack on civilian morale as such will not arise until it is generally believed even in Germany that the Nazi system is collapsing and that total defeat is imminent. This opportunity to enforce surrender may be a fleeting one; if it is not seized either the extremist elements may succeed in rallying the Army for a further stand or the collapse may spread so rapidly that central government ceases to exist.

SOURCE 2

An extract from a report presented to the War Cabinet in August 1944.

1 Make a list of the advantages and disadvantages of each option considered in Source 2.

Possible Methods of Attack

9. It is generally agreed that the greatest effect on morale will be produced if a new blow of catastrophic force can be struck at a time when the situation already appears desperate. The blow should be such that it cannot be concealed or minimised, and it should if possible imply a threat that it will be continued and intensified if surrender does not follow. The German attack on Rotterdam in May, 1940, was made in somewhat analogous conditions, and illustrates the effect which may be produced. Carefully co-ordinated propaganda is of course essential.

10. The following forms of attack have been suggested and considered:-

(i) Widespread strafing attacks by fighters on civilian objectives in Germany. Such attacks can undoubtedly do much to cause widespread uneasiness and confusion. They could not, however, be applied on a sufficient scale to produce any catastrophic calamity or threat to the civilian population as a whole.

(ii) Air Control. As a variant of the above proposal, it has been suggested that we should proclaim that from a given date all road and rail movement in Germany should cease and that all disobeying this order would be attacked. It would not in fact be practicable to execute this threat effectively throughout a country such as Germany, with the forces available.

(iii) Attack of small towns (say 20,000 inhabitants) Towns of 20,000 inhabitants represent small targets which can only effectively be attacked by visual bombing and this must normally be carried out by day.

There is no doubt that the sudden destruction of German small towns on a really large scale would have serious effects on morale. But the tactical conditions explained above make it very difficult to plan any such attack in advance with the certainty that it can be delivered effectively when the crisis comes. It is also difficult even in the best conditions to achieve a scale of attack of sufficiently catastrophic force. We cannot expect to do more than destroy 30 towns in as long a period as a month; even 100 towns of 20,000 people would contain only 3% of the population of Germany. In addition, the towns concerned are generally of little importance to the war effort; and the problems of police control and the suppression of publicity would be relatively simple in such small communities.

(iv) Berlin. The operational advantage of selecting Berlin as a target is that in view of its large size, attack is relatively free from restriction by weather conditions; the attack may be sustained over periods of bad weather by the use of blind bombing devices. It would thus be possible to arrange a heavy attack on Berlin at short notice and to maintain it for a number of consecutive days in all but the very worst weather conditions. It is also possible that considerable direct moral effect would be produced on the German Government. It is believed that its main administrative offices are still housed in Berlin and are likely to remain there; although provided with protected accommodation it would be most difficult for them to function effectively at the crisis of the war if the communications and public services of Berlin were in complete disorder. They would be still more seriously impeded by a general breakdown of public morale, affecting the large numbers of minor civil servants.

2 Choose the option which you feel is best suited to achieve the aims outlined in Source 1.

3 Imagine you are a member of the British government at the time and draw up a speech justifying your choice to the rest of the government.

35 HOW SUCCESSFUL WAS THE BOMBING OF THE GERMAN AIRCRAFT INDUSTRY?

British bombers kept up constant attacks on German industry throughout the war. One particular target was the aircraft industry.

SOURCE 1

A cartoon prepared by the British government (probably intended for dropping on Germany). The cartoonist has left the 'before and after' word bubbles blank – maybe because the message was undecided, or maybe because German text was going to be added.

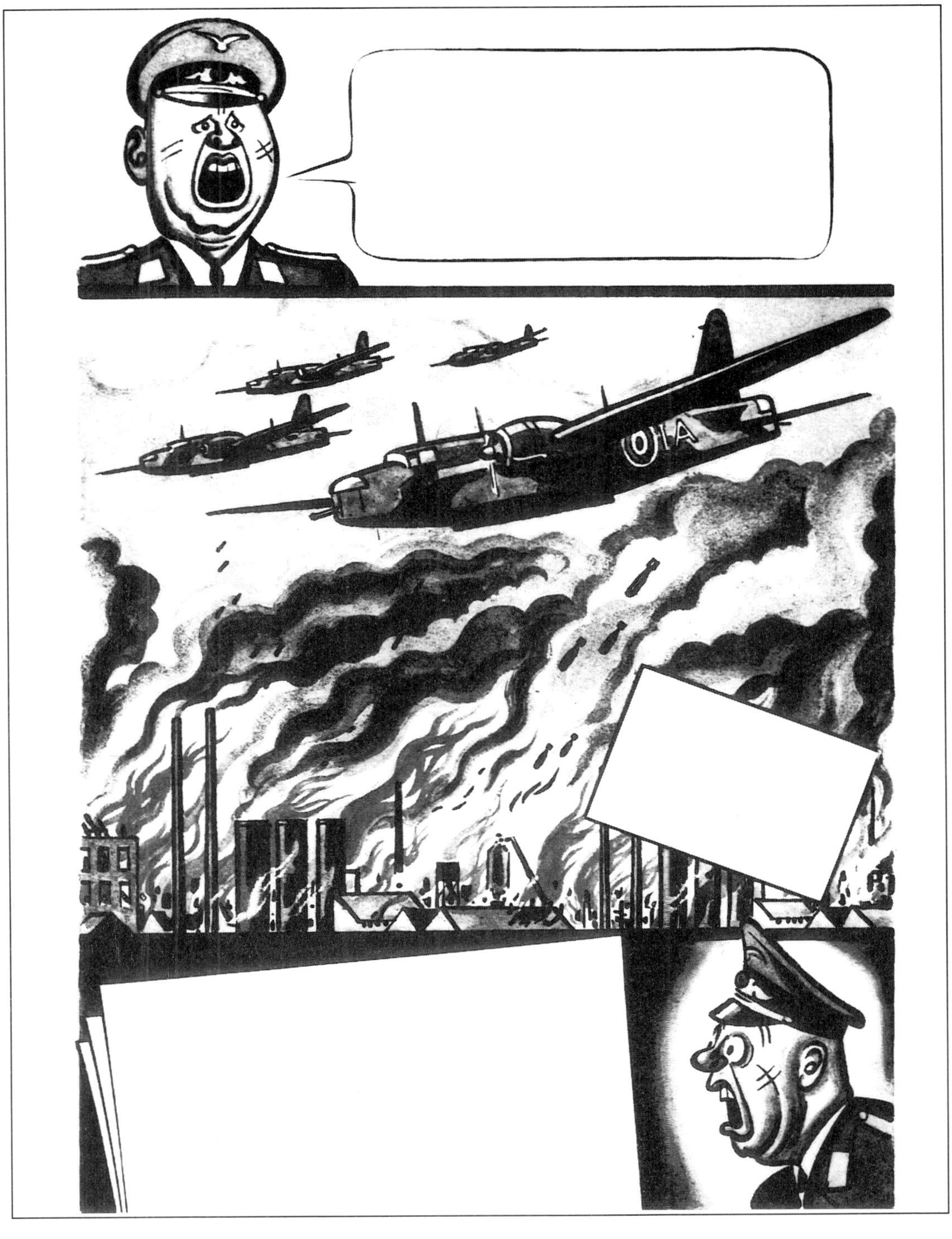

1 Write your own word bubbles to show what the British government hoped the bombing of German industry would achieve.

a) In the top bubble you should write what the German commander is saying before a bombing raid.

b) In the middle panel, write a caption that describes the scene.

c) In the bottom space, write what he is saying after it.

SOURCE 2 ▽

Extracts from a report prepared in 1945 to examine the effects of the bombing of the German aircraft industry.

1 Read extracts A and B of Source 2. Choose one example of a success in this bombing campaign.

2 Choose one example of a failure in the bombing campaign.

3 Source 2 suggests that German aircraft production failed for reasons other than Allied bombing attacks. Read extracts C–F of Source 2. What other reasons for its failure are given?

4 Compare the information given in Sources 1 and 2. Does Source 2 suggest that Allied bombing of the German aircraft industry was as effective as the cartoon seems to indicate?

A

5. To cut off the flow of usable aircraft to Hitler's fighting squadrons, the Combined Bomber Offensive applied every known form of attack. The Royal Air Force bombed cities and industrial areas by night to disrupt and to demoralize labor and to destroy such factories as might be located in the target area. The US Army Air Forces bombed air fields and factories by day to destroy as many finished aircraft as possible and to cripple further production. At the same time, rail centers, bridges and marshalling yards were under constant attack by both air forces and tons of bombs rained down on oil refineries, synthetic fuel plants and fuel dumps. In the end the total weight was too much. Germany's industrial machine could not endure such punishment and finally collapsed.

B

7. Of the **estimated** production loss, roughly 78 per cent or 14,000 aircraft were fighters. (Total reported fighter production for the period, 45,800 aircraft.) Whether or not the German Air Force could have used all these additional aircraft effectively (because of shortages of fuel or of pilots), it is obvious that the attacks against the German aircraft industry paid dividends. By keeping such a number of defensive fighters out of the air at times when the air war was critical, the job of wrecking Germany's manufacturing industries, her transportation system and her cities, was rendered that much easier and the war was probably shortened by some months.

8. The question is still open, however, as to how many of those accomplishments resulted from the direct attacks against the aircraft industry. The records which are presented in detail in this report point up the tremendous recuperative powers of Germany's aircraft production. Paradoxically, aircraft production appears, at first glance, to have been stimulated rather than retarded by the attacks. It must be remembered, however, that the great upswing in production that took place in the spring of 1944 had been **planned** and provided for during the six to nine months' period preceding. How much higher the production curve would have risen had the attacks not been made is only a matter for conjecture. It was not until the fall of 1944, after the aircraft industry <u>per se</u> had ceased to be a primary target for the Combined Bomber Offensive, that production began to lag.

C

12. **Prior** to the end of 1944 there is little evidence that lack of engines or of necessary equipment or of basic materials led to any critical shortages of finished aircraft. Even the widely publicized attacks against the ball bearing industry, which were supposed to pinch off a vital accessory to the building of aircraft and aircraft engines, failed to produce even a temporary setback. The costly raid on Schweinfurt did cut heavily into ball bearing production. The stock bins and the pipe lines to airframe and aircraft engine plants, however, were so well filled, redesign of equipment to eliminate ball bearings progressed so rapidly, and the increased output of unbombed bearing plant was so great that the situation never became critical to the point of denying finished aircraft to the GAF.

D

15. Physical damage studies point to the fact that machine tools and heavy manufacturing equipment of all kinds are very difficult to destroy or to damage beyond repair by bombing attacks. Buildings housing such equipment may be burned down and destroyed but, after clearing away the wreckage, it has been found, more often than not, that heavy equipment, when buried under tons of debris may be salvaged and put back into operation in a relatively short time and with comparatively little difficulty. Electrical equipment associated with heavy tools suffers most severely. A good fire in the vicinity of such equipment will destroy motors, control equipment and so forth. It has been generally observed, therefore, that incendiary attacks against airframe and aircraft engine parts are more effective than the equivalent amount of HE on the target.

E

18. Hitler frequently interfered with the aircraft planning programs because of his belief in the effectiveness of "secret" or "wonder weapons". Although no great percentage of the V-1 or the V-2 production was subtracted directly from the aircraft industry, Hitler insistence on such weapons interfered seriously at times with material and labor supplies to the aircraft industry and caused dissension and disputes with respect to the relative importance of the two classes of weapons on the priority schedule.

F

30. The basic error made by Germany was probably Hitler's failure to increase the aircraft program at the time the Allies began to build airplanes for the Combined Bomber Offensive. It is known that accurate information as to the plans and programs for building of aircraft in the United States was available to him, but he and Goering dismissed the figures as false and impossible, and thereby underestimated their eventual requirements to meet the Allied attack.

36 CASUALTIES

BRITISH ARMY (MALE) CASUALTIES IN WAR AGAINST GERMANY

Type of Casualty	Offrs and ORs	Defended Ports and Garrisons	East Africa	France	Italy	Middle East	North Africa	Norway	Persia/Iraq	Sicily	U.K.	W. Europe & S. France	At Sea	Miscellaneous	Balkans & Greece	TOTAL
Killed and Died of Wounds	Offrs	5	51	671	1641	1215	698	25	4	256	191	2640	377	50	37	7861
	ORs	14	266	10528	18480	11583	7264	257	20	2466	2456	30093	9789	5	255	93476
Deaths from Injury and Accident	Offrs	31	34	30	93	194	82	2	14	8	661	129	12	8	10	1308
	ORs	228	61	347	1729	1918	1264	12	129	133	8402	1770	122	16	84	16215
PW Deaths from Disease	Offrs	–	–	24	3	29	5	–	–	1	1	5	–	4	–	71
	ORs	–	–	766	100	1458	66	22	–	1	1	89	–	50	–	2553
TOTAL DEATHS	Offrs	36	85	725	1737	1438	785	27	18	265	852	2774	389	62	47	9240
	ORs	242	327	11641	20309	14959	8594	291	149	2600	10859	31952	9911	71	339	112244
Missing NETT:	Offrs	–	–	1	–	10	–	–	–	–	–	32	2	16	–	61
	ORs	–	–	63	28	45	11	–	–	–	3	96	309	51	4	610
Missing REJOINED	Offrs	–	–	479	71	264	62	–	–	8	–	202	5	41	–	1132
	ORs	–	–	12813	1935	5946	1501	–	–	305	–	4648	132	172	–	27452
TOTAL MISSING GROSS	Offrs	–	–	480	71	274	62	–	–	8	–	234	7	57	–	1193
	ORs	–	–	12876	1963	5991	1512	–	–	305	3	4744	441	223	4	28062
Wounded	Offrs	8	110	743	4042	2241	1441	32	9	462	218	6641	30	12	119	16108
	ORs	26	798	13333	52898	23244	17569	329	36	5837	4556	87960	602	3	1128	208319
Prisoners of War NETT:	Offrs	–	–	–	1	8	3	4	–	–	–	1	–	–	–	16
	ORs	–	–	110	57	284	23	29	–	10	5	42	3	–	–	563
PW repatriated under Geneva Conv.	Offrs	–	–	–	–	–	–	–	–	–	–	–	–	–	–	436
	ORs	–	–	–	–	–	–	–	–	–	–	–	–	–	–	6759
PW escaped and liberated by Allies	Offrs	–	–	–	–	–	–	–	–	–	–	–	–	–	–	5085
	ORs	–	–	–	–	–	–	–	–	–	–	–	–	–	–	106905
Total PW: Gross	Offrs	–	–	–	–	–	–	–	–	–	–	–	–	–	–	5537
	ORs	–	–	–	–	–	–	–	–	–	–	–	–	–	–	114227
TOTAL BATTLE CASUALTIES	Offrs	–	–	–	–	–	–	–	–	–	–	–	–	–	–	32078
	ORs	–	–	–	–	–	–	–	–	–	–	–	–	–	–	462852
	ALL RKS	–	–	–	–	–	–	–	–	–	–	–	–	–	–	494930

Offrs: officers
ORs: other ranks (ordinary soldiers)
PW: Prisoners of war
Geneva Conv: the Geneva Convention, an international agreement signed by most countries setting rules for the treatment of prisoners of war.

SOURCE 1

Casualty figures for the war against Germany prepared for the British government, March 1946.

1 Study sources 1 and 2 carefully. On a map of the world, shade in the areas where British soldiers were in action.

2 Draw a bar chart to show the total of ordinary soldiers (ORs) who died in each theatre of war (area) against Germany and against Japan.

BRITISH ARMY (MALE) BATTLE CASUALTIES IN WAR AGAINST JAPAN

SOURCE 2

Casualty figures for the war against Japan prepared for the British government, February 1946.

Type of Casualty	Offrs and ORs	Burma	Ceylon	China	India	Malaya	Netherland – East Indies	Far East (Misc.)	TOTAL	ALL RANKS
Killed and Died of Wounds	Offrs	909	–	53	13	227	11	7	1220	
	ORs	7242	11	351	92	2407	107	12	10222	
LESS Deaths after end of War	Offrs	2	–	–	–	–	–	–	2	
	ORs	32	–	–	–	–	36	3	71	
TOTAL: Killed and Died of Wounds	Offrs	907	–	53	13	227	11	7	1218	
	ORs	7210	11	351	92	2407	71	9	10151	11369
Died from Injury and Accident	Offrs	20	–	6	116	5	3	–	150	
	ORs	205	7	25	777	48	–	–	1062	
PW Deaths from Disease	Offrs	5	–	20	–	154	20		199	
	ORs	255	–	324	–	7537	1699		9815	
TOTAL DEATHS	Offrs	932	–	79	129	386	34	7	1567	
	ORs	7670	18	610	869	9992	1770	9	21028	22595
Missing: NETT	Offrs	13	–	–	–	32	7	2	54	
	ORs	581	–	70	–	757	123	11	1542	
PLUS Missing Rejoined	Offrs	40	–	25	–	280	1	2	348	
	ORs	749	–	103	–	1832	18	6	2708	
TOTAL: MISSING GROSS	Offrs	53	–	25	–	312	8	4	402	
	ORs	1330	–	173	–	2589	141	17	4250	4652
LESS Missing after end of War	ALL RANKS		*No split by ranks or theatres yet available*						136	
Missing at 14 Aug 45										4516
Wounded	Offrs	1584	–	1	15	32	–	20	1652	
	ORs	13352	6	2	145	65	1	38	13609	15261
LESS wounded after end of war	Offrs									
	ORs		*No split by ranks or theatres yet available*							113
Wounded at 14 Aug 45										15148
Prisoners of War: NETT	Offrs	–	–	11	–	85	10	–	106	
	ORs	2	–	41	–	231	116	–	390	496
PW repatriated under Geneva Conv.	Offrs	–	–	–	–	–	–	–	–	
	ORs	–	–	–	–	–	–	–	–	
PW escaped and liberated	Offrs								2453	
	ORs		*No split by theatres yet available*						29363	31816
TOTAL: Prisoners of War	Offrs								2559	
	ORs								29753	32312
TOTAL BATTLE CASUALTIES.										74571

3 On sources 1 and 2:
a) underline the total number of prisoners of war in the war against Germany and the war against Japan
b) highlight the figures for the deaths of prisoners of war in each source
c) calculate what percentage of the total number of prisoners of war died in each area.

4 From your knowledge of the Second World War, can you account for any differences in casualties in different parts of the world?

37 DUNKIRK: *they were there*

Sources 1–5 show photographs of various service personnel who have returned from France and Belgium following the evacuation from Dunkirk. The photographs all appeared in the *Illustrated London News*, 8 June 1940.

SOURCE 1

SOURCE 4 ▷

SOURCE 5

SOURCE 2 ▽

SOURCE 3

1 Match Sources 1–5 with these original captions from the *Illustrated London News*.

- A scene at a wayside station. Day and night train-load after train-load of men were given food, tea and cigarettes.
- *Poilus* (French soldiers) resting on the railway line immediately after reaching England and writing news of their safety to dear ones across the Channel.
- Comrades-in-arms brought from Flanders packed like sardines. Tens of thousands of French troops were evacuated with our own.
- French women telephonists arriving at a British port from Dunkirk. They remained gallantly at their posts up to the last.
- Though some – not all – of these Tommies just back from the most terrible battle of all time appear dishevelled and tired, all were clearly 'in the pink'.

2 For each photograph, explain why the British government would be pleased to see the picture published in the British press.

3 Are there any captions that the government might have wished to change at all?

Captain Gardner.

Sources 1–4 describe the exploits of four servicemen in North Africa who have been recommended for medals.

Awards (in order of status)

Officers	Other ranks	Service
Victoria Cross	Victoria Cross	Army, Navy and Airforce
Distinguished Service Order	Distinguished Service Medal	Army, Navy and Airforce
Military Cross	Military Medal	Army

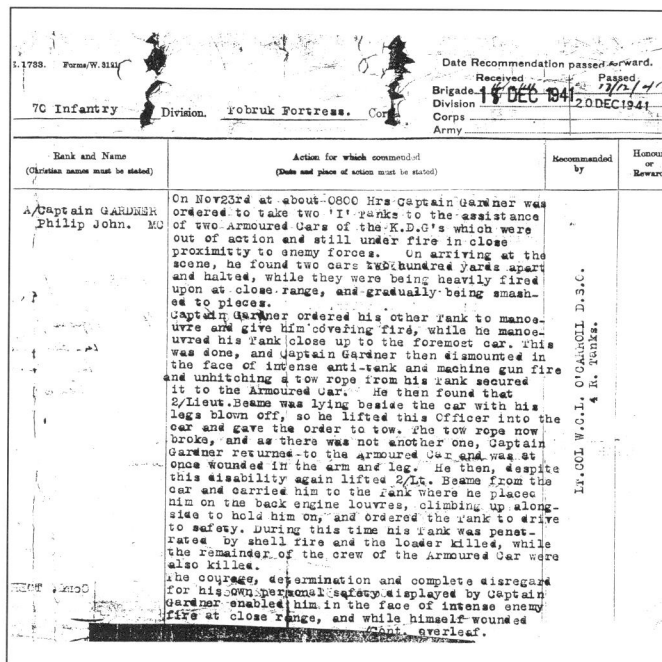

S.1783. Forms/W.3121.

70 Infantry Division. Tobruk Fortress. Corps

Date Recommendation passed forward.
Received — Passed
Brigade 16 DEC 1941 20 DEC 1941
Division
Corps
Army

Rank and Name (Christian names must be stated)	Action for which commended (Date and place of action must be stated)	Recommended by	Honour or Reward
A/Captain GARDNER Philip John. MC	On Nov 23rd at about 0800 Hrs Captain Gardner was ordered to take two 'I' Tanks to the assistance of two Armoured Cars of the K.D.G's which were out of action and still under fire in close proximity to enemy forces. On arriving at the scene, he found two cars two hundred yards apart and halted, while they were being heavily fired upon at close range, and gradually being smashed to pieces. Captain Gardner ordered his other Tank to manoeuvre and give him covering fire, while he manoeuvred his Tank close up to the foremost car. This was done, and Captain Gardner then dismounted in the face of intense anti-tank and machine gun fire and unhitching a tow rope from his Tank secured it to the Armoured Car. He then found that 2/Lieut.Beame was lying beside the car with his legs blown off, so he lifted this Officer into the car and gave the order to tow. The tow rope now broke, and as there was not another one, Captain Gardner returned to the Armoured Car and was at once wounded in the arm and leg. He then, despite this disability again lifted 2/Lt. Beame from the car and carried him to the Tank where he placed him on the back engine louvres, climbing up alongside to hold him on, and ordered the Tank to drive to safety. During this time his Tank was penetrated by shell fire and the loader killed, while the remainder of the crew of the Armoured Car were also killed. The courage, determination and complete disregard for his own personal safety displayed by Captain Gardner enabled him in the face of intense enemy fire at close range, and while himself wounded /Cont. overleaf.	Lt.COL W.C.L. O'CARROLL D.S.O. 4 R. Tanks.	

1 Working in groups, you must decide who has made the most valuable contribution to the war effort, and who will receive which of the above awards. Explain your choice.

in two places, to save the life of 2/Lieut. Beame in circumstances fraught with such difficulty and danger as has rarely been equalled in the history of the Service.

Witness to the above.

2/Lieut. F.H. Gearing, 4 R. Tanks.
7901807 AP/L/C.McTier. D.
7901730 Tpr. Cooper. H.A.G.

Lt. Col. Cmdr. 4 R. Tanks.

This officer's name was a by-word amongst the crews of the A.Cs or Tanks as they came back to rally.
Very strongly recommended

Brig.
Comdr. 32 Army Tk. Bde.

Schedule No. (to be left blank)	Unit	Regtl. No.	Rank and Name (Christian names must be stated)	Action for which commended (Date and place of action must be stated)	Recommended by	Honour or Reward	(To be left blank)

875/PMES/2/70000/4/41

Brigade._____ _____Division._____ _____Corps._____

Date Recommendation passed forward.
Received

Brigade_____
Division_____
Corps_____
Army_____

Passed

Army Form
W. 3121.

| GR 3483 | C Bty. 4 RHA | 1095630 | L/Bdr. HASLER Arthur Herbert | L/Bdr. HASLER escaped with two others from a Prisoner of War camp at BENGHAZI on 10 October 41. They had previously managed to secrete a store of tinned food and water and with this they intended to cross the desert to the Egyptian Frontier. Assisted by friendly Arabs they succeeded in reaching a place where they were found by one of our patrols. They brought back with them information of the greatest value which provided very welcome confirmation of our theories and filled in many gaps in our knowledge. They also provided accurate information on the location of dumps and other installations. In the Prisoner of War camp all prisoners pooled information with the idea that anyone who succeeded in escaping would be able to supply us with the maximum of information. These three men were apparently the prime movers of this system. L/Bdr. HASLER and his comrades not only did their duty in escaping from BENGHAZI and providing most accurate and intelligently collected information, but they were influenced in their action by unselfish motives. The definite impression was gained that their object in escaping was largely as a result of their appreciation of the importance of the information they had to impart and of the necessity of transmitting it by the only means possible - themselves, regardless of the hazards and dangers they knew they must face in attempting to reach Egypt through the desert from BENGHAZI. Their action provides an outstanding example of what intelligent and courageous men can achieve when placed in an apparently hopeless situation. | | | 2834 |

5/11/41 C-in-C.
Middle East Forces

General

SOURCE 2

Lance-Bombadier
Arthur Hasler.

SOURCE 3
Lieutenant-
Colonel Birley.

Army Form W.3121.

Wt. 42828/126. 300m. 2/40. W.S. Ltd. 51-6138 Forms/W.3121/6.

			Date recommendation passed forward
			Received	Passed

22 'nd. Brigade 7th nd. Division Corps

Brigade **3 JAN 42**

Unit 2 R.G.H.

Division

Schedule No. (to be left blank) Maj. Corps **3 Jan 4 Jan**

Army No. and Rank P/10922 (T/Lieut.-Colonel) Army **5.1.42 9.1.42**

Name Normand Addison Birley
(Christian names must be stated)

Action for which commended (Date and place of action must be stated)	Recommended by	Honour or Reward	(To be left blank)
On 19.11.41. at BIR EL GUBI when the Regt. was attacked by an overwhelming number of enemy tanks Lt. Col. N.A. Birley disposed his Regt. in the best way possible and held his ground for nearly two hours until the enemy tanks had almost overrun the position. Throughout the action he was right up with the leading Sqn. and by his own example did much to help the leading troops hold their ground. Towards the end of the engagement his own tank was put out of action and he had to climb on to the outside of another tank. At this time he was hit and had his arm badly broken. In spite of the fact that he was hit and must have been in great pain he continued to remain right up with the leading tanks sitting on the front of a tank under extremely heavy fire with no protection. When he wanted the Regt. to withdraw he went round – still on the outside of the tank – to other tanks in the vicinity ordering them to pass a wireless message to the leading Sqn. Leader telling him to withdraw. These messages came through, but Lt.-Col. N.A. Birley	*L.A. She[...] Major OC 2RGH* *J. Cockburn Brigadier*		2334

Army Form W.3121.

Wt. 42828/126. 300m. 2/40. W.S. Ltd. 51-6138 Forms/W.3121/6.

			Date recommendation passed forward
			Received	Passed

2 Armd. Brigade 7th rmd. Division Corps

Brigade **3 JAN 42**

Unit 2 R.G.H.

Division

Schedule No. (to be left blank) Maj. Corps **5.1.42 7.1.42**

Army No. and Rank P/10922 (T/Lieut.-Colonel) Army

Name Normand Addison Birley
(Christian names must be stated)

Action for which commended (Date and place of action must be stated)	Recommended by	Honour or Reward	(To be left blank)
Sheet 2. refused to leave until he was quite certain that all tanks had heard the order and were actually returning. Even then he waited until they were out of immediate danger. He then set about organising a new battle position with the remaining tanks, in case the enemy should advance further. He refused to allow himself to be evacuated until he had seen all his remaining tanks into close leaguer that night and issued instructions and handed over his command. Throughout the whole action his fine example and complete disregard for his personal safety was an inspiration to all under his command.	*N.M. Ritchie, Lt. Gen. G.O.C. in C 8 Army* *A.R. Godwin-Austen Lieut. General, Commander, 13 Corps.* *C. Auchinleck General Commander-in-Chief Middle East Forces*		

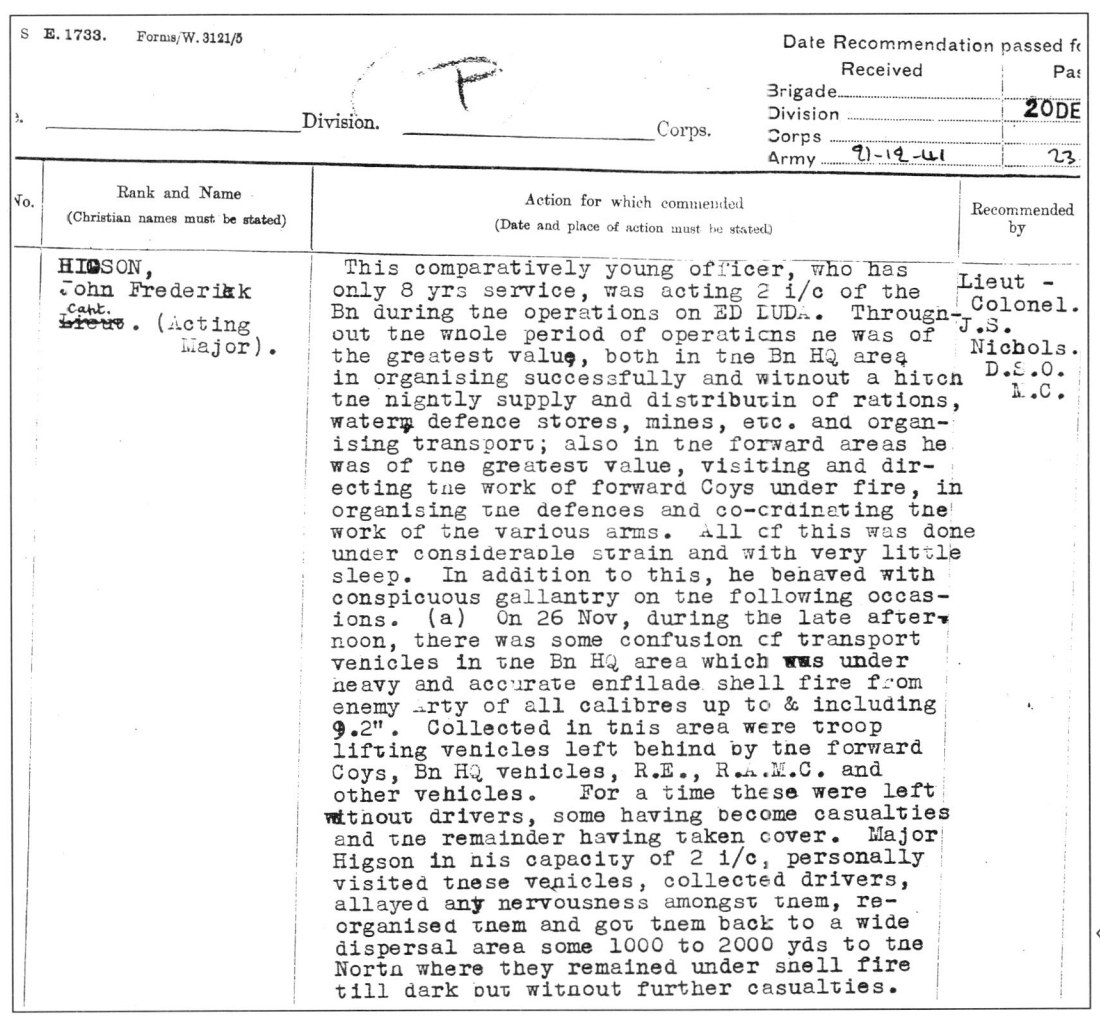

S E. 1733.   Forms/W. 3121/5

Date Recommendation passed f[...]
Received   Pas[...]
Brigade................
Division.........................   20DE
Corps...........................
Army.......9)-12-41..........   23

No.	Rank and Name (Christian names must be stated)	Action for which commended (Date and place of action must be stated)	Recommended by
	HIGSON, John Frederick Capt. Lieut. (Acting Major).	This comparatively young officer, who has only 8 yrs service, was acting 2 i/c of the Bn during the operations on ED DUDA. Throughout the whole period of operations he was of the greatest value, both in the Bn HQ area in organising successfully and without a hitch the nightly supply and distributin of rations, water, defence stores, mines, etc. and organising transport; also in the forward areas he was of the greatest value, visiting and directing the work of forward Coys under fire, in organising the defences and co-ordinating the work of the various arms. All of this was done under considerable strain and with very little sleep. In addition to this, he behaved with conspicuous gallantry on the following occasions. (a) On 26 Nov, during the late afternoon, there was some confusion of transport vehicles in the Bn HQ area which was under heavy and accurate enfilade shell fire from enemy Arty of all calibres up to & including 9.2". Collected in this area were troop lifting vehicles left behind by the forward Coys, Bn HQ vehicles, R.E., R.A.M.C. and other vehicles. For a time these were left without drivers, some having become casualties and the remainder having taken cover. Major Higson in his capacity of 2 i/c, personally visited these vehicles, collected drivers, allayed any nervousness amongst them, reorganised them and got them back to a wide dispersal area some 1000 to 2000 yds to the North where they remained under shell fire till dark but without further casualties.	Lieut - Colonel. J.S. Nichols. D.S.O. M.C.

◁ SOURCE 4
Major Higson.

[MS4224] W7670/M2618 2000m 9/17s 191 G & S E. 1733.   Forms/W.3121/5

Date Recommendation passed forward.   Army Form W. 3121.
Received   Passed
Brigade.....13 Dec 41.....14 Dec 41
Division.....15 DEC 1941.....20DEC1941
Corps........91-12-41.....23-12-41
Army.........91-12-41.....23-12-41

_____ Brigade. _____ Division. _____ Corps.

Schedule No. (to be left blank)	Unit	Regtl. No.	Rank and Name (Christian names must be stated)	Action for which commended (Date and place of action must be stated)	Recommended by	Honour or Reward	(To be left blank)
				(b) On 29 Nov after the enemy had penetrated the Bn position with tanks and infantry, it became urgent to get up two Coys of 2/13 Australian Inf Bn for counter attack. These at the time were dispersed and dug in some 2000 yds away NE of 4 R.Tanks. A considerable force of enemy tanks was in position about 400 yds from Bn HQ and enemy Inf was digging in half way between in bright moonlight. I sent Major Higson in a 15 cwt truck to guide up Coys of the 2/13 Aust Bn. During the journey he was heavily fired at from enemy tanks with M.G's and guns, but luckily was not hit. He eventually guided up the Aust Coys to Bn HQ ready for the counter attack. (c) Immediately after the counter attack, I sent Major Higson in a carrier to supervise consolidation and reorganisation. Whilst moving in the forward area, he saw two enemy lorries moving west to east about 100 yds South of the F.D.L's. He immediately attacked the two lorries in his carrier; the Bren gun jammed however, so he jumped out of the carrier, rushed up alone, stopped one lorry and took the driver prisoner. The conduct of this officer and work of this officer undoutedly had a considerable influence on the course of the operations on ED DUDA.			

Lieut-General.
G.O.C. in C. Eighth Army.

Ronald M. Scobie
Maj.-Gen.,
Comd. TOBRUK FORTRESS

J.S. Nichols Lieut-Colonel
Comdg. 1 ESSEX Regt.

3.1.42

Brigadier,
Comdg. 23 Inf Bde

14. 12. 21

It was the duty of all captured soldiers to try to escape and return to their unit. Many soldiers took enormous risks in attempting to do so. If they did eventually return, they were interviewed at length to find out if they had discovered any information that might be useful to the Allies.

Throughout May 1941 the Allies fought a losing battle with German forces on the Greek island of Crete. Crete lies between the Greek mainland and the North African coast. The Allies evacuated all the soldiers they could, but their evacuation stopped on 1 June 1941. Most of the British soldiers left behind fell into German hands as prisoners of war. Source 1 tells the story of Lance Bombadier Robinson.

SOURCE 1 ▷

Report on the escape of Lance Bombadier Robinson, a prisoner on Crete, from an interview in January 1944.

1 Draw a timeline from June 1941 to January 1944 to show Lance Bombadier Robinson's experiences.

2 To begin with, how did the Germans manage to recapture prisoners?

3 How did their tactics change?

4 What evidence is there in Source 1 that German rule in Crete became more harsh towards civilians between 1941 and 1943?

MOST SECRET
M.I.9/S/P.G./MISC/INT/184.

The information contained in this report is to be treated as MOST SECRET

ACCOUNT OF ESCAPE OF

890184 L/Bdr. ROBINSON, S. 106 Regt. R.H.A.

Date of Birth: 19th December, 1920   Escaped: July 1941

Date of Enlistment: 5th July, 1939

Captured: 1st June, 1941

Peacetime Profession: Liverpool Corporation as a Gardener.
Private Address: 14, Alexander Street, Waltham, Liverpool, 4.

1. **Capture.**   Taken prisoner in Crete on 1 Jun 1941 after the evacuation had ceased.

2. **Camps in which imprisoned.**

Source was taken to a prison camp at Gallatos.

3. **Escape.**

The camp at Gallatos was then just a wide area with no barbed wire on which 10,000 prisoners were in camp. The Germans were very short of food and for the first few days allowed them to go to Canea, the nearest town, for food. They took a sack, collected food, and came back. Then the Germans began putting up barbed wire.

Source got to know an old lady in Canea who told him that if he escaped she would look after him. She gave him a Greek pass, so before the wire was completed on 5 Jun 1941 Source got out at night time, in company with Gnr. Kent and Gnr. Hamilton. The old lady, however, could only look after two men and so Kent left them. Gnr. Hamilton and Source stayed at her house in civilian clothes and with forged Greek passes for about a month. One day when they were walking in the town, Source heard someone say from behind "Hallo chaps", and it was a German who spoke perfect English. Across the road was another German holding a pistol. They, therefore, had to surrender.

He said he was sorry to have to take them, but his job was his job, and told them that his father was a White Russian. On the way Source managed to put his hand in his pocket and destroy the Greek pass. They were taken to the German Kommandanten, where they found 15 other prisoners in civilian clothes, who had been captured by the same man in the same way. He had been sent round the town to round up the prisoners.

They were kept in a cell for five days and then taken before the Kommandantur, who said that he would overlook it this time, but that if they were caught again in civilian clothes they would be treated as spies and be liable to be shot. They were taken back to Gallatos by truck and put back into Military uniform. The camp was then well protected and guarded.

They were put in a small compound to serve a sentence of 14 days on bread and water, but after two days they put our own Military Police — minus their red caps — on to guard them — three men and an N.C.O., who said they would get into trouble if the P/Ws escaped. However, they told the Military Police that they were going and went out that night. Source escaped again with Gnr. Hamilton and Kent and also Gnr. Savage.

By this time the people in the town had been told that they would be killed if they harboured prisoners of war, and so they told them to get to the hills. The same old lady put them in touch with a Greek

Source: Lance Bombadier Robinson

continued ▷

Escape. (Contd.)

who was taking a party of eight prisoners in a bus. He took Source and his companions as well, making twelve. They had again put on civilian clothes. The driver took them 25 miles to a village in the hills where they were given food at a man's house, but he could not look after them all. They, therefore, split into pairs and Source went with a New Zealander, Pte. Finley, to a little village higher up where they stayed with some people for a month.

The Germans then started a terrorist campaign throughout the villages, blowing up places and setting fire to others. The reason they gave was that the Greeks were supporting the British. They, therefore, had to keep moving and started living in caves. They begged for food in villages, which was not easy to get. They went from place to place and Source ran into Kent again. The New Zealander subsequently left them in company with another New Zealander, and Kent and Source remained together. By this time it was getting on for Christmas 1941 and they had been sleeping in caves for about seven months.

One evening just before Christmas Source was sleeping in a house and Kent was in another house near by, when three Germans arrived in the village about midnight, posing as Englishmen, and they went to a house and asked for food, which the woman gave them. They asked if any English were there, and she pointed to the house where Kent was sleeping. They then entered that house and caught Kent in bed. The old woman was beaten up and left on the floor in a terrible state and the old man was given twelve months' imprisonment. Kent was taken off and Source has not seen him since. He was in civilian clothes and possessed a Greek pass. (He was in Source's Regiment and came from Liverpool).

Source, therefore, carried on and lived alone for quite a time. He was fourteen months near a village called Pervalycher. This was the Headquarters of the escapers and was full of Australian and New Zealanders and other Colonials. He slept in the barn of a house belonging to a family of a girl named ELEFTERIA BONATOS, who looked after them all.

Subsequently this girl escaped with Source and about 50 others, in company also with another woman who was working for British Intelligence. Word had come through by Greeks that a British Naval vessel might arrive and take them off. They made for a point between Sfykia and Sujar, and a British Intelligence Officer was waiting for them with an armed guard. He spoke Greek, but was an Englishman and came from London. The vessel eventually arrived and they got away from the island on the 14th May, 1943, landing at Tobruk the next day.

Before they left Crete Source married the girl Elefteria Bonatos, and they were again married before the British Consul in Cairo. She had to go to hospital in Cairo and Source stayed there at a Base Depot for a time, coming back by boat from Port Tewfik in company with other escapers from Italy and arriving in England about the end of October. Source's wife is here with him now, but her people are still in Crete. She did more than anyone else to help British and Colonial soldiers. Everyone knew her and it was well known that she was helping the British. On two occasions she had to take to the hills because Fifth Columnists had reported on her. She was given warning by the Greek Police, who said that the Germans might come up and take her. Her address is the same as Source's.

NOTE: Gnr. Robinson states that in the course of his experiences he learned Greek and speaks the language well. He says that he is well-known in the island and that he knows so much about the people that he feels that he might do valuable work in this connection. He knows, for example, who are the Fifth Columnists, who are those who have arms, and who have not. He wishes his case to be considered if possible with a view to having his experiences utilised.

INTERVIEWED: 5 Jan 1944.
DISTRIBUTION: O.C., I.S.9.
M.I.9 (2 copies), File.

L. Challen 9/Lt.
for Lt.Colonel.
O.C., I.S.9.

5 Make a list of anything that you think the Allied forces might have found useful in this report about the situation in Crete.

6 Either:
a) write four diary entries for Lance Bombadier Robinson for 1 June 1941, 5 June 1941, Christmas 1941 and May 1943, or
b) pick four moments in this story and draw a picture to illustrate each one.

7 Lance Bombadier Robinson asks that the experiences he gained in two years in Crete might be used by the Allies. How could they be useful? Write a note to accompany this report written by Lieutenant Challen. Your note should suggest how Lance Bombadier Robinson's skills could now be used by the Allies.

40 THE CAPTURE OF 'HILLMAN': D-Day

After months of preparation and planning, the Allies finally landed on the beaches of Normandy on 6 June 1944. This was known as D-Day.

The Germans were expecting an invasion, but the Allies had kept the exact place of their attack a careful secret. Early on the morning of 6 June, waves of Allied soldiers poured ashore all along the coast. They managed to land a massive amount of equipment and immediately set about establishing their hold on the area. Source 1 is the story of one incident in this massive operation.

1 What do you think the D of D-Day stands for? Discuss this in class.

SOURCE 1 ▷
A report on the capture of 'Hillman' on 6 June 1944.

2 Do you think this report was written for:
a) a newspaper
b) army officials
c) the British government
d) the ordinary soldiers in the army?
Explain your choice.

3 What was 'Hillman' (point 2)?

4 How would you recommend that the British forces should capture it?

5 What went wrong with the attack before it had even started (point 3)?

6 Who was killed in the attack?

7 What were they doing when they were killed?

8 Make a list of all the weapons and equipment mentioned as having been used in the attack.

9 How do you think this equipment was transported to Normandy?

10 Why do you think it was so important to capture 'Hillman'?

11 Pick one example of great bravery, one example of a bad mistake and one example of clever planning from the report.

Appx A to Div 8/G
dated 16 Jul 44

THE CAPTURE OF "HILLMAN" BY 1 SUFFOLK ON 6 JUN 44

1. "A" Coy under the command of Capt R.G. Ryley with a breaching platoon of "D" Coy under command (Lieut Russell) and 3 mine clearance teams of RE (Command Lieut Heal) were given the task of attacking and capturing the HEDGEHOG position known as "HILLMAN" which was just to the SOUTH of the village of COLLEVILLE-SUR-ORNE.

2. "HILLMAN" covered an approx area of 600 yds by 400 yds and consisted of deep concrete shelters and pillboxes and 3 cupolas and a complete system of connecting trenches about 7 ft deep. The armament consisted of 2 infantry guns, several machine guns with AA and ground roles. There were also normal riflemen of approx strength of one platoon and the Bn HQ of the unit guarding the beach defences. The position was surrounded by two belts of wire between which were Anti-tank and Anti-Personnel mines.

3. The whole posn was very well equipped with modern instruments, telephones and every comfort possible in the circumstances. It was in fact a very much stronger and better guarded and equipped than had been supposed prior to the operation. It was not known that there were any of the deep concrete shelters etc. In addition the fire of a cruiser was to have been brought down onto HILLMAN prior to the attack but the FOB was unfortunately wounded in the early stages of the operation and the naval programme never materialised.

4. Capt Ryley went forward to make his recce at about 1130 hrs on June 6th, while the coy moved up through the village to its FUP and in doing so it sustained a number of casualties from BOCHE mortaring in COLLEVILLE. One section of No 9 Platoon were almost wiped out.

5. After a short recce the coy plan was put into action and the D coy platoon moved forward under cover of HE and smoke and breached the two belts of wire and with the help of the RE detachments a sheeptrack eas made through the minefield. This was carried out successfully under fire.

6. 9 Platoon under command of Lieut J. Powell was the first platoon through the gap which was effected under cover of a squadron of 13/18 Hussars, SHERMAN tanks, 2 batterys of RA and 2" mortar smoke from "A" and "D" Coys. No 8 section got through the gap and immediately come under heavy machine gun fire and Cpl Jones was killed while trying to get his section forward. The platoon commander now came forward and got the PIAT team forward and into action so as to be able to fire three shots at a cupola which was the cause of most of the trouble.

7. A message was sent back to the company commander that the pl were pinned down. The platoon runner was killed in trying to get this message back and a second runner then had to be sent.

8. A further concentration of fire (HE and smoke) was put down and the rest of the coy were then led in by the company commander. Once again machine-gun fire again held up the advance and only four men (Capt Ryley, Lieut Tooley Lt Powell and Cpl Stares) managed to get through and went forward for about 200 yds and took a few prisoners. As it was obviously impossible to continue this without further assistance Lt Powell went back while the others remained until his return. He was only able to get one sergeant (Sgt Lankester) and two men and they again went forward and found that Lieut Tooley and Cpl Stares had both been badly wounded. Capt R.G. Ryley was killed very shortly afterwards when returning for assistance.

9. The position was now a stalemate and a further plan on a Bn level had to be made. It was decided to call up two flails and about 8 or 9 extra tanks. The flails were too long in arriving and the attack went in immediately the tanks had fired again onto the position. The tanks moved into the perimeter followed by 8 and 9 platoons who moved out and mopped up the area by using 75 and 36 grenades. One platoon D coy also moved in to assist, while one platoon C coy acted as a left flank protection. A number of the BOCHE surrendered others died in the emplacements and the success signal was given.

10. The assault which started at about 1130 hrs was not completed until about 2000 hrs and even then occasional sniping shots were still coming from some areas. About 50 Germans were taken prisoner during the day. Our own casualties were killed 2 Officers 4 other ranks. Wounded 8 other ranks. The two officers were Capt Ryley and Lieut T.J.F. Tooley.

Coy: abbreviation for military company
RE: Royal Engineers
cupolas: revolving domes to protect mounted guns
Bn HQ: Battalion Headquarters

recce: reconnaissance (examination of a region to discover certain features, position of enemy etc.)
HE: high explosives
RA: Royal Artillery
pl: platoon
Boche: German

41 THE GERMAN GENERALS

As the Allied advance proceeded, many German officers, including their highest-ranking generals, were captured. Each of the generals was interviewed to find out:
   a) what they thought of Hitler and the Nazi régime
   b) what they thought the prospects were for the Nazi war effort.
Sources 1–5 are extracts from the reports on five very different German generals.

 General von Schlieben.

Generalleutnant Karl Wilhelm
von SCHLIEBEN

Commander of CHERBOURG Defences, captured
CHERBOURG 26 Jun 44

Arrived: No.2 D.C.   29 Jun 44
           Camp 11   1 Jul 44

Left   :

Circumstances of Capture: PW refused repeated calls
to surrender. He had received a WT signal from the
FÜHRER to hold out to the last, and the situation
became hopeless owing to lack of material.

CAREER   Spent last war in 3rd Footguards Regt
           1925   7 Cavalry Regt
           Oct 29   Captain in 12 Cavalry Regt
           1932   12 Cavalry Regt
           1938   Staff of 13th Army Corps
           22 Jun 41 until 18 Oct 43 served in RUSSIA, at first with
              14 Pz.Div.
           Aug 38   Lt.Col
           Aug 41   Colonel commanding a Regt
           Mar 43   Awarded Knight's Cross for action N.W. of OREL
              commanding 208 Inf.Div.
           May 43   Promoted Generalmajor. Promotion to Generalleutnant
              presumably very recent

NOTES   Aged 49. Tall. Married. With his pink complexion, round
           boyish face, huge bulk and lumbering gait he gives the
           appearance of an overgrown, mentally under-developed school-
           boy type who will bully his inferiors and toady to his
           superiors. At first very truculent. Polite firmness proved
           successful. Has more bluff than guts. Like most prisoners
           of war he is much inclined to self-pity.

           Conversation with him revealed colossal ignorance. He said
           the Russians were a primitive people who had really achieved
           little. SCOTLAND was a completely unknown place to him.
           He asked if it were hilly or flat. He lacks sporting instinct
           and the guts to take his defeat like a man.

           Two fellow PW have stated to a BAO that they found von SCHLIEBEN
           very nervy and still shaken, though he had explained the
           circumstances of his capture to their satisfaction. Articles
           about him in the British press, which they had shown him, had
           upset him even further.

           As regards two orders alleged to have been given by von
           SCHLIEBEN to the effect that no prisoners were to be
           taken, and (b any attempting deserters should be shot,
           Oberst HERGELEIN (PW) stated that as regards (a) no such order
           was issued, and as regards (b) authority was merely given to
           junior commanders to shoot intending deserters if necessary.
           In fact no such shooting had taken place.

 General von Choltitz.

SECRET   von C H O L T I T Z

C.S.D.I.C.(U.K.)

General der Infanterie Dietrich
von CHOLTITZ

Commandant of PARIS; captured there 25 Aug 44

Arrived: No. 2 D.C.   27 Aug 44
   "   : No. 11 Camp 29 Aug 44

Left   :

Circumstances of Capture: Taken prisoner
when American forces entered PARIS, after
negotiations between him and the FFI for
an armistice had broken down.

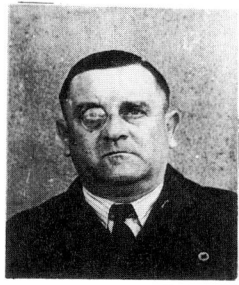

CAREER   By his own admission PW's rise in rank has been very rapid.
           According to his Soldbuch he seems to have been Generalmajor on
           5 Feb 43, promoted Generalleutnant 1 Feb 43(?) and promoted Ge-
           neral der Infanterie 1 Aug 44. He was at one time in command of
           five divisions in the CRIMEA and came to FRANCE early in Jul 44
           to replace General der Artillerie MARCKS as GOC LXXXIV Korps.
           For the first few days after his arrival he was placed in charge
           of XXV Korps in BRITTANY, replacing FAHRMBACHER. After two days
           with the XXV Korps he transferred to the command of the LXXXIV
           Korps, eight days after the death of General MARCKS. He was
           relieved of his command about 1 Aug and was posted as Kommandant
           to PARIS.

NOTES   PW is a cinema-type German officer, fat, coarse, bemonocled and
           inflated with a tremendous sense of his own importance. This
           latter quality causes him to talk freely and at times garrul-
           ously.   He is very much concerned with appearing in the most
           favourable light possible in the eyes of his captors and adopts
           the attitude that he had foreseen the outcome of the war because
           of his insight into historical necessities.

1 Work in groups of five. Each of you should write a brief physical description of one of the generals.

2 Swap your descriptions with another group and try to match their descriptions with the pictures.

3 Which of these descriptions apply to which of the generals:
   a) risen through the ranks
   b) pro-Nazi
   c) intelligent
   d) anti-Nazi
   e) ambitious
   f) proud
   g) suspected of involvement in war-crimes?

4 Underline examples where the sources are expressing an opinion.

5 Which of these generals do the Allies seem to:
   a) most respect
   b) most distrust
   c) most dislike?

6 Make a list of reasons why these sources may not provide reliable evidence of what these generals really thought or believed.

SOURCE 3
General
Schaefer.

SECRET

C.S.D.I.C.(U.K.)

General der Fallschirmtruppen
Hermann Bernhard RAMCKE

Commandant BREST: Captured BREST 19 Sep 44

Arrived: No. 2 D.C. 21 Sep 44
          Camp 11   27 Sep 44

Left   :

Circumstances of Capture: Captured in his 'bunker'
in BREST.

CAREER   A regular soldier, risen from the ranks. 39½ years' service.
         From 1905 till 1915 he served in the German Navy. Won the 'Pour le
         Mérite' in the Great War.   Organised and took part in the capture of
         CRETE by German Paratroops.

NOTES   RAMCKE is inordinately vain and has a most extensive knowledge of
         distorted history; ambitious, ruthless yet naive, an opportunist. As
         the Nazi Party is on the decline he is beginning to change his views.

         He is the author of a book entitled 'From cabin boy to Paratroop
         General'.   This book became a best-seller in GERMANY due to Party
         influence and the author claims to have made RM 800000 out of it.

         When captured RAMCKE was found to be in possession of a large **quantity**
         of French brandy and liqueurs, also a complete dinner service, probably
         looted.

         RAMCKE makes no bones about the fact that **he** was determined to win the
         highest decorations and has described to British officers how he
         recommended his subordinates for high decorations, knowing full well
         that the High Command would have to recommend him for a higher award.
         He was awarded the 'Swords and Diamonds' for his defence of BREST and
         his last act was to send a WT message to HITLER recommending himself
         for the award of an estate. He received no reply to this signal.

         In the opinion of his fellow PW RAMCKE is the man to lead an under-
         ground movement if he thought he would get anything out of it for
         himself. He has **five** sons whom he proposes to bring up to revive a
         'free' GERMANY.

SOURCE 4
General Ramcke.

7 Taking these five case-studies as examples,
write a brief summary of the attitudes of the
leaders of the German army to:
   a) the Nazis
   b) the conduct of the war.

8 Each source gives the date and place of
capture of the general in its report. Plot the
places and the dates of capture on to a blank map
of France. Use your map to write a paragraph
describing the progress of the Allies in their
reconquest of France.

Generalleutnant Hans SCHAEFER

Cmd. 244 Inf. Div.; captured
          MARSEILLES 28 Aug 44

Arrived: No. 2 D.C. 26 Dec 44
          No. 11 Camp 1 Jan 45

Left   :

Circumstances of Capture: unknown.

CAREER

1912   Joined the German Army.
1940   Served in the French campaign; at the end of it had command of a
          'Regiment' at ORLEANS.
1941-43   Served on the Russian front during this period; was wounded;
          spent about nine months convalescing in GERMANY.
1944   Before completing his convalescence, was posted to MARSEILLES as
          garrison commander which he remained until his capture.

NOTES   SCHAEFER is a regular officer, 52 years of age, and a Protestant.
          He was last in GERMANY in April 1944. His home is at ZWEIBRÜCKEN,
          just outside the SAAR.

          SCHAEFER maintained that he had never had anything to do with
          politics; he had, however, absorbed the Nazi arguments and seems
          to have been ready to benefit by Nazi successes as long as they
          continued. He said he now blames the Nazis for losing the war, because
          they waged it as a political and not a military one, and thinks
          steps should be taken to induce the Wehrmacht to give up the
          struggle; at the same time he does not believe any such approach
          has hope of success as long as the Wehrmacht remains one fighting
          whole. He fears the spread of Bolshevism in a harshly-treated
          GERMANY, but believes the Germans, if generously treated, would of
          themselves eradicate the Nazis from their midst.

          SCHAEFER was PW at C.S.D.I.C.(WEST) for some months and created a
          rather bad impression on arrival at No. 11 Camp. He appears to be
          self-centred and self-satisfied, adopting the air of a spoilt child.
          He seems not to be a good mixer and is rather intolerant. He
          appears to be anti-Nazi.

SOURCE 5
General Kittel.

Generalleutnant Heinrich KITTEL

Commander, METZ Fortress; captured METZ 22 Nov 44

Arrived: No. 2 D.C. 27 Dec 44
          No. 11 Camp 6 Jan 45

Left   :

Circumstances of Capture: Was captured in a field
hospital at METZ, having been wounded in the knee ,
while fighting as a rifleman during the last hours
of the defence of METZ.

NOTES   Generalleutnant KITTEL is a professional soldier of exceptional
          intelligence, who in the course of his career has been connected
          with most major political happenings in GERMANY. He is strongly
          opposed to the Nazi 'State within the State' and he detests the
          Police, SS, SD and administration camarilla which advanced in the
          wake of the German Army. However, because of his oath to HITLER
          and what he believes to be his duty towards GERMANY, he will not do
          or say anything which might damage the war effort of the REICH.

          He has a strong sense of humour and takes a philosophical outlook
          on life.

          KITTEL, who was Commandant of ROSTOV until its evacuation, is on
          the Russian list of war criminals and held responsible for the
          poisoning of 16000 Russians. (cf. S.R.C.G.1089(C)) He was at
          MESCHEPS(?) SPA, north of DVINSK (LATVIA) when the SS or SD carried
          out mass executions of Jews near DVINSK. (cf. S.R.G.G. 1086(C)).
          He denies responsibility for these acts.

Keeping up the morale of soldiers during the war was especially important when servicemen and women were thousands of miles from home. After the declaration of victory in Europe in May 1945 – VE Day – it became particularly important to boost the morale of those who were still fighting in the Far East. The following sources discuss what life was like for soldiers in southeast Asia, India, Ceylon and the Pacific.

SEAC

THE SERVICES NEWSPAPER OF SOUTH EAST ASIA COMMAND

No. 501   One Anna.
SATURDAY, 26 MAY, 1945.
Printed by Courtesy of
THE STATESMAN in Calcutta.

'I Accuse Mr Amery'

THERE are thousands of men in the British Army in India. There may soon be many more. Yet the information I have convinces me that the conditions under which many of them are serving are so bad as to be nothing short of scandalous.

They are short, in many cases, of medical supplies. They are short of nurses, and they are denied most of the elementary comforts that Service men in this country, in France and in Italy have come to expect as their right.

Mr Amery: Secretary of State for India

SOURCE 1

A feature in the *Sunday Pictorial* by Captain F.J. Bellenger, MP, August 1944. The article criticised the conditions under which the British Army had to serve in India.

Good Morning..

In our feature pages and Letter Bag this week we have drawn attention to two subjects which are causing a good deal of disquiet among forward troops.

The first concerns entertainment. Six months ago the position was steadily improving. Now it is deteriorating rapidly. Troops are asking: Where are the stars, and where are the shows? They are entitled to an explanation.

The second subject is more important, because it concerns the day-to-day life of the soldier. It is the cigarette situation in the forward areas.

Last Wednesday SEAC printed letters from a chaplain, two soldiers and an airman pointing out (a) that men forward are not getting their entitlement of 50 cigarettes a week, and that their chances of getting 100 a week, promised for June, seem remote. (b) that the ration still consists mainly of the old-type De Reszke and Woodbine of Indian manufacture, despite a promise that more American tobacco would be introduced into future issues.

SOURCE 2

An extract from SEAC, a newspaper for servicemen in southeast Asia. It has been retyped.

1 According to Source 2, what are the main complaints of servicemen in the Far East?

2 How reliable do you feel evidence from Sources 1 and 2 might be in describing the quality of life for servicemen in the Far East? Give reasons for your answer.

A

2.   As you well know, service in the Far Eastern theatre is bound to be unpopular for reasons which do not admit of a cure.   The men are thousands of miles from home, the climate is bad, the white population is small, cities are few and crowded, and the rural amusements available are not such as appeal to the troops.   It is more than ever important, therefore, that in those matters over which control can be exercised high class standards should prevail.

B

The shortage of doctors is a major source of trouble: if men think that they will not get proper treatment if they are sick or wounded, the effect on morale is immediate.   The shortage of nurses is equally serious.

<u>We recommend that</u>:-

you should direct that in assessing the rival claims for doctors and nurses of civilians and of men serving in the Far East, greater weight should be given to the requirements of the latter.

C

<u>Accommodation and amenities in leave centres and static camps.</u>

6.   The standard of accommodation provided for British troops in India and Ceylon is wholly inadequate.   The buildings being erected cannot be made fly-proof, with the result that dysentery cannot be checked.   The resources of India in building labour and materials are limited, but there is no reason why they should not be employed to create buildings of modern design rather than, as at present, structures in which no American commander will allow his men to be lodged; nor why the houses of prominent civilians should not be requisitioned to provide premises for Service clubs and canteens.

Similar improvements are needed in the furnishing of these buildings. Refrigerators, shower-baths, ample fly-proofing material, decent furniture and adequate sanitary appliances are all a necessity.

D

<u>Beer.</u>

8.   You are aware of the shortage of beer for troops in Italy: the shortage is even more acute in the Far Eastern theatre.   The only ways in which the problem can be solved are:-

(a) by increasing the supply of barley and hops so as to enable greater quantities of beer to be brewed locally, including, possibly, in ships for the Fleet.   We are unlikely to receive more from America, and other world sources should be explored; but the majority must come from the U.K.;

(b) by reducing the quantity available for civilian consumption in this country, and increasing the amount exported.

We realise that these measures involve a considerable shipping commitment, but this, in our view, must be accepted.

<u>We recommend that</u>:-

you should give a directive to the Minister of Food and the Minister of War Transport that the export of barley, hops and beer itself should be increased, at the expense of the civilian consumption in this country.

E

<u>Cinemas and wireless.</u>

10.   Orders for cinema and wireless equipment have been placed in America and in this country, and the American authorities concerned have been asked to do what they can to accelerate production.   We feel almost certain that your personal intervention with America will be required.   Meanwhile, an approach by you to the Minister of Production as regards equipment being produced in this country would be of great value in ensuring that deliveries are made to programme and that future requirements are met.

<u>We recommend that</u>:-

you should approach the Minister of Production on the lines indicated above, and in due time also the American authorities concerned.

SOURCE 3

Five extracts from a report to the Prime Minister by Government Ministers, 31 October 1944.

1 According to Source 3, why is it particularly important that attention should be paid to morale amongst servicemen in the Far East?

2 Does Source 3 support or contradict the claims made in Source 1 about the quality of life for servicemen in the Far East? Give evidence to support your answer.

3 Does Source 3 affect your opinions about the reliability of Sources 1 and 2? If so, explain why.

4 Study the suggestions made in Source 3 for improving morale. Put them in an order of priority for action. Are there any with which you do not agree?

5 You are a member of the Government Committee looking into the morale and welfare of servicemen in the Far East. What other actions would you like to suggest the British government should take? With a partner, make a list of ten suggestions. Put them in order of priority and explain your reasons for each choice.

A

Winston Churchill took over from Neville Chamberlain as Prime Minister early in 1940. He had two very different roles to play during the war years. Within government he was the central decision maker. Around the country British propaganda showed him as a symbol of British patriotism and resistance. His 'bulldog' spirit and his determination to win the war whatever it cost was used to inspire the British people. Throughout the war Churchill kept up a hectic round of visits to military and civilian sites, both around Britain and overseas.

1 Write down three words that you associate with Winston Churchill from your study of the Second World War.

SOURCE 1 ▽▷

Three images of Winston Churchill distributed by the *Illustrated London News* (A) and the Ministry of Information (B and C).

B

C

PRIME MINISTER'S CALL

TO MASTERS, OFFICERS AND MEN OF THE MERCHANT NAVY

"We never call on them in vain and we are confident that they will continue to play their part in carrying out men and their equipment and munitions to any place that may be required and under whatever conditions may exist at the time."

Winston S. Churchill

2 Write down another three words to describe the impressions given of Churchill by the pictures in Source 1.

SOURCE 2

An itinerary for Churchill's visit to Liverpool in April 1942. This is a transcript.

SOURCE 3

An itinerary for Churchill's visit to East Sussex in May 1941.

PROGRAMME

0755 hrs.	*Regional Commissioner meets Prime Minister and his party at Lime Street Station.*
0800 hrs	*Leave Lime Street for Adelphi Hotel for breakfast.*
0925 hrs.	*Lord Mayor, Town Clerk and Admiral Sir Percy Noble arrive at Adelphi.*
0933 hrs.	*Atherton Street. Inspect damaged property.*
0948 hrs.	*Adlington Street. Inspect A.R.P. personnel and air raid damage.*
1010 hrs.	*Lord Mayor and Town Clerk of Liverpool take leave of P.M.'s party.*
1015 hrs.	*Mersey Tunnel.*
1025 hrs.	*Erskine Road. Meet Mayor and Town Clerk of Wallasey. Inspect A.R.P. personnel and Parachute Mine damage.*
1050 hrs.	*Dock Road. Inspect damage to Flour Mills.*
1100 hrs.	*Meet Mayor and Town Clerk of Birkenhead. Meet representative of Mersey Docks and Harbour Board, and walk to see damaged mammoth crane.*
1120 hrs.	*Mallaby Street. Inspect A.R.P. personnel and damaged property.*
1135 hrs.	*Inspect Bratton Road where 3 Parachute Mines fell.*
1145 hrs.	*Arrive Cammell Laird's [shipbuilders].*
1230 hrs.	*Leave Cammell Laird's.*
1245 hrs.	*Arrive Adelphi for lunch.*
1300 to 1345 hrs. }	*Lunch*
1345 to 1430 hrs. }	*Rest*
1430 hrs.	*Mrs Churchill and Lady Haig proceed with Miss Dart to inspect W.V.S.*
1445 hrs.	*Arrive West End of N.Shed Gladstone Dock. Inspect Naval personnel and Merchant Ships' crew.*
1530 hrs.	*Leave Dock Estate. En route view damage to Railway Goods Yards, etc., and see typical blocks of warehouses.*
1545 hrs.	*Arrive East Side Brunswick Dock. Inspect Merchant Ships' crews.*

PROGRAMME – FRIDAY 12 MAY

85

2nd Army Commander is Lt.-Gen. M.C. Dempsey.
12 Corps Commander is LT.-Gen. N.M. Ritchie.

2.53 P.m. Arrive Lydd. Met by Maj.-Gen. G.I. Thomas, Commanding 43 Division and Brig. G.H.L. Mole, Commanding 129 Brigade.
Denje Marsh. Demonstration of Wasp action by 4 Somerset Light Infantry.

3.25 p.m.
Camber. Demonstration of Matt Bridges or Assault Raft for A.T.K. gun by 43 Division Royal Engineers. (Brig. H.E. Pike, – C.R.E.)

4.0 p.m.
Northiam. Demonstration of Sports by 94 Field Regiment, R.A. (Brig. G.W.E. Heath. – C.R.A.).

4.20 p.m.
Sedlescombe. Demonstration involving clearing road demolitions and mine clearance by 5 Dorsets. (Brig. N.D. Leslie. Commanding 130 Brigade).

4.55 p.m.
Bexhill. Demonstration of booby traps by 4 Dorsets.

5.10 p.m.
Rocks. Demonstration of cliff casualty evacuation by 130 Field Ambulance (Col. K.A.M. Tomory, A.D.M.S.)

5.40 p.m.
Depart Hastings by train.

The train will arrive at Ascot at 8.25 p.m. when General Eisenhower joins the party for dinner.

1 Choose three events listed in Sources 2 and 3 and explain why each was an important thing for the Prime Minister to do.

SOURCE 4 ▷▽

Extracts from a report by one of Churchill's assistants describing the Prime Minister's visit to Canada in September 1944. These are transcripts.

DIARY September 1944

Tuesday, September 5.
. . . The QUEEN MARY, with 4,000 other passengers, including American wounded, in addition to the OCTAGON party, weighed anchor at 8.30 p.m. and steamed southwards through the Irish Channel.

Wednesday, September 6.
The Prime Minister spent most of the day in his cabin reading 'Phineas Finn'. Mrs. Churchill, Mr. Martin, Commander Thompson and Mr. Colville lunched with him. General Ismay and Brigadier Whitby were invited to dinner.

Friday, September 8.
. . . In the morning, the Prime Minister discussed with Lord Cherwell the question of increases in Service pay, and subsequently attended a meeting of the Chiefs of Staff about the future of operations in Italy and in Burma.

Saturday, September 9.
The weather remained oppressively hot in the morning, but by noon the Queen Mary, in spite of altering course to avoid a submarine, had left the Gulf Stream and the skies and the atmosphere cleared. Mr. Churchill developed a slight temperature, but this subsided in the evening and he read and worked in bed until 1 a.m.

Sunday, September 10.
The Prime Minister attended a meeting of the Chiefs of Staff at noon, and they and Lord Cherwell subsequently lunched with him.

The Queen Mary docked at Halifax shortly after 2 p.m. Mr. Malcolm Macdonald and the Prime Minister of Nova Scotia came on board to welcome Mr. Churchill. The Party disembarked and left by train for Quebec at about 3.30 p.m. Before the train left, a crowd assembled round the Prime Minister's coach and there was some community singing. Mr. Churchill made a short speech thanking them for their welcome.

Tuesday, September 12, 1944.
At 11.30 a.m. a photograph was taken on the Terrace of the Governor-General and Princess Alice, the President and Mrs. Roosevelt, the Prime Minister and Mrs. Churchill, and Mr. Mackenzie King, all of whom subsequently lunched together.

Wednesday, September 13, 1944.
. . . After dinner the Prime Minister saw General Ismay about strategy in the Far East, Lord Cherwell about financial arrangements for stages II and III and Mr. Richard Law about U.N.R.R.A. Mr. Law had arrived by train from Montreal.

Tuesday, September 14, 1944
The Prime Minister saw the C.I.G.S. at 9 a.m. At 11 a.m. he had a meeting with the President and Mr. Law, chiefly connected with the administration of Italy and the question whether Italy should be a beneficiary from U.N.R.R.A. At 11.30, the President and the Prime Minister had a discussion about Lease-Lend in stages II and III at which Mr. Moregenthau and Lord Cherwell were present.

. . . Mr. Eden arrived in time for dinner and after dinner there was a film, possibly the worst ever made in Hollywood.

Saturday, September 16.
. . . After luncheon Honorary Degrees of McGill University were conferred on the President and the Prime Minister. The ceremony took place on the Sun Roof and was opened with a speech by the Visitor of the University, Lord Athlone. The Chancellor (Mr. Morris Wilson) and the Vice-Chancellor (Dr. Cyril James) then conferred the Degrees and both recipients made a short speech.

When the ceremony was over the President and the Prime Minister held a Press conference lasting about half an hour. Over 100 reporters and Press photographers assembled for this on the Sun Roof and the proceedings were opened by a few words from Mr. Mackenzie King.

Wednesday, 20th September.
After a night spent in the train the Prime Minister and his party embarked on a tender at Staten Island and at 9.30 a.m. boarded the QUEEN MARY which had sailed from New York an hour earlier.

Thursday, 21st September.
QUEEN MARY was routed further to the south than had originally been intended, owing to the position of submarines. She therefore entered the Gulf Stream and, as on the outward journey, the weather was hot and sticky. The Prime Minister started writing his speech for the Debate in the House of Commons next week. After luncheon he saw a number of news reels in the main ballroom.

Friday, 22nd September.
After luncheon the Prime Minister saw the first half of a film about the life of President Wilson, and then went on to the bridge for half an hour.

After dining alone with Mrs. Churchill, the Prime Minister played bezique till 3 a.m.

bezique: a card game
U.N.R.R.A.: a United Nations fund
C.I.G.S.: Chief of Imperial General Staff

1 Read Source 4 carefully. What do you think was the purpose of the Prime Minister's visit to Canada?

2 Certain extracts in the report describe what Churchill liked to do in his time off from official duties. Why do you think the assistant recorded this detail?

3 Choose three 'official' events on Churchill's visit. Explain why each was important.

4 In 1944 there was still a risk of a ship being sunk by torpedoes in the Atlantic. Why do you think Churchill risked the journey?

5 Do you think Churchill would have risked sailing to Canada in 1941? Explain why.

44 A NUCLEAR FUTURE

Although the war in Europe ended in May 1945, the war in the Far East dragged on into the summer. The Japanese were in retreat, but they were fighting to the death to defend territory they had conquered earlier in the war.

In August 1945 an American bomber dropped the first atomic bomb on Hiroshima. The second bomb was dropped on Nagasaki three days later. The next day the Japanese government surrendered.

DRAFT STATEMENT BY THE SECRETARY OF WAR

ATOMIC FISSION BOMBS

1.   The recent use of the atomic bomb over Japan, which was today made known by the President, is the culmination of years of herculean effort on the part of science and industry working in cooperation with the
5   military authorities. This development which was carried forward by the many thousands who participated with the utmost energy and the very highest sense of national duty, with the greatest secrecy and the most imperative of time schedules, probably represents the greatest achievement
10 of the combined efforts of science, industry, and the military in all history.

2.   The military weapon which has been forged from the products of this vast undertaking has an explosive force such as to stagger the imagination.
15 Improvements will be forthcoming shortly which will increase by several fold the present effectiveness. But more important for the long-range implications of this new weapon, is the possibility that another order of magnitude will be evolved after considerable research and
20 development. The scientists are confident that in a matter of years atomic bombs may well be developed which may be many thousands of times more powerful than the atomic bombs now at hand. It is abundantly clear that the possession of this weapon by the United States even in
25 its present form should prove a tremendous aid in the shortening of the war against Japan.

herculean: great, huge

◁ **SOURCE 1**
A draft statement to be made by the British Secretary of War to Parliament following the dropping of the first atomic bomb over Japan, August 1945.

1 Why do you think the development of the atomic bomb and the first drop on Hiroshima had been kept secret (line 8)?

2 The first atomic bomb dropped on Hiroshima killed fewer people outright than earlier saturation bombing of Tokyo by conventional means. Why do you think the atomic bomb brought the war to an end so quickly?

3 According to Source 1, what is the main result of the possession of the atomic bomb by the United States?

4 **Using your wider knowledge of the Second World War, list other consequences of the development and dropping of the first atomic bomb.**

During the war millions of people in Europe were forced to leave their homes. In many cases this was primarily to move away from the fighting; in others they were forcibly removed. One group who found themselves in a foreign country at the end of the war in 1945 were called the 'Baltic Cygnets'. A cygnet is the name of a young swan, but in this case the name refers to young women.

At the end of the war Germany was split up and governed by the four victorious powers: Russia, America, Britain and France. In the British zone camps were established for 'Displaced Persons' or DPs as they were called. These aimed to ensure that refugees could be sheltered, fed and clothed in an organised way until their final destination could be decided upon. The new Labour government in Britain at the end of the war was faced with a chronic shortage of workers. The 'Baltic Cygnets' were recruited to work in sanatoriums and hospitals.

SOURCE 1
An article in the *Manchester Guardian*, 21 October 1946.

Some of the Balts—formerly "displaced persons"—who arrived in Manchester yesterday to do domestic work in hospitals. ("Manchester Guardian" Copyright)

Eighty-five women from displaced persons' camps in the British zone of Germany who are going to do domestic work in sanatoriums and hospitals in the North-west region arrived in Manchester yesterday. Altogether a thousand volunteers are coming to this country to meet the urgent needs of the hospitals, and if this first party to arrive can be regarded as typical then the benefit derived from the arrangement should be mutual. The women—Estonians, Latvians, and Lithuanians—were delighted to be in England and warmly appreciative of the welcome they have received. Each one could tell a personal story of hardship and of sorrow. All have either parents or other relatives in Europe who still remain untraced. Yet, while it was impossible to ignore this fact—and, indeed, it should not be forgotten—it was encouragingly obvious that these women are facing the future with cheerfulness and with confidence. Most of them were conscripted by the Germans and put to work, mainly in factories and on the land. A few are elderly, but the great majority are young—strong-looking and healthy and just as much interested in their personal appearance as any other girls of their years.

Wages and conditions of service will be the same as those for British workers employed on similar duties. The women are being sent to the hospitals in parties of four to about twelve, and in each party there will be one girl who speaks English.

1 From which countries did the 'Baltic Cygnets' originally come?

2 Why did the Cygnets come to Britain?

3 Many of the women left behind relatives and friends, yet they volunteered to come to Britain to work. Why do you think they may have done this?

4 What jobs did the Baltic Cygnets do in Britain?

5 Why do you think British people were not able to do these jobs?

6 By what criteria did the officials judge the women?

7 Why do you think they chose those criteria?

8 Take each of the criteria that you wrote down in answer to question 6. What evidence is there in Source 1 that these criteria were applied to the Baltic Cygnets who were brought to Britain?

An extract from a memorandum about 'Displaced Persons' working in British hospitals. The memorandum was discussed by the Cabinet Committee on Foreign Labour.

C A B I N E T

Foreign Labour Committee

Recruitment of Displaced Persons from Germany
for work in British Hospitals.

Memorandum by the Parliamentary Secretary to the Ministry
of Labour and National Service.

2.   One of our officers, who recently visited a number of the
Camps in the British Zone in connection with the scheme, reports
that the women from the Baltic provinces, from whom volunteers are
being sought, are of very good type, and that it should be
possible to recruit from among them suitable persons for employment
in this country in numbers considerably in excess of the limit of
1,000 under the scheme already agreed by the Committee.   Indeed, out
of a total of employable women of Baltic origin estimated by the
Authorities in the British Zone at about 20,000 it is thought that there
may be no difficulty in selecting as many as 5,000 very suitable
volunteers for work in this country.

3.   A good response to the offer of employment in British Sanatoria
has already been shown and there is reason to believe that many more
of these women would be willing and eager to volunteer for similar
work.   They are generally of good appearance and habits and have been
well looked after in the Camps.   The general standard of
education is good;   most of them speak German as well as
their own language, while many already speak English quite
well,   especially the younger ones, a number of whom have
previously had a full course of secondary education.
Careful selection, combined with strict medical examination
of the kind which is being undertaken under the supervision
of the Medical Director of U.N.R.R.A., should produce a
substantial number of women of useful qualifications and of
good health who would form a valuable addition to our man-power
and a not undesirable element in our population.

1 What evidence can you find in Sources 1 and 2 that suggests that the Cygnets:
  a) wanted to come to Britain
  b) were made to feel welcome in Britain
  c) filled gaps created by a severe shortage of labour?

2 Why do you think that the government decided to use volunteers from the DPs camp?

46 DID BRITISH SOLDIERS TREAT BELSEN VICTIMS CRUELLY?

With the collapse of Germany in May 1945, the Allied military authorities faced many difficult tasks. One of these was how to deal with the many millions of 'Displaced Persons' (DPs) who were found in ex-enemy territories. By October 1945 most of these DPs had been repatriated. This left 550,000 who were in the British zone. Of this total, only a relatively small number were Jews.

SOURCE 1 ▷

A telegram reporting the text of a full page advertisment placed in the *New York Post* on 7 December 1945. The advertisement was placed by an organisation called 'The American League for a Free Palestine'.

[EN CLAIR]
WR.3650/4/48.

GENERAL DISTRIBUTION
FROM WASHINGTON TO FOREIGN OFFICE

Earl of Halifax
No. 8252

D. 8.05 p.m. 10th December, 1945

There are no arabs in Bergen Belsen. One incident Bergen Belsen and the whole British policy towards the Hebrew peoples stands revealed. The date is November 16th 1945 seven months after the Nazis surrendered the notorious Bergen Belsen camp to the democracies. The place is that very camp where thousands of Hebrews died and where today the survivors are still compelled to live. The incident occurred not under the Swastika but under the liberating Union Jack, under the aegis of the Four Freedoms. On that day the representatives of the Hebrews in Bergen Belsen voted to submit a protest against the statement of Foreign Secretary Bevin which was designed to keep them in the valley of death in Europe and to prevent them from being repatriated to the only place in the world where they could be safe - their national territory Palestine. However, the German administrator of the camp one G. Grande, learning of the plan, appeared with British military police who arrested Marian Lipke the President of the Hebrew committee of the camp and several of its members. In the course of their interrogation by a British officer some of them were beaten by German policemen. All this is a matter of report by outraged but thoroughly dependable correspondents of American news services. When the British M.P's arrived they removed under the supervision of the German administrator banners bearing inscriptions in English "Open the Gates of Palestine" and confiscated typewriters and files of the offices of the Hebrew Committee of the camp. Then they tore down the blue white Hebrew flag and threw it on a pile of garbage. These events caused many of the Hebrew internees of the camp to gather and voice their protest against the German administrator and British officers. The military police then let loose with their rubber truncheons striking indiscriminately at men, women, and children. Remember these were British officers not German Nazis, the victims were men and women and children who had managed to survive this sort of treatment over a period of many years and who thought that at last half a year after VE-day they had finally been liberated. Why must the British carry on the Nazi horror?

It is true that the British Government does not pursue its end through mass executions in crematoriums they are too smart for that, besides there is no longer any need for it since the Germans had succeeded in exterminating more than five million, and only a remnant remains and the British are too subtle for such flagrant methods. They advance toward their goal by a less obvious process not neglecting such co-operative forces as hunger, disease, cold and above all the native anti-Semitism in Europe which now rages wilder than ever before, and in places where it had never existed before. We therefore appeal to you to join the movement of righteous indignation and of action demand of President Truman and of your congressmen that (a) all Jews in Europe and the Middle East who so desire should be regarded as Hebrew nationals and be immediately given Palestinian citizenship, (b) the United States Government give full assistance to the immediate repatriation of these Palestinians to their own territory, (c) the United States Government forbid the British Government to use lend lease materials in its unholy war against Hebrew survivors in Europe or Palestine.

1. Read Source 1 carefully. At which camp is the 'incident' said to have taken place?

2. According to Source 1 where is 'the only place in the world' where Jews could be safe?

3. What acts of violence are described by the writer?

4. This advertisement says that the incident described has been reported by 'thoroughly dependable correspondents of American news services' – yet no names are mentioned. Does this necessarily mean that Source 1 is unreliable?

5. How would you begin to check on the details in this advertisement?

6. Why do you think Source 1 was placed in a newspaper by 'The American League for a Free Palestine'?

repatriated: sent back to their native or original country
indiscriminately: without selection, not choosing anyone or any particular group
liberated: freed
Congressman: member of the American Congress (the American parliament)

SOURCE 2▷

A reply to the advertisement in the *New York Post* from British officials in charge of DPs ('Displaced Persons') in the zone of Germany under British control.

1 Source 2 describes the contents of the advertisement as 'garbled, exaggerated and incorrect'. How does Source 2 explain what happened?

2 What do you think might have caused the report of the incident to be 'garbled, exaggerated and incorrect'?

SOURCE 3 ▽

The same incident was discussed in the House of Commons during a Parliamentary Debate. These are three extracts from Hansard dated 20 December 1945. Hansard is a report of all the speeches that are made in Parliament. The first speech is made by Mr J.B. Hynd MP.

PRESS REPORT IN TEXT IS GARBLED EXAGGERATED AND INCORRECT BOTH AS TO FACTS AND PLACE. HOHNE WHICH IS THE NEAREST DP ASSEMBLY CENTRE TO BERGEN BELSEN PROCESSION OF JEWS MARCHED TO OFFICE OF MIL GOV DET TO PRESENT A RESOLUTION TO BE PASSED TO PRIME MINISTER. OC MIL GOV DET ACCEPTED RESOLUTION FOR PASSING TO AUTHORITIES THROUGH APPROPRIATE CHANNELS. THERE WERE NO INCIDENTS AND NO ARRESTS AND MR ROSENSHAFT ACTIVE PRESIDENT OF JEWISH COMMITTEE IN DP CAMP HOHNE REPORTS HE HAD NO COMPLAINTS AS TO THIS PROCEDURE. INCIDENTS ALLEGED IN AMERICAN PRESS REPORT PROBABLY REFER TO A POLITICAL DEMONSTRATION STAGED BY JEWISH SUB-COMMITTEE IN A CAMP AT HANOVER CONTAINING EX-CONCENTRATION CAMP INMATES OF SEVERAL NATIONALITIES. THIS DEMONSTRATION WAS PROBABLY ORDERED BY THE CENTRAL JEWISH ORGANISATION UNDER MR ROSENSHAFT ALTHOUGH THIS NOT YET PROVED. THIS DEMONSTRATION LED TO DISORDERS WHICH RESULTED IN THE ARREST OF TEN JEWISH DEMONSTRATORS BY BRITISH MILITARY POLICE. TRIAL BY MIL GOV COURT IS ARRANGED FOR 10 DEC. LEGAL DIVISION CONSIDER ADEQUATE FACILITIES FOR LEGAL AID AVAILABLE LOCALLY UNDER NORMAL PROCEDURE. CONSIDER THAT TRIAL IS BEST MEANS OF CLARIFYING ISSUE. INCIDENTS NOT OF GREAT GRAVITY AND NO FURTHER COMMENTS CAN BE MADE AS MATTER IS SUB JUDICE. RESULTS OF TRIAL WILL BE COMMUNICATED WHEN KNOWN. YOU MAY THINK IT WORTH WHILE TO MAKE ENQUIRIES AS TO THE OUTSIDE SOURCE OF THE STATEMENT ABOUT THE INCIDENT AT HOHNE. IF REFERRING PUBLICLY TO THIS MATTER YOU MAY CARE TO POINT OUT THAT SUCH INACCURATE AND TENDENTIOUS STATEMENTS ARE NOT LIKELY TO FURTHER THE CAUSE OF THOSE WHO MAKE THEM.

Mil Gov Det: controller of the camp
OC: Officer commanding the Detachment
resolution: petition
tendentious: designed to promote a particular viewpoint

A

There is no censorship of newspapers within the centre and complete freedom of movement in and out of the camp is permitted. No restriction is placed on Zionist activities. Contrary to statements which have been circulating in the Press overseas there was no disturbance at this centre on 15th November. Nor has there been a procession of Jewish displaced persons from the centre marched to the office of the military government detachment to present a resolution to be passed to the British authorities. The command-ing officer of the detachment accepted the resolution for onward trans-mission. There were no incidents and no arrests and the acting president of the Jewish committee at the centre reports that he has had no complaints about the procedure.

The facts are that recently a procession of Jewish displaced persons from the centre marched to the office of the military government detachment to...

B

MR. LINDSAY: May I ask the Minister how these completely inaccurate reports are put about? I have received reports about the work of the British Red Cross.

MR. HYND: I obviously cannot say how these inspired Press statements in other countries originated. The fact is that they have been published and, therefore, I am glad to have this opportunity of repudiating them.

C

MISS RATHBONE: Is the Minister aware that as far as I have been able to make out -- and I have been making inquiries since I first heard of these violent criticisms -- the particularly unfair criticisms which he has answered to-day do not seem to have originated in any of the well-known Jewish bodies in this country? They did not even know that the criticisms had been made.

MR. HYND: I am glad to say that, so far as I am aware, such stories have not appeared in the British Press.

Zionist: someone who believes in the establishment of a Jewish state in Palestine.

3 What evidence does Mr Hynd put forward to argue that the incident described in Source 1 never took place?

4 What in Mr Hynd's reply matches what you read in Source 2?

5 Using Sources 1, 2 and 3 write an advertisement of your own in reply to the one placed by 'The American League for a Free Palestine'. Your reply should include:
a) what you think was inaccurate in the *New York Post* advertisement
b) what you think did actually happen at the camp
c) why you think the incident became garbled.

47 · WHERE SHOULD THE UN HEADQUARTERS BE?

At the end of the Second World War, many important problems remained to be tackled. Most European countries badly needed help for reconstruction. Refugees and prisoners of war had to be returned home. The Nazi leadership had to be put on trial.

The United Nations was involved in all of these problems to some extent. However, the wartime Allies – Britain, America and the Soviet Union – began to argue soon after the war was over. Since they, together with China, had set up the United Nations in 1942, they had the most power within it. The disagreements between the Allies threatened the organisation almost before it started.

The temporary headquarters of the UN was set up in New York, but many people expected it to move once Europe had recovered from the war. The dispute over where to put the headquarters, though not the most important problem after the war, shows us some of the difficulties faced by this new organisation.

SOURCE 1 ▷

Extracts from a British government document produced in 1945 to encourage discussion about the site of the UN.

1 Read the extracts in Source 1 carefully. What 'essential freedom' does extract A believe to be necessary for the site of the United Nations?

2 Why, according to extract A, was this freedom so vital?

3 This extract mentions five other general considerations in setting up the UN headquarters. Choose two of them, and explain why you think each was important.

4 In which area of the world does extract B want the UN headquarters to be? Suggest why.

A

Where should the Headquarters of the World Organisation be?

(a) *Desiderata.*

4. A large number of desiderata have been drawn up. Considerations which must be taken into account include guarantees for freedom of communication and discussion, climate, buildings, amenities, language. The only absolutely essential one is freedom of communication and discussion. It is necessary that all countries should be able to send their representatives without hindrance and that the latter should be able to express themselves with complete freedom without reference to local conditions. Attention has also been drawn to the advantage of security in case of armed operations against a disturber of the peace.

desiderata: considerations to be taken into account

B

(b) *Should the Headquarters be in the territory of a Great Power?*

5. There will probably be general agreement that this would be undesirable. Any Great Power in whose territory the Organisation was situated might be suspected of wielding a disproportionate influence on the Secretariat. Moreover the suggestion would not be agreeable to the bulk of the smaller nations. However, if there were any general desire to establish the Organisation in the United Kingdom we should presumably welcome and encourage it.

Secretariat: the officials who ran the UN from day to day. In this case the Secretariat includes the Secretary General, the most senior post at the UN
Great Power: powerful countries such as the USA, the USSR, Britain, France and China

C

(e) *If in Europe, where?*

10. If it is agreed that we should press for Europe, there is some reason to suppose that we should get support both from Soviet Russia and even from the United States—and presumably also from France. Many suggestions have been made, but for practical purposes these reduce themselves to Brussels, The Hague, Lisbon, Prague, Vienna, Copenhagen and Geneva. Short of some unexpected development the first three may be ruled out, since the Russians would probably not be prepared to come to Western Europe, and would certainly not be prepared to come to Lisbon. Of the remaining four, *Vienna* has much to recommend it by reason of its building amenities. It has also been suggested that its selection might simplify the solution of the Austrian problem. But there are obvious disadvantages in choosing a German-speaking country and one only recently detached from the enemy. Security objections alone, for instance, might prove overwhelming. *Prague* might have fewer objections and is a serious candidate, but it might well be objected here that it was in the Russian " sphere of influence." *Copenhagen,* on the other hand, has very little to be said against it, except possibly that the climate is not ideal. It is very well situated geographically, its hotel accommodation should be quite sufficient and the population would be extremely well-disposed.

Geneva: the site of the UN's predecessor, the League of Nations. The Swiss government refused to have the UN in Geneva.

For several reasons, but mainly because there was no agreed alternative, New York remained the UN headquarters. Attention then turned to designing a permanent building to house the UN.

United Nations	Nations Unies	RESTRICTED
GENERAL ASSEMBLY	**ASSEMBLEE GENERALE**	A/HQC/M.20/Rev.2 1 July 1946 ORIGINAL: ENGLISH

HEADQUARTERS COMMISSION

SUMMARY OF THE REQUIREMENTS OF THE UNITED NATIONS

BASED ON THE REPLIES TO THE QUESTIONNAIRE

A. ASSEMBLY:

A.1 - The Assembly meets once a year in general session, do you foresee this will always be in the month of September?

Assembly meets in September, occasionally otherwise.

A.3 - How many committees, besides the ten standing ones, do you foresee during the annual session?

6 Committees with 60 members in future.
1 Committee with 14 members in future.
1 Committee with 9 members in future.
2 Committees with 10 members in future.

Average 7 temporary committees.

Provide for 7 large committee rooms varying from 300-500 persons, one with cinema (Average 400 persons).

10 committee rooms, varying from 30-100 persons.

A.6 - How many journalists, radio broadcasters, film and photographic representatives should be provided for?

Provide for 800 in Assembly Hall (balconies)

A.7 - How many diplomats and how many distinguished visitors, general public and representatives of non-governmental organizations should be provided for?

Minimum 1000 - maximum 2500. Provide for 2000 on balconies Assembly Hall.

A.11- Should the Assembly Hall be provided with a lobby?

Yes.

A.12- What auxiliary accommodation (President's - Vice-President's- Secretary-General's offices, Delegates' Lounge, etc.) should be provided for?

15 offices and waiting rooms. Delegates' Lounge and waiting room. Lounge for Assembly staff, two restaurants with bars.

A.13- What working facilities - apart from the press gallery in the hall should be provided for?

On main floor: First aid, Public address, Press, Working room with facilities.
On special balcony: Radio, Film,

B. SECURITY COUNCIL:

B.1 - How frequently do you foresee the Security Council's meetings, besides the bi-weekly statutory ones?

The Security Council will require a special hall per annum.

B.2 - How many members should normally be provided for (Permanent Representatives, Foreign Ministers and especially interested States and Secretariat)?

Main floor: 100 seats
100 elsewhere
200 total (Main floor)

B.6 - How many journalists, radio-broadcasters, film- and photographic representatives should be provided for?

Press: 425 seats.

B.7 - How many diplomats and how many distinguished visitors, general public and representatives of non-governmental organizations should be provided for?

(VIP) Special guests - 300 seats on balcony
Other 200 seats
balcony
balcony: 500 seats

◁**SOURCE 2**

Results of a survey carried out by United Nations staff in 1946 to find out what sort of building the UN needed. The questions asked are on the left, replies are summed up on the right.

1 Extract C in Source 1 suggests the UN should be based in Europe. Look at a map of Europe in 1945. Using all the information you have gathered about the Second World War, explain which of the following places you think would be the best site for the UN in Europe at that time:
  a) Vienna
  b) Copenhagen
  c) Prague
  d) Paris.
Explain your choice. What are the problems with the other cities?

2 Why was the site of the UN headquarters so important? Write down as many reasons as you can. Which reason do you think was the most important?

3 Read Source 2 carefully. Use it to draw a plan of the ideal UN building. You will need to work out how many people you must fit into the main hall, and how many other rooms you will need.

You are responsible for the PRO archives for the Second World War. The war has left you with a difficult task. Which of the following records are to be kept and which ones are to be destroyed?

SOURCE 1 ▷

A note written by Churchill's private secretary, November 1941.

SOURCE 2

The Munich Agreement signed by Hitler and Chamberlain, October 1938.

11th November, 1941.

Dear Way,

Attached is a list of the tickets required for the Prime Minister's train 5th – 8th November.

Yours sincerely,

C.R.T.

R. G. Way Esq.
War Office.

Circulated to the Cabinet by direction of —
The Secretary of State for Foreign Affairs
THIS DOCUMENT IS THE PROPERTY OF HIS BRITANNIC MAJESTY'S GOVERNMENT

ARCHIVES   218

CENTRAL (GERMANY).   October 1, 1938.

CONFIDENTIAL.   SECTION 1.

[C 11508/42/18]   Copy No.   8

Declaration signed by the Prime Minister and Herr Hitler at Munich on September 30, 1938.—(Received in Foreign Office, October 1.)

WE, the German Führer and Chancellor and the British Prime Minister, have had a further meeting to-day and are agreed in recognising that the question of Anglo-German relations is of the first importance for the two countries and for Europe.

We regard the agreement signed last night and the Anglo-German Naval Agreement as symbolic of the desire of our two peoples never to go to war with one another again.

We are resolved that the method of consultation shall be the method adopted to deal with any other questions that may concern our two countries, and we are determined to continue our efforts to remove possible sources of difference, and thus to contribute to assure the peace of Europe.

A. HITLER.
NEVILLE CHAMBERLAIN.

September 30, 1938.

---

1 Study each source carefully and place them in order of importance.

2 Why did you select this order?

3 Source 2 is quite important. Where are you going to keep it?

4 Does it make any difference to historians if records like these above were selected by someone with no interest in what historians of the future might need?

SOURCE 4

A government poster, 1942.

SOURCE 3

Government publicity, November 1941.

THEME 1: WHAT DID BRITAIN THINK OF HITLER?

INVESTIGATION 1 • *two pages*

'A MAN OF SIMPLE TASTES'

The title is a quote from Source 1.

In the 1930s the Foreign Office in London received regular briefings about the leading political personalities in Germany. The biography of Hitler in Source 1 was prepared by the British Embassy in Berlin in 1937.

As some of the historical detail in the third and fifth paragraphs is quite complicated, you may need to explain the key events to pupils.

The language is also somewhat complex, but in this first investigation it is worth reminding ourselves that one by-product of working with the original source material in this book is to develop pupils' language skills – including their vocabulary, spelling, grammar and even, in some cases, their handwriting.

Source 1: The PRO reference is FO 408/67.

Questions 1–4: These give some opportunity for differentiation. Pupils could work in pairs (each given just one page of Source 1 to investigate) and then pool their answers.

Question 2: One object of this question is to help pupils skim read what is after all a long and dense document. To prepare for this exercise you can highlight or underline some or all of the dates for pupils beforehand. If you only use selected dates then pupils' timelines can be made a good deal simpler. For example, you could pick out Hitler's birth, his experience of the Great War; his imprisonment; his election; his elevation to the German Chancellorship.

This timeline can be kept and be extended to include other events as pupils study the sources in investigations 3–11 or the events of the war itself.

Question 4: Explain what a turning point is. And possibly pre-select four moments for pupils to choose from: eg poverty in Austria, fighting in the Great War, writing Mein Kampf, the 1930 election, the death of Hindenburg.

Question 5: This question will get pupils to identify the elements of the document which express opinion rather than fact. There are some quite subtle ways in which opinion is expressed. Point pupils to the tone in which his childhood is described, or the implications of the final paragraphs, as well as the more obvious judgements on his political career in lines 111–118.

Question 6: Have a range of textbooks available for pupils to trawl for a suitable picture of Hitler. Compare pupils' answers afterwards.

INVESTIGATION 2 • *four pages*

WHY WAS HITLER SO POPULAR IN GERMANY?

The Foreign Office was not only dependent on its own officers for assessing the changing situation in Germany. It also received reports and letters from personal friends, business people, and from many other contacts in Germany. Pupils can consider why the government would want to receive such a range of reports. This investigation brings together a number of different reports and letters to look at the overall question of how Hitler achieved such widespread popularity.

It will help pupils to investigate not only the role of the Depression – and Hitler's measures to combat it – in Hitler's popularity, but also the part played by censorship, the Hitler Youth, foreign policy successes and policy towards the Jews.

Sources 2–4 come from July–December 1937. The PRO reference is FO 371/20733.

Source 2: In an aside in this document the author records a conversation with a factory worker who described Hitler as a 'Mussolini'. The author later goes on to say in his conclusion that *in the short run* he regarded Mussolini as a greater threat to the British Empire than Hitler: 'He is certainly a more tenacious hater, and he bears us a more serious grudge'.

Source 5: This can be used on its own alongside the later investigation into the *Anschluss*. The PRO reference is FO 371/21750.

INVESTIGATION 3 • one page

GERMAN REARMAMENT

Investigations 3–11 take pupils through the various incidents that finally led to war in 1939. As you use them, get pupils to place each event on a timeline for 1933–1939.

The PRO archives are particularly helpful in shedding light on how Britain responded to German territorial expansion and rearmament. As we study these 'steps to war', two themes in particularly underlie the investigations:
- a study of Britain's policy of appeasement
- a study of how the legacy of the First World War and the Treaty of Versailles affected events in the 1930s.

This first investigation examines the announcement of German rearmament in March 1935.

Sources 1 and 2: The PRO reference is FO 371/18849.

Question 1: The aim of this question is for pupils to extrapolate information from that specifically presented in the source itself. This is best tackled in a class discussion.

INVESTIGATION 4 • one page

WHY DID THE REOCCUPATION OF THE RHINELAND CAUSE SO MUCH WORRY?

Question 1: This predictive question is to be tackled before pupils look at Source 1. It would be best if you write these options on the board and ask pupils to consider this question before giving them the investigation.

Source 1: FRO reference is FO 371/19891. This document is a telegram to the Foreign Office in Britain. We have omitted the first part of the document which summarises the early discussions. Evidently the Italians tabled proposals which would allow the German troops to remain in the Rhineland. The French were appalled. Their representatives consulted their own government, and returned with the view given in the first sentence of the extract.

Questions 2 and 3: Pupils could work in groups of three, taking one country each.

Question 4: The document offers the possibility of sanctions as a means to eject the German troops. Pupils may be aware how often this strategy is proposed or derided as a solution to international political problems today. Thinking about the modern day may help them in framing their answers to Question 4.

INVESTIGATION 5 • two pages 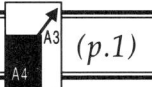 (p.1)

'EUROPE'S SAVIOUR FROM COMMUNISM'

In this investigation we study a number of extracts from a report by Arnold Toynbee, a leading British intellectual of the period. He had been granted an interview with Hitler, just two days before Hitler decided on the move to remilitarise the Rhineland. However, his report was delivered to the government some days **after** German troops had marched into the Rhineland.

The investigation serves two related purposes – first to highlight Hitler's attitude towards Communism; second to show how he sought to present himself to Britain. Hitler's opposition towards Communism appealed to many British leaders who in the past had been more worried about Communism than about Fascism.

Source 1: The PRO reference is FO 371/19891.

Question 1: If you wish, you could assign pupils just one of the extracts to work on.

Question 4: Compare pupils' answers with the caustic tone of the two Foreign Office officials who wrote on this report:

'Knowing Mr Toynbee personally I have great respect for his learning, but none for his judgement'.

'Mr Toynbee suggests that much can be achieved by treating Herr Hitler with courtesy and being responsive from the English side to his overtures. Twice in the last 15 months we have made two separate series of the most obvious advances to him. That of February 1935 produced the conscription decree. That of this autumn and winter ended in the reoccupation of the Rhineland.'

INVESTIGATION 6 • one page

'HMG DISLIKES BLOCS'

The 'Anti-Comintern' pact faced the British government with a dilemma. They were worried about Communism, so might be expected to approve its objectives. However, they were also worried about the rising influence of Japan as they felt their empire in the Far East could be under threat. They were worried still more about the implications for Europe of closer ties between Germany and Italy. So they might be expected to disapprove of the pact. Add to this the legacy of the Great War – and the memory of how the alliance system dragged Europe into war in 1914 – and you have a classic foreign policy problem. Source 1 is one straightforward example of Britain's response. Most of the documents relating to this pact are very difficult and inaccessible for Key Stage 3.

Source 1 on the other hand has the advantage of being very clear and therefore more accessible.

Source 1: The PRO reference is FO 371/21028.

Question 1: You could partially shade in the map beforehand to help some pupils. (NB Durazzo was the capital of Albania.)

Question 2: Encourage pupils to consider the gerographical location of the countries.

INVESTIGATION 7 · three pages

'A PASSIONATE LUNATIC'

The policy of appeasement depended to a large extent on the British believing that the Germans could be trusted. This investigation highlights Britain's increasing fears about Hitler (the investigation title 'a passionate lunatic' is an assessment of Hitler from Source 2), as well as their increasing fears about the state of their own rearmament. In Febrary 1937 one Foreign Office official described British rearmament as 'a dreadful record of all-round improvidence . . . 48 long-range bombers against 800 German . . . if ever a country has gambled its existence we have done so.'

Sources 1–4: The PRO reference is FO 371/20733.

Question 1: These statements could be considered as a whole class activity.

Question 2 (third page): This can be extended into a major piece of work if you have used earlier investigations such as 'A man of simple tastes' or 'Why was Hitler popular?' A 'Foreign Office' template can be made up for pupils to write their report on.

A paper was prepared on this very subject 'Can Hitler be trusted?' by the British Embassy in Berlin in December 1938. Unfortunately, the paper is too wordy and abstract for it to be useful in class. The conclusion of the memo was, unsurprisingly, that Hitler could not be trusted. 'Hitler cannot be judged by ordinary standards; he is a law unto himself. He is able in the course of a discussion to utter a palpable untruth with every appearance of sincerity . . . All agree in attaching no importance to Hitler's latest declaration that he has no further territorial claims to make in Europe and the [German] nation is awaiting with anxiety or exaltation, according to their outlook, the beginning of the next drive which, it is confidently anticipated, will take place in the course of the coming year.'

Pupils could be given a structure for their answer based on that of the British Ambassador in Berlin:

a) Hitler's attitude to truth/propaganda
b) Nazi beliefs about the use of force
c) Broken promises
d) Attitude to treaties and agreements.

INVESTIGATION 8 · two pages

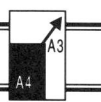

THE 'ANSCHLUSS'

The first page of this investigation can be used on its own. The second page is extension material using further extracts from the letter.

Source 1: The PRO reference is FO 408/68.

Sources 2 and 3: The PRO reference is FO 371/21750. The language is difficult in this source. You may wish to supplement our annotation.

Question 5: You could write each of the listed results on a separate card yourself i.e. Hitler is more popular than ever in Germany; six and a half million Germans have been added to the German population; the area of Germany is greater than before the First World War; stocks of gold, foreign currency, raw materials and agricultural produce have fallen into German hands; extra troops have been added to the army; German influence abroad will increase.

Questions 1–3 (second page): These questions are designed to look at the difference between fact and opinion. To get pupils started you might like to underline some sentences for them to consider, before you make photocopies.

INVESTIGATION 9 · four pages

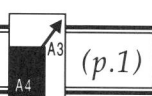

(p.1)

THE SUMMER AND AUTUMN OF '38: ARP and Munich

The aim of this investigation is to focus on the Munich crisis. The strategy is to use extracts from the *Illustrated London News* to help pupils appreciate how likely war seemed to the British people prior to the Munich crisis, and therefore how immensely relieved the population was when the crisis appeared to be settled. The Munich Agreement gave Germany the *Sudetenland* in return for Hitler's promise that he had 'no further territorial ambitions'.

As one of the most famous examples of appeasement in action, it brings into focus many of the themes in the previous investigations.

All Sources are taken from the *Illustrated London News*, Volume 193.

Source 1: They key to the numbered items was as follows:

1. Blankets
2. Camp-beds.
3. Hammer.
4. String.
5. Adhesive Paper.
6. Gum.
7. Disinfectant.
8. Matches.
9. Candles.
10. Radio.
11. Gas-masks.
12. Gas-tight Door.
13. Privacy Screen.
14. Ceiling Supports.
15. Gas-tight Window
16. Protected Glass.
17. Heavy Curtain.
18. Lamp.

19. Sand-buckets.
20. Drinking-water.
21. Shovel and Rake.
22. Sand Container.
23. Cracks Covered.
24. Tinned Food.
25. Crockery.
26. First Aid.
27. Thermos Flasks.
28. Food Tin.
29. Bread Tin.
30. Water-buckets.
31. Water Pump.
32. Oilskins, etc.
33. Ventilator Covered.
34. Notice.
35. Telephone.
36. Clock.
37. Sealed Flue.
38. Electric Fire.
39. Toys, etc.
40. Books, etc.

Source 3: The caption of the top picture in the *Illustrated London News* read 'Holding the declaration (reproduced below) bearing his own and Herr Hitler's signatures: Mr Chamberlain addressing the crowd at Heston.'

Source 4: The actual descriptions of the events of each date were as follows:

a) 12 September: Herr Hitler's speech at Nuremberg: he declares that if others will not help the Sudetens to self-determination, Germany will.

b) 14 September: Mr. Chamberlain's message to Herr Hitler, suggesting a personal meeting in Germany.

c) 22 September: Mr. Chamberlain goes to Godesburg. Herr Hitler presents an 'unreasonable' memorandum to him. Change of Czech Government. Gen. Syrovy Premier. French security measures.

d) 26 September: Roosevelt's first message to European States. Sir Horace Wilson's message from Mr. Chamberlain to Herr Hitler. Herr Hitler's Berlin speech. Statement by Mr. Chamberlain on the speech.

e) 30 September: Mr. Chamberlain, Herr Hitler, Signor Mussolini, and M. Daladier sign an agreement as to the methods to be adopted in the transfer of Sudeten territory at 12.30 a.m.

INVESTIGATION 10 · one page

THE SUMMER OF '39: the Royal holiday

Since the Munich Agreement Hitler had taken over the rest of Czechoslovakia and in summer 1939 there was a clear assumption by the British government that Poland would be the next object. They had given an undertaking that if Poland was invaded they would come to its aid.

The aim of this investigation is to give a snapshot of opinion in the summer of 1939. The documents relate to a member of the Royal Family's holiday plans for the summer.

It can work well alongside investigation 11 as a two-page investigation to give a fuller picture. Alternatively, each one can be used on its own.

Sources 1 and 2: The PRO reference is FO 800/316.

Question 4: This reply is intended to be based on Source 2, but pupils may like to add ideas of their own from their wider study of the period.

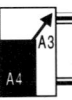

INVESTIGATION 11 · one page

'HE MAY CHANGE HIS MIND TOMORROW': Poland

This investigation can be used alongside investigation 10, or separately. The document is a letter from the British Embassy in Berlin, concerning the likelihood of a German invasion of Poland. It clearly illustrates the continued belief in the policy of appeasement even at this late stage.

The language is quite difficult in this source. Pupils may need additional help, or you may prefer to see this investigation as extension work only for the most able.

Source 1: The PRO reference is FO 800/316.

Have a map to hand so that pupils can see where Danzig and the Polish Corridor are.

INVESTIGATION 12 · two pages

'WHY WE ARE AT WAR'

The document in this investigation is the draft of a speech prepared by the War Cabinet for the Prime Minister to give to the House of Commons. It explains the British government's reaction to the peace proposals put forward by Hitler after the invasion of Poland.

It provides a useful summary of the way relations between Germany and Britain had evolved over the previous five years – and how the policy of appeasement had finally run its course.

Source 1: The PRO reference is PREM 1/395.

Question 6: Prime Minister's Question Time is at 2.00 pm on a Tuesday or Thursday afternoon. If appropriate you could tune in live instead of recording it.

Encourage pupils to take a range of approaches: some might choose this moment to criticise appeasement with hindsight, for example 'why did they not declare war years ago when Hitler was weak?' or 'why is the government so worried about Poland when it was not worried about the *Sudetenland* one year ago?' Others might praise the government for trying so hard to avert war; some might at this stage still advocate appeasement remembering the slaughter of the Great War, for example 'Why not accept Hitler's proposals – surely anything is better than another war?' or 'Have the government thought about the consequences of war for the British people?' Yet others might have their own original proposals to put back to Germany as an ultimatum.

An extension to stage c) is for a teacher or pupil to take the role of Prime Minister and role play the question time giving the answers written for the PM by the separate groups.

INVESTIGATION 13 • one page

SEPTEMBER 1939

The aim throughout the investigations into life on the Home Front is to supplement the many other excellent published resources about life in Britain during the war. The investigations illustrate how the available evidence at the PRO can provide:

a) insight into the reasons for the policies followed by the government

b) insight into what life was like for a range of people during the war.

This investigation sets up a simple decision-making exercise using a number of sources as stimuli. Each of these policies – rationing, evacuation, internment, ARP, censorship and protection from gas attack – will be returned to in subsequent investigations.

Questions 1–3: Pupils could work in pairs or small groups for this activity. In some cases you may wish to cut down the choice of options to just two or three for each group.

In practice some of the measures had been introduced before the outbreak of war. Gas masks had been distributed in 1938 prior to the Munich crisis. Air raid shelters had been distributed in the summer of 1939. Censorship was put into place almost immediately the war began, and children were evacuated from the first weekend of September 1939.

Large-scale internment of aliens took place in May 1940 when the threat of invasion by Germany was at its greatest. Rationing was introduced in stages between 1939 and 1942.

INVESTIGATION 14 • two pages

PROPAGANDA: believe it or not

The theme of propaganda underlies many of the investigations in this book, simply because we are publishing sources from the government's archive and inevitably a lot of material in the collection was created for a propaganda purpose (see page 5 of the introduction).

How can historians use such propaganda as evidence? The essential point to make to pupils about a historian's use of evidence is that, contrary to what many pupils believe, a biased piece of evidence is *not* useless. The value of any evidence, no matter how biased it may be, lies in the questions that are asked of it and how it is part of a collection of other sources. Propaganda is useful to the historian in respect of

understanding what the government considered to be important for the public to know, or for it to be persuaded of. So this investigation is a useful antidote to those students who would reject anything tainted by bias.

To generate clearer understanding of the concept of propaganda, one starting point is the parents' brochure for your school [if available]. It will be immediately recognisable to pupils and they will able to latch on to the idea that facts may be used selectively and do not always guarantee the truth.

Using this as a starting point, the idea of persuasion can be linked to other aspects of our culture such as advertising, the selling and buying of houses, the election poster or the party political broadcast and numerous other activities – with all of which pupils will be familiar.

Sources 1–4: The PRO reference is INF 3/400.

As there are four posters, this investigation might lend itself to work in groups of four, followed by a presentation to the rest of the class of the work each pupil has done on his or her poster.

The questions on the worksheet will gradually lead the pupils into thinking more critically about propaganda. An extension activity would be to consider the success or failure of the posters:

• Do they succeed in sending clear messages?

• Who would be the target audience for such messages?

• What makes for a successful poster: humour, cartoon characters, familiar faces?

Later in this book there are many examples of government propaganda produced for other purposes or audiences, eg for Allies such as the Russians or the Americans, or for dropping over German cities (see investigations 32 and 33).

Pupils can draw up their own definitions of what makes something into propaganda. They can also try to draw up their own rules for how to use such material in the classroom. The following questions can be used as a starting point for creating your own class 'Propaganda shredder':

The propaganda shredder

Background

1 Who wrote/made it?
   a) The government?
   b) A newspaper?
   c) An individual?

2 For whom was it written or made?
   a) People in Britain or people abroad?
   b) Women or men?
   c) Young people or old people?
   d) Soldiers or civilians?

3 Why was it written or made?
  a) To encourage people?
  b) To discourage people in enemy countries?
  c) To persuade people to do something?
  d) To attack an enemy's actions?
  e) To justify some British action that had been or was to be taken?

4 When was it written or made?
  a) What was going on at the time?
  b) Was the war going badly or well for Britain?

5 Where might it be used?
  a) In a newspaper or magazine?
  b) On an advertising hoarding?
  c) On the radio?

Content

6 What facts are given?
  a) Statistics?
  b) Places?
  c) Events?
  d) Information about people?

7 Can the facts be verified from another source?

8 Are opinions expressed in the words and pictures:
  a) about people
  b) about events
  c) about the way the war is going
  d) about the enemy
  e) about the British people
  f) about the people reading the poster?

9 Is the piece of propaganda supposed to cause:
  a) a change of behaviour
  b) a change of attitude?

Evaluation

10 Is it an effective piece of propaganda? Not does it work well now, but **would it have worked for people at the time?**

INVESTIGATION 15 · one page

FEAR OF INVASION: 'heads isolated from their bodies'

What did people expect the war to be like? Since the Great War, technology had advanced enormously. The Spanish Civil War had seen the first major civilian bombing in Europe – and gas and incendiary bombs had been 'tried out' as well as conventional explosive bombs. As the preparations for war in investigation 13 illustrate, the government were preparing for all these possibilities.

The early months of war also proved the devastating strength of the German war machine as the German armies swept through north west Europe. Source 1 examines how adequately the British government had prepared for an invasion.

Source 1 is not an 'official' document. The army officer is writing on his own initiative early in 1940 when the threat of an invasion seemed most imminent. The writer is even giving an exact week for the expected invasion – 'June 7/8–15'.

This investigation can be used in a number of ways: as part of an examination of the reasons for evacuation (alongside investigation 17), or of the reasons behind a whole range of civil defence measures taken in 1939 and 1940 (alongside investigation 24).

Pupils could also use this document to help them decide what the government should do to protect London. Pupils studying this topic often have only a vague idea of why London was targeted. This source brings out how London was important as the centre of government.

Source 1: The PRO reference is CAB 118/55.

Question 1: The order given by Source 1 (Careful bombing of selected areas; roads, rail and telephones cut; heavy bombing all over London; parachutists land; attacks on important buildings and people) is not the only possibility. There is room for discussion here about whether people might anticipate a different order of events.

Question 2: The attacks would be concentrated at night, so the moon was needed for visibility. Attacking at the weekend would give the German troops more chances of catching the defences off guard. A recent example of such tactics could be the 'Yom Kippur' attack by Egypt on Israel, 1973.

Question 3: The King was an important figurehead. His capture would affect morale and he would have great value as a hostage.

INVESTIGATION 16 · one page

FEAR OF INVASION: 'they may land anywhere'

Early in 1940 the army began a massive operation to place mines along the remaining unprotected coasts of southern and eastern Britain against the threat of German invasion.

This investigation looks at this operation from the standpoint of a single civilian. It can be used alongside the previous one as part of a two-page investigation, or it can stand in its own right. It paints an intriguing picture of the relationship between soldier and civilian. There is a 'sit-com' quality to the exchange – Mr Cleave comes across as something of a Victor Meldrew battling with British military bureacracy. This document is the culmination of a series of letters between Mr Cleave and the army authorities requesting them to remove the mines from the stretch of beach in front of his home. The reason for this, as he explained many times, was that at high tides in rough seas the mines were thrown against the embankments outside his house and exploded.

Source 1: The PRO reference is WO 199/94.

INVESTIGATION 17 • two pages

HOW SUCCESSFUL WAS EVACUATION?

The sources in this section look at evacuation from the government's standpoint. They are a useful adjunct to the many personal letters and accounts of evacuation available in other textbooks.

One of the government's constant needs was to persuade parents to part with their children in the first place or, when the threatened air raids failed to materialise, to try to prevent children from being returned home.

One of the questions posed by this investigation is how far the government propaganda worked and to what extent it was the bombing itself which eventually led people to accept widescale evacuation.

To start off this investigation, you could get pupils to plot the main evacuation areas on a map of the UK. These are described in a government report at the end of the war as follows:

The areas from which persons of the priority classes have been evacuated fall into four groups to each of which different considerations apply.

(A) the <u>London evacuation area</u> comprising –

  (a) the original (1939) Metropolitan Evacuation Area, i.e. London County, together with 29 adjoining County Boroughs and Boroughs and a group of districts on Thameside and the Medway (List A1).

  (b) 27 Boroughs and Urban Districts, mainly within the London Region and adjoining the original Metropolitan Evacuation Area, which were made evacuable on account of the Flying Bomb risk (List A2).

(B) The <u>"Bomb Alley" evacuation area</u> – a roughly triangular area with the apex at London and the base extending along the South Coast from Folkestone to Eastbourne – made evacuable on account of the Flying Bomb risk (List B).

(C) The <u>"Special Scheme" evacuation areas</u> – towns on and near the coast from Yarmouth to Littlehampton inclusive, made evacuable on account of the risk of invasion (List C). Evacuation from those areas were not restricted to the priority classes but was available for all persons other than essential workers.

(D) The <u>provincial evacuation areas</u> – large provincial towns made evacuable on account of the risk of air-raids (List D)

  {NOTE – groups B and C overlap to some extent.}

The wide area of the 'Bomb Alley' evacuation area is interesting. The flying bomb dropped wherever it ran out of fuel. Many fell far short of their intended target, London.

Source 1: The PRO reference is CAB 73/3.
Question 1: 87,000 children returned home in England.
Question 2: This could be answered both in numerical terms or in terms of the reactions in the receiving districts. In order to prevent a collapse in the evacuation system, the government had to increase allowances and improve services in the reception areas.
Source 2: The PRO reference is MH 101/3.
Source 3: The PRO reference is CAB 73/2.
Source 4: The PRO reference is INF 13/171.
Questions 1 and 2: Evidence in Source 3 suggests a change of attitude: '2000 people a day' were being evacuated; 'voluntary evacuation' of rich and poor. Evidence in Source 3 that attitudes had not changed: 'people preferred if they went at all to go to country districts', 'some return movement'.
Question 3: At the height of the Blitz, there was no time to organise unaccompanied evacuation, and as the government priority was to get all non-essential workers out of the worst affected areas, they saw that mothers taking their children away themselves was a good solution.
Question 5: This question is designed to test pupils' understanding of the issues raised by evacuation and 'propaganda'. An extended answer might consider the fact that hundreds of thousands of children were evacuated in response to the initial government campaign, but that the government propaganda failed later when there was no visible threat from the *Luftwaffe*. When the bombs did come to the cities, families still preferred to stay together, and still preferred to stay at home, but when homes and lives were destroyed or threatened, they would move.
Question 6: This can be a major class exercise bringing in pupils' wider knowledge of evacuation, and relating back to their study of propaganda in investigation 14.

An alternative extension exercise could be done before pupils see the actual government campaigns on evacuation. In groups, pupils could design a campaign to inform parents of the need to evacuate their children. Pupils will need to create leaflets and posters and to write a script for a radio broadcast. How can pupils persuade parents that evacuation is necessary without causing panic?

RMS RANGITATA

This is an investigation designed with two objects in mind. First, to study a less familiar aspect of evacuation – evacuation abroad – and to compare this with the experience of evacuation in Britain which pupils will have studied in their course. Second, to look at historical interpretations and the utility of various sources as evidence.

The documents are taken from the reports made to the Children's Overseas Reception Board who employed the escorts in charge of the evacuated children on the RMS *Rangitata*. They are a form of (biased) historical interpretation. There is little other evidence with which to compare the views expressed here, but a report by the ship's captain suggested the Chief Escort was tactless and ended up doing a disproportionate amount of the work as a result (although he did praise her attitude under stress). More revealingly, the captain suggested that the Chaplain was far too old to be doing the job and could not control the children!

The documents in investigations 18 and 19 serve an additional purpose in giving a passenger's or 'victim's' perspective on the Battle of Atlantic and the attacks on merchant shipping which so threatened Britain's shipping routes throughout the early years of the war.

To begin this activity, you could ask pupils to list the pros and cons of choosing evacuation abroad against evacuation at home.

Sources 1–4: The PRO reference is DO 131/5.

Source 3: This was taken on arrival at New Zealand. Note the reasons pupils give for their choice. How far have they been able to use the internal evidence in the picture to help them decide?

Question 8: Pupils can be given a structure for their diary entries as follows:

Entry 1. The day the ship leaves Liverpool. Write about your journey to Liverpool, your impressions of the other children and the escorts, your feelings as the ship left. Did anyone come to see you off?

Entry 2. The attack of the German 'U' boats'. Write about what you saw and felt, and about the time that followed. What did you think the next morning when all the other boats had gone?

Entry 3. Routine life on board.
Write about the lessons you have, your teachers and the other escorts, the changes in weather. How do you stop yourself getting bored?

Entry 4. Arrival in New Zealand. Write about your feelings on getting to dry land, the things you will miss and the things you look forward to. What do you fear about your new life?

Entry 5. (Extension). Find out about New Zealand. In what ways is life different from where you live? In what ways is it the same? Write a further diary entry about the time after you have been taken in by a local family.

 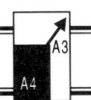
A DISASTER AT SEA – THE CITY OF BENARES

In this tragic story of the sinking of a ship carrying children on evacuation to Canada pupils will come face to face with the realities of the Battle of the Atlantic.

Sources 1–3: PRO reference is DO 131/20

Question 7: This is an extension question that gives pupils an opportunity to consider a wide range of evidence from this investigation and from their study of evacuation within Britain. Their answers can also be compared with their opinion expressed before their study of investigation 18.

THEME 5: HOW DID PEOPLE COPE IN THE BLITZ?

INVESTIGATION 20 • four pages

TAKING SHELTER

One of the enduring images of life on the Home Front in the Second World War is of the civilian population struggling to find shelter in the face of German air raids. Organising shelters, monitoring their use and encouraging people to use them were constant preoccupations of the government throughout the war. This four-page investigation sheds light on the use of shelters from both the civilians' and the government's perspective.

Source 1: The PRO reference is AIR 19/60. This is a description of British bombing capabilities, but the same problems applied to the German Luftwaffe.

Source 2: The PRO reference is HO 186/2247.

Question 1: This diagram could be prepared by the teacher as an introduction to the topic, to demonstrate how the further away from the target the bomber is when the bomb is released, the more likely it is to be affected by air currents or poor visibility. Many pupils will have an image of precision bombing gained from TV coverage of modern warfare. As Source 1 illustrates, in 1939 the technology was very new, and the inaccuracy of the bombers added to their danger for the civilian population.

Question 2: The pilots are inexperienced and

undertrained, the monoplane is not nearly as versatile as the biplane.

Source 4: The PRO reference is HO 205/14.

Question 2: Pupils should think about the problems of flooding, and the difficulties of erecting such a shelter if you were elderly or disabled, or living on your own. They may also consider the wider issues such as whether people really expected to be bombed when eight months into the war no bombs had fallen.

Question 3: It was at this time that the government's fear of invasion and of German bombing to prepare for it was at its height. The Germans had driven the Allies off European soil at Dunkirk in May, and it seemed as if Britain would be the next target. (See for example Source 1 of investigation 15).

Source 5: Incredibly we are told that the shelterers survived in this Anderson shelter. Pupils might observe how the placing of the shelter in relation to the house was different from the advice given in Source 3.

Sources 7 and 8: The PRO reference is HO 205/20.

Question 2: This could be tackled in groups. This is meant to make use of all the sources and is open-ended enough to allow for brief or extended answers.

As an extension exercise pupils could be allocated 'typical' family roles, discussing the type of shelter most suitable for their needs. The 'head' of the family could then report back to the whole class on his or her group's decision.

INVESTIGATION 21 • one page

WHAT USE DID PEOPLE MAKE OF AIR RAID SHELTERS?

Throughout the months of the Blitz, the government took a regular census of the types of shelter being used in London. The figures in Source 2 come from their censuses.

This investigation can be used alongside investigation 20 to follow up pupils' work on the final question, or as stimulus material in its own right.

Source 1: The PRO reference is INF 2/47.

Source 2: The PRO reference is HO 200/1.

Question 1: Pupils may need some more background on the events mentioned – for example the appointment of 'Bomber' Harris to Bomber Command. The dates are August 1940, June 1941, January 1942. You could follow this up by discussing relationships between the changed bombing pattern and the events marked on the graph.

Questions 3–4: The change is primarily because of evacuation.

Question 5: This question too could be answered by use of a line graph to indicate the peaks, troughs and turning points. Use the month on month grand total. Alternatively it could be an oral or written exercise.

Question 7: The scale will need to be quite big to show the small percentages. For example, a pie chart

should be 15 centimetres (six inches) in diameter. A divided bar chart should be 10 centimetres (four inches) in length.

You may also wish to bypass the maths for some pupils by supplying them with the percentages:

	November 1940	August 1941
Basement	7.4	6.6
Trenches	4.6	2.3
Surface shelter	2.9	1.6
Railway arch or tunnel	3.2	5.0
Andersons	71.5	70.0
Others	10.5	12.8

Question 8: Ask pupils to consider in particular why so many available places in the shelters were not used.

INVESTIGATION 22 • one page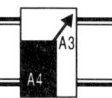

DOWN STREET

Clearly it was not just civilians who needed protection against German attacks. The administrative and political leaders also needed protection. Some government departments were evacuated out of London. Others were provided with special shelter in London itself. One such shelter – Winston Churchill's Cabinet War Rooms under Whitehall – is open to the public nowadays. Down Street Station is not, but this investigation gives you an opportunity to see the elaborate provision made for the effective functioning of the Railway Transport Executive in a disused tube station under Mayfair in central London.

Source 1: The PRO reference is HO 200/1.

Source 2: The PRO reference is AN 2/678.

Question 1: use a Tube map.

Question 3: Pupils can consider why this location was chosen and not one outside London.

Question 5: Talk through with pupils beforehand the priorities for their design – keeping safe, being in close touch with other government departments, access to doctors or to fresh air etc.

INVESTIGATION 23 • two pages

THE BETHNAL GREEN TUBE DISASTER

From the start of the Blitz, many Londoners had preferred the Underground stations to any other form of shelter. At first the government had resisted this. However, from late 1941 they set about organising it more effectively to ensure safety and adequate facilities for the shelterers. Each Tube station was to be provided with up to 46 staff including a doctor, a nurse, 16 wardens and 10 lavatory attendants.

However, this did not however prevent one of the major civilian tragedies of the war – the Bethnal Green Tube disaster when 173 people were crushed to death as they crowded into the Tube station when an air raid warning sounded. This investigation is a causation exercise which reveals not only the problems of organising shelter, but also the attitude of Londoners to the continued bombing of their city almost three years after the start of the Blitz.

It is worth pointing out that the use of the Underground as shelter increased as more dangerous weapons such as the flying bombs were used by the Germans.

Source 1: The PRO reference is CAB 73/7. We have used a transcript.

Question 2: You can write each one out on a separate card and use the cards for this 'prioritising exercise'. (**NB** pupils must be able to say *why* they have chosen these three. Why are these the most important causes?

Question 5: This might be best handled in class discussion.

The following is the list of causes as identified in the official report.

Dealing now with the contributory causes of the accident, they may, I think, be conveniently separated into two main groups – (i) a psychological change in the attitude of the population towards air raids and shelters generally and (ii) the physical causes.

(i) (a). *The borough has some 60% of its public shelter accommodation in this tube, a much larger proportion than any neighbouring borough. This has instilled in the minds of the people a marked preference for this type of shelter, to the exclusion of more easily reached shelters more widely dispersed. Apart from the regular users, a large number of people not in the immediate vicinity of this shelter had come to regard it as a desirable haven to resort to in the event of what might prove to be a heavy raid.*

(b) *A particularly strong apprehension of drastic reprisals for the recent heavy raid on Berlin. This apprehension was fostered by*

newspaper accounts of the effects of new types of bombs.

(c) *A realization that new bombing tactics allowed far less time to get under cover than formerly was the case, and that a raid might be expected to reach its maximum intensity in a very short time. In the new type of raid the air raid warning might precede the bombs by a very short margin.*

(d) *A wholesome respect for the danger from splinters from our new barrage. The mouth of the shelter stands, as I have said, in a somewhat exposed position.*

(e) *A lack of knowledge of the nature and appearance of the anti-aircraft rockets now in use.*

(f) *The desire of parents to get their children under cover quickly, which induced numbers of people, not hitherto users of the shelter to go there before a threatened raid. A very large number of children have fairly lately returned to the area. All these factors combined to produce –*

(g) *A loss of self control in some hundreds of people attempting to enter the shelter.*

(ii)(a). *The physical presence of large numbers of children who have come back recently to the area retarded the speed of intake into the shelter, and the speed at which people could reach it.*

(b) *The shelter has only one entrance. In this it is, if not unique, very exceptional in relation to its size.*

(c) *The lighting on the stairs was very dim, which not only increased the chance of a fall on the stairs, but was bound to produce confusion if one occurred. If a fall occurred, however, no lighting could, in the circumstances of the present disaster have prevented that happening which did happen.*

(d) *There were no handrails down the centre of the stairway. These might have enabled a person falling to save himself. If such a person was burdened with a child in arms and a bundle, as many were, their value would be problematical. If a jam happened despite their provision, they would almost certainly make matters worse. As a contributory cause I attach little importance to their absence.*

(e) *The absence of a crush barrier, allowing a straight line of pressure from the crowd seeking entrance to the people in the stairs. This was, in my opinion, the main structural defect at the time of the accident.*

(f) *The main and proximate cause was a sudden rush for the entrance by probably 350–400 people.*

THEME 6: HOW DID PEOPLE REACT TO WARTIME RESTRICTIONS?

INVESTIGATION 24 • two pages

SIGNPOSTS AND BEACHES

As with all investigations in this book, there is a strong emphasis on AT3 work. However, investigations 24 and 25 also encourage pupils to think about reasons for government action (AT1b) and to appreciate that different groups of people and individuals would have had varying responses to government restrictions (AT1c).

These documents also suggest a lighter side to the effect of government restrictions.

Sources 1 and 3: The PRO reference is WO 199/143.

Sources 4 and 5: The PRO reference is WO 199/2559.

Question 1: The purpose, of course, was to hinder any invader's progress,

Question 3: The wastage of rationed petrol that resulted from drivers getting lost due to the absence of signposts could cause considerable ill-feeling.

Source 5: This might be best read in class beforehand. Unusual phrases such as 'sauce for the goose . . .' in paragraph 3 should pose fewer problems once the overall tone of the letter is clear.

RATIONING

There is much good material published on rationing. And as many families include members who can still recall Second World War rationing, pupils may have the added opportunity of pursuing their family's oral history on this topic.

The aim of this investigation is to help structure a consideration of rationing and to supplement whatever other evidence pupils have at their disposal with a set of documents that allow pupils to find out for themselves:
 a) what items were rationed
 b) why they were rationed
 c) how rationing was supposed to work
 d) whether rationing got more or less severe as the war progressed
 e) how people felt about rationing.

Sources 1 and 5: The PRO reference is BT 1 31/40.
Source 2: The PRO references is INF 2/47.
Question 3: The reasons given were: bread and flour – 'rationing would be interpreted as the first sign of surrender'; vegetables – 'variations in supply, price, quantity, tastes and the absence of standard units make rationing impractical'; fish – 'supplies are down to 35 per cent of normal anyway, and many people do not eat it'; cheese – 'rationing is impossible due to widely differing consumption'; milk – 'of vital importance to children, nursing mothers and young people'; coffee – 'current supplies will last between 2 and 3 years'.

Source 8: The PRO reference is RG23/9A.
Sources 9–10: The PRO reference is RG23/16.
Question 1: Those questioned unanimously agreed with rationing in principle as it was seen to be a fair system: the feeling that nobody had more than anyone else gave people peace of mind. There was a general fear amongst those interviewed, based on experience of past wars, that war without rationing might mean starvation. It was felt that rationing prevented queueing, black markets, rising prices, under-the-counter deals and shortages. People might also have felt it their patriotic duty to answer 'yes' to the question whether they approved of rationing or not.

THEME 7: WOMEN AND WAR

'JOIN THE WOMEN'S LAND ARMY'

Investigations 26–30 look at various aspects of the role of women in the war – as industrial workers, as members of the Services, as farm workers and as internees.

The illustration below shows the extent of women's mobilisation in the war.

Even so, women's experience of war is often neglected by historians. These investigations will therefore complement pupils' general work on the war and can be slotted into their courses at a number of different points.

The three posters in this investigation are designed as stimulus material to raise pupils' interest in and awareness of the Women's Land Army.

Sources 1–3: The PRO reference is INF 13/140.
Question 3: With these posters as with all government propaganda, encourage pupils to consider who the target audience was. Source 3 has a more general propaganda purpose, whereas Sources 1 and 2 are more directly recruitment posters.

WHAT WAS IT LIKE TO BE IN THE WOMEN'S LAND ARMY?

Investigation 27 goes on to look in detail at the work of the Women's Land Army.

This investigation gives pupils a fuller insight than is usually possible in school textbooks into the kind of work women undertook in the WLA, and how they felt about their work.

Investigation 26 can be used alongside it to make up a six-page investigation of women's war experiences.

If you have also bought a copy of *Documents for Britain and the Great War*, it is possible to compare the operation of the WLA during the Great War with its operation during the Second World War.

The emphasis in this unit is on detailed work with the

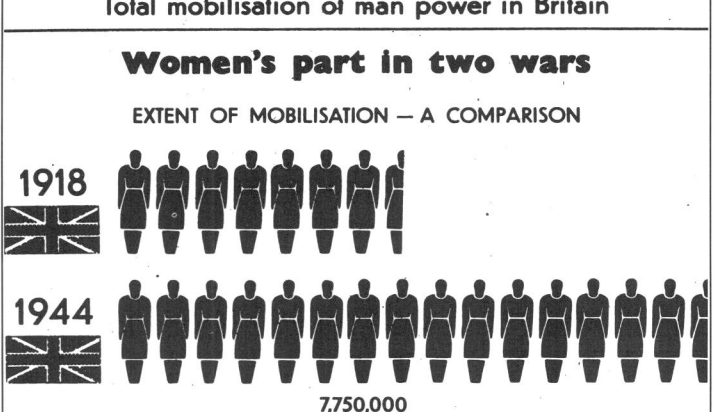

Total mobilisation of man power in Britain

Women's part in two wars

EXTENT OF MOBILISATION — A COMPARISON

1918

1944

7,750,000

All able-bodied women in Britain without children or family responsibilities between 19 and 50 years are mobilised in essential war work. There are also many thousands of voluntary women workers below and above these ages.

sources to help build up a rounded picture of the WLA.

Source 1: The PRO reference is INF 2/47.

Sources 2, 3 and 6–11: MAF 59/21

Sources 4 and 5: MAF 59/154.

Questions 1–4: Compare the images of the Land Girl presented by the posters used in investigation 26.

Sources 5, 6 and 7: There is opportunity here to discuss the wider question of men's attitude to women workers.

Question 9: An extension activity could be to ask pupils to imagine the war is over. Working in groups of four, one of them should be an interviewer and interview the other three, who will each play one of these roles:

a) a farmer who employed Land Girls

b) a Land Girl who enjoyed her work on the farm

c) a Land Girl who had a miserable time, but did not leave her job.

Ask each one to describe an incident in their wartime service and to say how the experience of the WLA has changed them.

INVESTIGATION 28 • *two pages*

'WHAT DID YOU DO IN THE WAR, MUM?'

This question was so often asked of fathers on propaganda posters that it seemed natural to apply it to mothers too. The investigation could be extended to use many of the documents in investigations 26–29.

Source 1 and 2 are taken from the *Illustrated London News*, Volume 196.

Sources 3 and 4: The PRO reference is INF 3/400.

Source 5: The PRO reference is ZPER 34/196.

Source 6: The PRO reference is INF 13/171.

Question 1: This investigation is intended as stimulus material and the task has been left deliberately open-ended so that pupils can bring in their knowledge from other areas. Have a range of textbooks handy for pupils to look at and refer to in their answer.

You may feel that some preliminary work with the visual material is necessary. If so, you could for example photocopy these pictures without captions and ask pupils to match up Sources 1–4 with the captions written on to a separate sheet, and then to write a detailed description of the work the women are doing in Sources 5 and 6.

INVESTIGATION 29 • *four pages*

WHAT WAS IT LIKE TO BE A FEMALE INTERNEE?

This investigation sheds light on a little discussed episode of the war – internment of aliens. It highlights the different experiences of internment suffered by the different parties and nationalities involved. The same premises in the Isle of Man had been used for exactly the same purpose in the 1914–18 war, and the official report from which the extracts are taken concludes that, although internment is to be regretted, the same premises with similar conditions would be recommended were it to be again necessary. Let's see what your pupils think.

Sources 1–3: The PRO reference is HO 213/1053. The language of the report is that of a Civil Servant and there are some obscure turns of phrase which pupils will need help with.

Source 1: You may also want to have a map of the whole of the British Isles to give context to this map.

Question 1: Pupils might consider both the government's fear that aliens might help an enemy, and their fear that Britons might harm German people living in Britain. In the Great War, after all, there were very vicious attacks on German people and businesses by British civilians.

Question 5: This is best done in groups – or in whole class discussion.

Question 6: A starting point for this exercise could be a playground incident which will be seen in different ways by different people, eg in the case of bullying, 'victims', perpetrators and spectators.

In thinking about the experience of the internees we have to remember that each is an individual. Their nationality, beliefs and values may be important, but so equally may their personality and individual identity, in determining how they deal with the experience of internment. Try to flesh out the individual characters a bit more in class discussion, so that they stand out from the stereotype.

After the reports are written they can be put on display. Pupils can try to work out from the report which of the three people is supposed to have written it, using the description of their experiences as evidence.

Extension exercise: internment is seldom described in any detail, if it is mentioned at all, in school textbooks discussing the Home Front. You could ask pupils to look through all the textbooks you have available and see how many of them cover the subject and in what depth. Ask pupils to consider reasons for this limited coverage. Is is too unimportant or too painful, or does it not fit the image we might like to maintain of Britain during the war?

'JOBS FOR GIRLS ... JOBS FOR BOYS'

This investigation has two main purposes. First to give pupils an insight into the way that children were encouraged to help the war effort; second to reflect on the assumptions about the roles of boys and girls that characterise this period.

Source 1: The PRO reference is INF 13/144. The posters from which the extracts were taken were probably intended for display in schools.

Question 3: Pupils can either just write the headlines or they can write a detailed paragraph description as well.

Question 5: There are plenty of opportunities for comparison with gender roles today. The breakdown was:

Jobs for girls	**Jobs for boys**
Snug slippers	new pane of glass
skirt renovation	refix handles
seating a skirt	choked sink
refix a loose handle	oil door locks
collect wood ash	mend a table leg
when a drawer sticks	sew on a button
SOS scrubbing bucket	how to darn
polishing pads	frayed flex

THEME 8: ALLIES AND ENEMIES

HOW MUCH DID THE ALLIES KNOW ABOUT THE HOLOCAUST?

The report in Source 1 was not only published in a magazine circulated in Britain and America, but also filed in the Prime Minister's office along with many other letters, for example a request from the leaders of the British Council of Jews to meet him. These leaders wished to discuss how the Allies might help bring to an end the terrible slaughter of the Jewish people.

Many pupils may believe that the Holocaust was a secret until the first death camps were overrun. Although it is true that the *scale* of the slaughter was only clear once the camps had been captured, it is certainly not true that the slaughter of the Jews and other groups such as gypsies was a secret. One of the main aims of this investigation is for pupils to see what kind of details the Allied governments had available to them.

Source 1: The PRO reference is PREM 4/51/8.

ENCOURAGING THE SOVIET PEOPLE

This is another propaganda exercise which can be used alongside or to contrast with investigation 14.

It would be possible to extend this investigation by comparing the 'GPD picturegraphs' prepared for circulation to the USA (see Source 2 in investigation 25 and Source 1 in investigation 27) with those in this investigation intended for circulation to the USSR.

Pupils could experiment by creating their own picturegraphs, for example to present information about the restrictions the British were accepting for the sake of the war effort, as in investigation 24. They should design the picturegraph in a form appropriate for the USA or the USSR.

Sources 1, 2 and 3: The PRO reference is INF 2/47.
Sources 4 and 5: The PRO reference is INF 2/31.
Questions 1–2: These are probably best handled in class discussion.

'BERLINERS: have you lost your minds?'

Once the war had turned the corner for the Allies, one of their major aims was to erode the morale of the German people. Ferocious air raids on civilians in German cities and towns increased in intensity as the Allied positions improved. One of the aims of such raids was to overwhelm the German people and to shorten the war by destroying civilian morale (see investigation 34). Many millions of leaflets such as Source 1 were dropped on German cities as well. The *Luftwaffe* had dropped similar German propaganda on Britain. (Some of this is also in the PRO, but unfortunately the reproduction was too poor for use.)

This investigation is an ideal introduction to investigation 34, which looks at the wider context of the bombing campaigns.

Source 1: The PRO reference is PREM 4/99/5. The English translation is not that good. For cross-curricular language work you could ask your pupils to try to do better!

WHY DID THE ALLIES BOMB GERMAN CITIES?

The belief has been widely held that Allied bombing of Germany did not have the considerable effects which were hoped for. The material contained here and in investigation 35 gives pupils an opportunity to investigate contemporary accounts to see if this was indeed the case. The investigations will involve pupils in evaluating evidence closely and in examining the causes and consequences of the bombing.

Sources 1 and 2: These are from a memorandum presented by the Chief of Air Staff to a War Cabinet Committee. The PRO reference is CAB 122/831.

Question 1: This is best handled in a class discussion. Try to list as many possible consequences of the bombing as you can and then decide which are the main aims.

Comparisons can be made with how the German air raids on Britain earlier in the war affected British morale. Would this experience influence the British leaders planning the bombing of German cities?

Questions 1 and 2: These are best tackled in groups. In the actual Committee discussion, the bombing of Berlin was decided on.

Question 3: This can be done in groups or individually. If in groups the speeches can be read out to the class by one member of the group acting as spokesperson.

HOW SUCCESSFUL WAS THE BOMBING OF THE GERMAN AIRCRAFT INDUSTRY?

The effectiveness of civilian bombing was almost impossible to assess. Almost, but not quite, as difficult was the bombing of military and industrial targets. This investigation looks at the government's assessment of the success of its campaign against the German aircraft industry.

Source 1: The PRO reference is INF 3/1433.

Question 1: This provides scope for individuality and humour! A display could be made of the better efforts. This could be tackled in class then questions 1–4 on the second page could be used for homework.

Source 2 has the PRO reference AIR 48/2.

Questions 1–4: Whilst questions 1–3 are straightforward comprehension exercises, question 4 calls on pupils to assess the range of sources together and think about:

a) whether the consequences were as intended

b) whether the attacks were still successful even if not precisely as intended.

Extension: as follow-up work, pupils could find out more about the British bombing campaigns, or write a profile of 'Bomber' Harris considering whether attitudes towards him have changed over time (AT2), and if so why.

THEME 9: WHAT WAS LIFE LIKE ON THE FRONT LINE?

CASUALTIES

The next seven investigations attempt to pull together some case studies of the combat that are:

a) representative of the range of records held by the PRO

b) representative of the many different arenas in which Allied troops were operating throughout the war.

This first investigation begins with the casualty lists prepared for the government. The PRO reference is CAB 106/319. The table is an extract from the original statistical table.

It serves two main purposes. First, it shows the many different theatres of war in which British troops were involved, in this truly global war. Second, it highlights

the fact that the risks they faced varied between one theatre of war and another. In some areas the main risk of death was ill-treatment as a Prisoner of War, in others disease, in others active combat.

Questions 1–3: Given the maths involved in this, you might choose to help some pupils or do this a class exercise.

Question 4: This will probably best be handled as a class discussion.

DUNKIRK: *they were there*

These pictures taken from the *Illustrated London News* of June 1940 demonstrate the popular view of Dunkirk which was advanced immediately after the evacuation.

'BEYOND THE CALL OF DUTY: medal citations'

Throughout the war tens of thousands of individuals – from both the Allied and Axis side – were commended for acts of bravery. In this investigation we look at four British medal citations. All are from a single theatre of war over a short period, but drawn from a range of ranks and representing a range of awards from the Military Medal to the Victoria Cross.

The task of the pupils is to decide which of four possible awards the soldiers should receive. This involves pupils:

    a) developing a basic understanding of the hierarchy of the medals they have to choose from

    b) thinking in detail of how each of the actions cited showed personal courage and how the action contributed to the war effort.

Detailed interrogation of the sources has been left very much up to the individual teacher. Some pupils may need more structure than others. If you need to guide pupils through the task, then take one citation as an example and begin by making the name and rank clear. Point out to pupils how some of the medals are intended for officers, and others for other ranks. Then take pupils through the citation showing how the details are laid out. It would also be helpful to discuss what the various abbreviations and the more formal language means, for example 'fraught with difficulty', 'provided very welcome confirmation' etc.

Then ask pupils to list anything in the citation which shows the soldier's outstanding personal bravery.

Deciding who has made the most valuable contribution is quite difficult because it involves pupil appreciation of, for example, the way in which actions that boost the morale of other troops, or build up teamwork and loyalty within a group of combat soldiers, make as great a contribution to the war effort as a heroic individual attack. You may wish the class to work in groups – one to consider each medal citation.

Sources 1–4: medal citations are on microfilm. The PRO reference is WO 373 (Reel 9).

The medals actually awarded were: Lance Bombadier Hasler: Miliary Medal; Captain Higson: Military Cross; Major Birley: DSO; Captain Gardner: Victoria Cross.

The photo of Captain Gardner comes from the *Illustrated London News* of 18 July 1942. The *Illustrated London News* regularly featured all recent recipients of the Victoria Cross.

TWO YEARS IN CRETE: *prisoners of war*

It was the duty of every prisoner of war to try to escape and to return to his unit. Many pupils will have images of prisoner of war camps obtained from films such as *The Great Escape* or *The Bridge over the River Kwai*.

However, as this investigation will make clear, many prisoner of war camps were in practice much more 'ad hoc' and escapes far more spontaneous and chaotic than such popular images lead us to expect. One group of POWs got out of their Italian camp by bribing the sentries with their underwear!

Every prisoner of war – once he returned to his unit – was throughly debriefed about how he escaped, how he travelled back to his unit, who helped him and how. The 'helpers' were listed by name and address if possible, as they could potentially create a network of contacts for other escapees or for mounting attacks with enemy-held territory.

POWs were also asked for any information about enemy activities that might help the Allied operation, and had to sign a solemn undertaking not to reveal any details at all about their escape – even extending to the countries through which they had travelled.

Source 1 is the report on the debrief of Lance Bombadier Robinson from Waltham in Liverpool. The PRO reference is WO 208/3343.

Question 1: Robinson spent two years on the run in Crete after escaping, so the debrief is necessarily long and detailed. Question 1 will help pupils to piece the story together. You may wish to underline certain dates before you photocopy the worksheet.

Questions 2–4: Use the report to offer evidence that the German control of Crete became harsher and more punitive over the period of occupation.

Question 6: This gives opportunity for differentiation, as pupils can choose the manner of response. It would be possible for pupils to work in pairs for this exercise – one to write diary entries, the other to draw pictures to illustrate these moments.

Alternatively, pupils can work in groups of four. One pupil could work on a diary entry and picture for each date.

THE CAPTURE OF 'HILLMAN': D-Day

'Hillman' was a small gun emplacement on the coast of Normandy. The capture of 'Hillman' was one small incident amongst hundreds that made up D-Day itself. Part of the purpose of this investigation is to help pupils see how the major, famous events of the war, which we look back to and describe in very broad terms, are themselves made up of many smaller events. This investigation also helps pupils relate to the experiences of ordinary soldiers involved in the Normandy landings.

The logistics of even this small attack seem quite horrendous. Multiply this by several hundred, and you can begin to see why the reconquest of France took many months, even years to plan.

There are many films of the events of D-Day, for example 'The Longest Day', which can be used for AT2 work. The impression of events conveyed by such films can be compared with the impressions gained from sources such as Source 1.

Hillman was a code name for a gun emplacement. All the individual features on this coastline were given code names – those of other features included Morris, Daimler, Hedgehog, Eel, Bass, Gin and Rum.

Although many of the questions are quite straightforward, this is undoubtedly one of the more difficult documents to read and work with. The investigation may be most appropriate for the most able pupils or for class discussion.

Source 1: The PRO reference is CAB 106/999.

Question 2: The report in Source 1 was written for army officials as part of the commanding officer's routine reporting of all military activity. Pupils might use the evidence of the technical details or the frequent abbreviations to infer this. However, Source 1 was also used separately as an appendix to a report sent to the British government to summarise events of the first two days of the Normandy landings.

Questions 3 and 9: These questions are intended to get pupils to consider the logistics of mounting such an attack.

INVESTIGATION 41 · two pages

GERMAN GENERALS

Once the Allies had landed in France, their progress across the country was relatively swift. As the Allies progressed they captured many high-ranking German officers. The five sources in this investigation are taken from reports compiled on five German generals by Allied officers, both British and American.

One aim of the interviewers who wrote these reports was to establish the generals' attitude to Hitler and the Nazis, and to German military prospects overall. However, the interviewers clearly hold strong opinions on each general's character and conduct, and this investigation therefore provides an unusual approach to work on differentiating fact and opinion.

The generals seem resigned to German defeat. As early as 1942, the first captured generals were indeed talking not about whether the Germans would lose the war, but how long it would take.

Sources 1–5: The PRO reference is WO 208/3433.

Questions 1–2: These questions can either be done in groups, or you can write the descriptions and ask the class to guess to whom they apply. These questions are purely designed to stimulate pupils' interest in the documents.

INVESTIGATION 42 · one page

'I ACCUSE MR AMERY': soldiers' morale in southeast Asia

In this investigation pupils analyse, compare and evaluate different sources to find out about the situation of British soldiers in the Far East.

Possible starting points might be what pupils know about the living and working conditions of soldiers on active service, either today or in other spheres of combat in the past eg in the trenches during the First World War.

Source 1: The headline comes from the *Sunday Pictorial*, a popular newspaper of the time. The PRO reference is WO 32/11194. Captain Bellenger had a regular feature in the *Sunday Pictorial* called 'Voice Of The Services'.

Source 2: The PRO reference is WO 32/11194. This newspaper was produced specifically for the Forces serving in southeast Asia.

Question 2: Ensure that pupils are well aware of the need to consider the bias of the newspaper report. They should also consider how investigating bias in two different types of newspaper means that different questions must be asked of each one.

Source 3: The PRO reference is WO 32/11477.

Question 5: The problems and recommendations included in Source 3 are only a sample of the many in the report. Other recommendations were:

a) indoctrination (to convince servicemen that they are valued and not forgotten)

b) more effective air transport (to enable rapid evacuation of casualties and regular delivery of fresh meat, mail and other amenities)

c) more white women to work in India and Ceylon in leave centres and welfare work

d) priority for ex-servicemen in acquiring houses and furniture on return to civilian life.

Compare these with pupils' responses to question 5.

INVESTIGATION 43 • three pages

DAYS IN THE LIFE OF WINSTON CHURCHILL

The Programme of Study for this unit requires an investigation of four main wartime leaders. The PRO naturally has a lot of documentation on Churchill, but much less on the other three.

This investigation shows the range of tasks performed by the Prime Minister at various stages of the war. It also aims to help pupils get a picture of the kind of man Churchill was, by looking behind the scenes of his official duties.

Source 1: (B) INF 2/46, (C) INF 2/73.

Source 2: The PRO reference is PREM 4/38/L. This document has been reset to exclude the travel directions which were included in the original itinerary.

Source 3: The PRO reference is PREM 4/38/P.

Source 4: The PRO reference is PREM 10/3.

INVESTIGATION 44 • one page

A NUCLEAR FUTURE

The aim of the final investigations in this book is to study some of the immediate consequences of the war. The section begins with the consequences of the dropping of the first atomic bombs.

Most of the PRO documents relating to the development and testing of the atomic bomb remain closed to public scrutiny. This investigation therefore uses the first public government statement of 'the nuclear age' to stimulate pupils into thinking about what kind of future the development of the atomic bomb had created. In class discussion it will be possible to discuss the tone of Source 1. Is it with too much hindsight that we read Source 1 as having a sense of gravity and tension in it – a sense of awe and fear rather than a sense of relief? Or is it an expression of unqualified admiration for the scientific achievement? See what you think.

Source 1: The PRO reference is PREM 3/139/8A.

INVESTIGATION 45 • two pages

WHY DID BRITAIN WELCOME THE 'BALTIC CYGNETS'?

The focus of this investigation is on a group of immigrants who were invited to Britain. It could be fitted into work about the effects of the war on Britain and how the new government went about rebuilding the country after six years of war. The 'Baltic Cygnets' were not the only immigrants to be invited to work in Britain after the war, and it is important here to place black and Asian immigration of the 1940s and 1950s in

its proper economic and imperial context. The peoples of the British Empire did not only contribute to the victory over the Fascist Powers. They were also to contribute significantly to the rebuilding of the post-war British economy. The influx of people from many different countries marks an important point in the development of multi-cultural Britain.

You will have to provide pupils with any necessary background to the division of Germany after its defeat in May 1945. A map showing Germany and the Baltic countries mentioned in the sources would be a useful aid for pupils' understanding.

Sources 1 and 2: The PRO reference is HO 213/1000.

Activities that could supplement the questions in the investigation include:

a) role-play interviews with a 'Baltic Cygnet'

b) a discussion of the criteria used to select the most suitable volunteers

c) writing to the various Embassies of the Baltic countries in London in order to trace any former 'Baltic Cygnets' who might be still alive and willing to be interviewed.

Finally, it is interesting to relate this historical episode to British immigration policy today, with a quick look at our attitudes towards refugees from the world's current trouble spots.

INVESTIGATION 46 • two pages

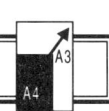

DID BRITISH SOLDIERS TREAT BELSEN VICTIMS CRUELLY?

This is a short investigation which confronts pupils with clear contradictions and disagreements within a set of sources. The sources are not particularly easy to read, so additional annotation has been provided.

This investigation could form a valuable part of

pupils' work on the Holocaust.

Sources 1–3: The PRO reference is FO 945/596.

Source 1: Some brief background information about the situation in Palestine and the historical reasons behind Britian's responsibility for it will be necessary for pupils to understand the advertisement in the *New York Post*.

Contradictions in evidence often lead pupils to reject one side and accept the other. However, it is important that pupils are introduced to the idea that if sources are viewed alongside other evidence, rather than in isolation, it is possible to make judgements about their veracity. By questioning the provenance of a source, pupils can be shown how sources often provide interpretations of events rather than factual information.

INVESTIGATION 47 • *two pages*

WHERE SHOULD THE UN HEADQUARTERS BE?

This investigation looks at Cold War tensions through the early history of the United Nations, and in particular at the problem of finding a site for the UN headquarters acceptable to both the Soviets and the Americans.

This investigation can easily follow on from pupils' work on the wartime conferences at Yalta or Potsdam, or work on the origins and aims of the UN. Some knowledge of the structure and functions of the UN is also appropriate. The investigation should be preceded by general class discussion about the conditions in various countries at the end of the war. The situation in the USA, for example, can be compared with the USSR, Britain, France, Switzerland and Germany. Discuss how that country in particular was affected by the war, and what the post-war political and economic situation was

like. A map showing the political divisions of the world – along with its population and military strength – would also be a useful reference tool.

Sources 1–2: The PRO reference is FO 371/59721.

The writer of Source 1 assumes that Britain is a Great Power. Pupils could discuss how accurate this perception was in 1945. They could also discuss the possible distinction between 'a Great Power' and 'a superpower' (remembering the Soviet Union's disadvantages at this time).

Question 5: None of the sites listed here is ideal. The important point is that pupils understand that both Western and Eastern Europe were unacceptable. Geneva might seem to have been the ideal location (the empty League of Nations buildings were available and Switzerland was a non-aligned country). However, there was an understandable desire to break with the past, and the Swiss government vetoed the idea as a possible breach of their neutrality.

Better answers will identify several reasons for their choice including good climate and facilities, but also stressing the problem of pleasing both the USSR and the USA.

British officials expressed surprise in 1945 that the Soviet government accepted New York as the temporary headquarters. They seemed unclear about what the USSR really wanted. Stalin's main concern seemed to be that the UN was not located in Western Europe.

During 1946, there were increasing signs of Soviet dissatisfaction with New York. For example, the Soviet Union was angered by the hostility of the American press towards it.

Question 3 (second page): This activity can follow on from or can be done separately from the other questions. It is designed to reinforce pupils' understanding of the functions and importance of the UN. A picture and plan (see below) of the real UN building will make a useful comparison with pupils' designs.

CONCLUSION

INVESTIGATION 48 • *one page*

CHOOSING HISTORY

This is intended as a very flexible exercise which can be extended to use or include any of the documents reproduced in this book.

We have selected four to show the exercise working in practice. The documents used here do not require much reading. If you choose documents which do have to be read, the exercise becomes a good deal more sophisticated.

Pupils can work in groups or independently. The task can be briefed orally or in writing.

Source 1: The PRO reference is PREM 4/38/H.
Source 2: The PRO reference is FO 371/21658.
Source 2: The original (see page 30) has gone to the Imperial War Museum. The PRO archives now include only a transcript of the text.
Source 3: The PRO reference is HO 186/2247.
Source 4: The PRO reference is INF 3/227.